# Criteria for Philanthropy at Its Best®

Benchmarks to Assess and Enhance Grantmaker Impact

# Acknowledgements

Over the past year, numerous people contributed to the development of this report.

Project Co-Directors: Aaron Dorfman
  and Niki Jagpal
Primary Author: Niki Jagpal
Contributing Authors: Aaron Dorfman,
  john a. powell, Julia Craig and Lisa Ranghelli
Research Assistance: Julia Craig,
  Matthew P. Maronick, Charles M. Fernández
Primary Editor: Kristina C. Moore

NCRP is especially grateful to the NCRP Board of Directors, Research Advisory Committee and staff.

Special thanks to the following for their additional substantive assistance:
Lori Bartczak, Rick Cohen, Kathleen Enright, Andrew Grant-Thomas, Robert Grimm, David Harder, Nathan Henderson-James, Mark Kramer, Steven Lawrence, J. McCray, Larry McGill, Chuck McLean, Ron McKinley, Barry Knight, Spence Limbocker, Marcy Murninghan, Terry Odendahl, Rob Reich, Mark Rosenman and Michael Seltzer.

And also thanks to the more than sixty different grantmakers that provided unrestricted core operating support, which made this project possible. A list of funders is available at www.ncrp.org.

## ABOUT THE AUTHOR

Niki Jagpal joined NCRP in 2008 and has a broad range of experience working on research and policy advocacy in the nonprofit sector. Most recently, she was a member of the Research Department at Media Matters for America, a web-based progressive research and information center. Previously, Niki worked for several years at Ipas, an organization that works to enhance women's reproductive rights and health. She helped expand the organization's region-wide work in Asia and the United States. She has extensive experience organizing and mobilizing grassroots participation in local and national advocacy campaigns, and also has worked with local groups to increase bipartisan civic engagement and improve election protection. She has worked at the Center for Community Change, the Center for Juvenile Justice Reform at Georgetown University, and the Fannie Mae Foundation. She led workshops and given presentations at local and national universities to engage the next generation of nonprofit leaders.

Niki holds a bachelor's degree in history and cultural anthropology from Duke University and a master of public policy from Georgetown.

Copyediting: "Editor-in-Chief" of Edit Avenue • Book Design and Layout: Dominic Vecchiollo
Printing: VMW Printing Inc.

# Table of Contents

*(Continued on p. vi)*

# Table of Contents

(continued)

# Challenging Grantmakers to Strengthen Communities

## WHY THESE CRITERIA? WHY NOW?

Our nation is at a critical moment. The economy is in crisis, the private sector is in turmoil and the civic sector already is feeling the negative spillover effects. But, as is true of all crises, this moment presents philanthropy with an opportunity. As White House Chief of Staff Rahm Emmanuel said recently, "You never want a serious crisis to go to waste, and what I mean by that is an opportunity to do things that you didn't think you could do before." The current challenges present grantmakers with a chance to critically analyze persistent problems that have been ignored for too long. These difficult decisions and choices now have become urgent issues.

A crisis of this level compels us to consider new, sometimes radical, solutions. Americans recently elected the nation's first African American president, reminding us all that our country is unique. It's one premised on opportunity, progress and constant change. Yet, as we celebrate this historic moment, our public and private sectors are engaged in critical self-analysis and reconsidering their practices to seek out bold solutions. The time is now for philanthropy to do the same. Grantmakers, their nonprofit partners and communities nationwide must heed this call and consider altering current norms and practices significantly. Now more than ever, it's vitally important for innovative and rigorous self-assessment to ensure that the civic sector is part of the solution to the pressing issues we face as a nation. And that's exactly why our Criteria for Philanthropy at Its Best is especially needed at this time.

The private, public and civil society sectors all contribute to nurturing the public good. Government is obliged to protect its citizens and provide services to those in greatest need. Private enterprise provides jobs and the economic engine that fuels our nation. Civic sector organizations—including both institutional grantmakers and non-grantmaking nonprofits—play a crucial role in improving lives and strengthening communities, often filling a void where government and free enterprise fail to adequately meet public needs. As the public and private sectors reassess their institutional practices, grantmakers must do so, too. We need to ensure that foundations remain relevant and maximize the impact of their work, which supplements the other sectors in important ways.

Now is the moment when opportunity and need intersect in a way that is unprecedented in modern history. Current philanthropic practice accomplishes many needed and beneficial things, but philanthropy is not sufficient in its current form to play the kind of substantive role required to help solve the most urgent problems facing our nation and the world. Grantmakers simply are not delivering as much social benefit as they could or should be, raising the important question of why this is so.

Our sector never can be a substitute for either the public or private sector, but grantmaking institutions must do all that is within their power to ensure that the civic sector becomes the highest performing complement to government and free enterprise. But what, specifically, should foundations and other institutional grantmakers do to maximize their impact and best serve nonprofits, vulnerable communities and the common good? That is the central question this document seeks to answer. As the world focuses on meeting the current challenges, institutional philanthropy must ask itself some long overdue, perhaps difficult, questions. The National Committee for

Responsive Philanthropy (NCRP) has developed a set of criteria to provide grantmakers with the tools to do precisely that.

There's a popular but overused saying in philanthropic circles: "If you've seen one foundation, you've seen one foundation." People use that phrase to emphasize how different each foundation is from the next. Anyone familiar with the sector knows that there is, indeed, great variability among grantmaking institutions. But many people also use the phrase to deflect criticism, arguing that the unique nature of each foundation makes it impossible to compare one foundation to another or to hold grantmakers to any standards more rigorous than those that are within bounds of the law. But that's simply not true: comparison is possible and valid, provided that it is done appropriately and with sufficient flexibility.

Just as profit is the bottom line for the private sector, impact is the most important measure for the civic sector. A foundation serves the public good if it has impact on important societal issues. It is almost impossible, however, to examine each of the nation's more than 70,000 grantmaking institutions and determine the extent to which that foundation is enhancing the public good, creating positive social benefits or advancing the public interest. Our criteria offer a meaningful tool to begin addressing this very challenge. A foundation that meets the criteria is not guaranteed to have positive impact, but it is more likely to do so than a foundation that doesn't operate in ways consistent with the criteria.

Some grantmakers are being risk-averse while waiting out the financial storm, but in this time of crisis, philanthropy should do more, not less. Conscious analysis and inclusive discussions can help us address these challenging times. I don't pretend for a minute that this will be easy for anyone, but important choices almost never are. If we see this crisis as a genuine opportunity to confront difficult issues directly, our nation's grantmakers will emerge stronger and better equipped to serve our ever-changing world.

What differentiates an exemplary grantmaker from an underperforming one? What can a foundation do to improve its relevance to nonprofits, vulnerable communities and the public? These are the challenges we've attempted to address. It's my hope that the pages that follow will inform much needed discussions and help ensure that our sector truly is meeting its tremendous potential.

## DEVELOPING THE CRITERIA

NCRP just celebrated its 33rd anniversary. As the only independent watchdog of foundations and institutional grantmakers, one of our primary roles since our founding has been to bring the voice of nonprofits and the marginalized communities these groups often serve into deliberations about philanthropic priorities and practices. The criteria clearly and intentionally reflect that history and NCRP's values as an organization. We always have been uncompromising in holding the field to a high standard. The voices of nonprofits and of vulnerable communities too often are missing when grantmakers reflect on their practice. With these criteria, we're bringing back their voices.

Our vision is that philanthropy contributes in meaningful ways to the creation of a fair, just and democratic society. It does so by serving the public good, not private interests, and by employing grantmaking practices that help nonprofits achieve their missions most effectively. Philanthropy, at its best, also strengthens democracy by responding to the needs of those with the least wealth, opportunity and power.

To develop the criteria, we used an iterative process that involved rigorous research and literature reviews, original data analysis to understand current practices, and numerous rounds of discussions and debate among a group of about 50 people over the period of approximately 15 months. We intentionally did not use a broader process because we didn't want to produce a "least-common-denominator" set of criteria. Plenty of those already are available, but they clearly haven't solved some of our most persistent challenges. We wanted the end result to be a set of criteria that truly challenges grantmakers to strengthen communities. The people involved included the NCRP board of directors, our research advisory committee, staff, and a dozen or so external advisors.

## KEY CONCEPTS

The criteria focus on values, effectiveness, ethics and commitment. We focus on values because who benefits from philanthropy does matter. Effectiveness is important because grantmakers and their nonprofit partners need to maximize impact, regardless of what issues they're addressing. Our concern with protecting the public trust, ensuring compliance with the law and maximizing the social benefit of philanthropy led to criteria focused on ethics and commitment.

The concept that foundation dollars should be viewed as "partially public" dollars is woven throughout the text. The generous tax subsidies provided to donors and to foundations make the government and the public partners with philanthropists in pursuit of the public good. NCRP believes that foundation trustees are stewards of these partially public dollars. Especially now, donors need to understand that once the funds have been placed in a foundation, it's not their money anymore.

Another key concept throughout the criteria is the idea of maximizing social benefit or impact. Everything we advocate for in this document is intended to generate the greatest amount of social good possible with limited philanthropic funds. Foundation spending is dwarfed by government spending, so it is especially important that grantmakers be strategic to maximize the community-wide benefits of their work.

> Everything we advocate for in this document is intended to generate the greatest amount of social good possible with limited philanthropic funds. Foundation spending is dwarfed by government spending, so it is especially important that grantmakers be strategic to maximize the community-wide benefits of their work.

Another theme that's woven throughout many of the chapters is a call for grantmakers to rethink the issue of "credit." What foundation doesn't want to be able to say that it supported important work with demonstrable results? That's only fair. But at the same time, it's equally relevant to reconsider whether credit should go to only one grantmaker when many others supported the same work. NCRP believes that institutional philanthropy can benefit greatly from looking at "credit" through the lens of contribution rather than attribution. We're all in this together and share many of the same goals.

## FLEXIBILITY AND LEADERSHIP

Philanthropy is nuanced and complex, but these criteria set concrete and measurable benchmarks. Some funders may view the criteria as overly prescriptive—but we don't see it that way. The criteria were developed to highlight the most important issues in philanthropy and to challenge grantmakers to assess their current practices critically and determine if and how to change the ways they do business. Flexibility, courage and leadership are crucially important for these criteria to have meaning-

ful impact on philanthropic practice. This is particularly true in light of the current challenges our sector is facing.

To be clear, this is not a rankings system and shouldn't be viewed as such. A foundation that meets eight of the 10 measurable benchmarks isn't necessarily better than a foundation that meets only five. We recognize that there may be good reasons for a particular grantmaking institution not to live up to certain benchmarks we put forward. But the four criteria and the 10 associated benchmarks are, in our view, the most critically important issues for foundations to consider if they want to contribute to the common good to the greatest extent possible.

We intentionally haven't created a scoring system to go along with the criteria, and we haven't assigned relative weight or importance to the benchmarks. Additionally, there isn't enough quality data available at this time for us to be able to rank or score foundations based on the criteria. And even if there were enough data available, ranking would be extremely difficult without creating perverse incentives to reward the wrong behaviors in some situations. The appendix lists what we call "field leaders," or those foundations that we're aware of and have access to information from that appear to meet or exceed the benchmarks. It's important to understand when looking at these lists that we might have excluded a particular grantmaker not because it isn't practicing exemplary philanthropy or even because it doesn't meet that particular benchmark. It might be an outcome of data limitations—an important reason to view these lists as illustrative rather than exhaustive. Still, I think it's important to highlight those grantmakers that we do know practice Philanthropy at Its Best, and it's also a reason we want to engage in dialogue with funders that believe they should be listed so we can acknowledge them in other ways.

Some grantmakers will find that the current economic crisis makes it challenging for them to live up to some of these criteria. But the financial crisis also makes the practices we recommend all that much more important. We also understand that smaller foundations, or foundations with particular trust restrictions, will find some of the benchmarks espe-

> A criterion that seems challenging is a vital starting point for truly intentional and robust debate about why this is so; we want grantmakers to wrestle with these issues. It's our role as the sector's watchdog to push for a real transformation in philanthropy. We don't, however, intend to be dogmatic or inflexible in pursuit of compliance with the criteria.

cially challenging to meet. And here's where courage and leadership come into play. A criterion that seems challenging is a vital starting point for truly intentional and robust debate about why this is so; we want grantmakers to wrestle with these issues. It's our role as the sector's watchdog to push for a real transformation in philanthropy. We don't, however, intend to be dogmatic or inflexible in pursuit of compliance with the criteria.

Ultimately, it's up to the leadership of each institution to decide how it's going to operate and whether or not it makes sense to meet or exceed the benchmarks for each criterion. We've made what I believe is a compelling case for each criterion, and we've shown that the benchmarks are achievable by giving examples of grantmakers that already meet or exceed them. Foundation trustees, then, as stewards and protectors of the public trust, have the responsibility to consider what course of action they will take, and it is my hope that trustees and executives at foundations will engage courageously in vigorous discussions and debate about these important issues. These conversations will help each grantmaker clarify why it operates the way it does and will encourage examination of why certain practices are or are not consistent with a foundation's mission and with the broader public interests.

## REGULATION

Regulation, when crafted properly, is hugely beneficial to our society. It also is clear that deregulation and a lack of oversight can have disastrous consequences—simply consider the current economic crisis as an example. Former Federal Reserve Chairman Alan Greenspan stated in congressional testimony in October 2008 that that he "made a mistake" in trusting that free markets could regulate themselves without sufficient government oversight.

It's no different for philanthropy. NCRP believes that regulation of grantmaking institutions is essential. Over the years, NCRP has engaged in efforts to influence the regulation of foundations, and we surely will be involved in such efforts again in the future. Foundations remain some of the most loosely-regulated institutions in the country; this has both positive benefits and serious negative consequences. This particular document, however, is not a call for regulatory action on these issues. Instead, we view these criteria as central to informing meaningful self-regulation for foundations and other institutional grantmakers. If foundations don't do a better job of regulating themselves with integrity and rigor, and if more grantmakers don't demonstrate their relevance to nonprofits and marginalized communities by meeting the benchmarks set forth in this document, the likelihood of more government regulation of the sector will increase.

## HOW TO USE THE CRITERIA

Each chapter provides a compelling case for one of the criteria, citing the latest research and providing original new data in some cases. We put a tremendous amount of time and effort into ensuring that these criteria reflect the most current qualitative and quantitative analyses available to us. Various institutions and individuals will find value in the criteria and each will use this document in different ways.

As stated before, we hope grantmakers will find the criteria helpful in examining their work. There are discussion questions at the end of each chapter so that executives and trustees can explore deeply how each criterion applies to their foundation. For example, a family foundation board might want to discuss one chapter at each of its next four meetings. Because we identify funders that currently meet or exceed the benchmarks we've established, grantmakers can compare their own practices to those of their peers. We also have an interactive online self-test so that foundations can measure their performance based on our criteria.

Journalists will find the criteria helpful when writing stories about foundations or other grantmakers in their communities. Often, journalists assigned to cover stories about philanthropy have little prior experience in the sector, so we hope that this will be a useful tool for them. In cases of suspected abuse, for example, a journalist can consult the ethics chapter to determine whether or not the suspected abuser has been following the recommendations or meeting NCRP's benchmarks.

Nonprofits will find much value in these criteria as well. We hope that grantees will use the criteria as a tool to empower themselves to raise critical issues in thoughtful ways with program officers and foundation leaders. The document is full of information that grantees can use to make compelling arguments to their funders about why they need support for their advocacy work or a multi-year grant, for example.

Policymakers, too, will find the benchmarks and the mapping of current practices informative when considering issues related to philanthropy. The growing number of academic centers focused on philanthropy also surely will find value in this text.

And finally, NCRP will, of course, use these criteria for years to come in our work. We'll highlight grantmakers that exceed the benchmarks, and we'll criticize, when appropriate, funders that fall short. That's the role of a watchdog, after all. We're challenging grantmakers to strengthen communities and we believe that these criteria provide the right tools to do just that. Our goal when criticizing grantmakers is to maximize the net benefit of philanthropy to society, which is the bottom line for ensuring that our sector remains viable, relevant and sustainable.

As more grantmakers live up to these criteria in the coming years, they will increase their impact on important issues, enhance the public good and strengthen the public trust. This will benefit not only the whole nonprofit sector, but our entire society.

Aaron Dorfman
Executive Director
National Committee for Responsive Philanthropy
March 2009

## RESEARCH ADVISORY COMMITTEE

# Criteria for Philanthropy at Its Best

## CRITERION I: VALUES

A grantmaker practicing Philanthropy at Its Best serves the public good by contributing to a strong, participatory democracy that engages all communities.

a) Provides at least 50 percent of its grant dollars to benefit lower-income communities, communities of color and other marginalized groups, broadly defined

b) Provides at least 25 percent of its grant dollars for advocacy, organizing and civic engagement to promote equity, opportunity and justice in our society

## CRITERION II: EFFECTIVENESS

A grantmaker practicing Philanthropy at Its Best serves the public good by investing in the health, growth and effectiveness of its nonprofit partners.

a) Provides at least 50 percent of its grant dollars for general operating support

b) Provides at least 50 percent of its grant dollars as multi-year grants

c) Ensures that the time to apply for and report on the grant is commensurate with grant size

## CRITERION III: ETHICS

A grantmaker practicing Philanthropy at Its Best serves the public good by demonstrating accountability and transparency to the public, its grantees and constituents.

a) Maintains an engaged board of at least five people who include among them a diversity of perspectives—including of the communities it serves—and who serve without compensation

b) Maintains policies and practices that support ethical behavior

c) Discloses information freely

## CITERION IV: COMMITMENT

A grantmaker practicing Philanthropy at Its Best serves the public good by engaging a substantial portion of its financial assets in pursuit of its mission.

a) Pays out at least 6 percent of its assets annually in grants

b) Invests at least 25 percent of its assets in ways that support its mission

# Chapter I: Values

# Criterion I: Values — At A Glance

A grantmaker practicing Philanthropy at Its Best serves the public good by contributing to a strong, participatory democracy that engages all communities.

a) Provides at least 50 percent of its grant dollars to benefit lower-income communities, communities of color and other marginalized groups, broadly defined

b) Provides at least 25 percent of its grant dollars for advocacy, organizing and civic engagement to promote equity, opportunity and justice in our society

> Philanthropic support for people and communities that historically have been marginalized is extremely low. Although serving disadvantaged communities is not the only purpose of philanthropy, it should be a much higher priority than it is. In the aggregate, only 33 percent of grant dollars can be classified as benefitting marginalized communities, even very broadly defined.[1] This is cause for concern in spite of the fact that philanthropy and the charitable sector are not a substitute for public programs; the government has an obligation to assist the country's underserved populations.

> By intentionally elevating vulnerable populations in their grantmaking, foundations benefit society and strengthen our democracy. Prioritizing marginalized communities brings about positive benefits for the public good. "Targeted universalism" is one of the most effective strategies for doing this.

> Income and wealth inequality impact the entire U.S. economy negatively. Grantmakers that pursue social inclusion for the economically disadvantaged help not only the poor, but broader society as well. Race persists as a significant barrier to social inclusion and to achieving the American Dream. Grantmakers that prioritize racial and ethnic minorities see benefits accrue to people of all races.

> Overcoming social problems for any marginalized group is complicated and multifaceted. Grantmakers that use systems thinking to guide their work recognize this and are leading the way, helping philanthropy be more relevant in addressing pressing social needs.

> Advocacy, community organizing and civic engagement have played essential roles in the development of our society and our democracy. They are among the most effective strategies for implementing a systems approach and for achieving a significant, measurable impact on a variety of issues. These efforts advance democratic renewal and enhance civic engagement.

> Leading the field, 108 foundations (13.35 percent of our sample) provided at least 50 percent of their grant dollars for the intended benefit of marginalized communities. Also noteworthy, 56 foundations (6.9 percent) provided at least 25 percent of their grant dollars for social justice. These are the benchmarks for Philanthropy at Its Best.

# Chapter I: Values

Social inclusion is based on the belief that we all fare better when no one is left to fall too far behind and the economy works for everyone. Social inclusion simultaneously incorporates multiple dimensions of well-being. It is achieved when all have the opportunity and resources necessary to participate fully in economic, social and cultural activities which are considered the societal norm.

– Heather Boushey et al.,
Center for Economic and Policy Research & Inclusion[2]

Many foundations play an extremely important role in the civil society sector by prioritizing marginalized communities in their grantmaking and thus enhancing substantive, participatory democracy. Contributing to the public good in this way is in keeping with what Alexis de Tocqueville identified in the 19th century as the feature that distinguishes the United States from Europe. Citing the power of the "voluntary association" he observed during his travels throughout the country, he contended that the freedom of U.S. citizens coming together united by a common purpose would connect them to civil and political society in which they shared common democratic values.[3] Tocqueville argued that such connections made U.S. democracy truly participatory and inclusive, identifying the relationships between social equality and democracy and between that equality and voluntary association.[4]

By focusing intentionally on the most marginal in their grantmaking, foundations can promote greater equality and enhance the ability of underserved populations to contribute meaningfully to the democratic process and improve social capital nationwide. Importantly, by elevating vulnerable populations in

philanthropy, everyone in society benefits and our inclusive democracy is strengthened, with positive benefits that extend well beyond marginalized communities. Unfortunately, too few foundations take advantage of their independence and accumulated wealth to enhance the common good in this way. Instead, they often practice patronage giving by providing grants to large educational or cultural institutions that primarily serve the elite, eschewing the needs of the most vulnerable in our society.

Philanthropic support for people and communities that historically have been marginalized is extremely low. Although serving disadvantaged communities is not the only purpose of philanthropy, it should be a much higher priority than it is. NCRP acknowledges that grants to promote the eradication of disease, to advance higher learning, to promote excellence in the arts, or to protect the environment often have substantial benefit for all people, including those who historically are or have been marginalized. Yet, there are many reasons for foundations and institutional grantmakers to prioritize giving for struggling communities in their grantmaking. Many of the great American philanthropists have used their surplus wealth to benefit underserved populations and groups that are marginalized; indeed, focusing on underrepresented populations is an important part of the American philanthropic tradition. The belief that philanthropy ought to give precedence to the economically disadvantaged persists today among some modern-day U.S. grantmaking institutions. Disappointingly, the vast majority of foundations do not prioritize underserved communities in this way.

This chapter provides background and rationale for why every foundation has an obligation to direct some of its funding to benefit those with the least wealth, opportunity and power. A brief overview of the evolution of institutionalized grantmaking in the United States grounds this analysis, and human development and social inclusion offer persuasive reasons for philanthropy to rethink economic well-being. Next, a review of the macroeconomic effects of income and wealth inequality makes the case for philanthropy's special role in focusing on the economically disadvantaged. Race persists as a significant barrier to equality of achievement in the United States, compelling philanthropy to lead by example by prioritizing racial and ethnic minorities in grantmaking. Finally, advocacy, community organizing and civic engagement are presented as important ways to see an inclusive, participatory democracy in action. They are demonstrated as among the most effective strategies to address the special needs of vulnerable communities. Importantly, adopting this criterion and elevating marginalized populations in grantmaking results in broad community-wide benefits. This increases the impact of philanthropic giving, maximizing the return on investment and generating sustainable benefits enjoyed by all members of our society.

vide services to underserved populations. But philanthropy has a special responsibility to nurture and strengthen democracy, and the nonprofit sector is positioned uniquely to promote the health of our pluralistic and diverse society. By enhancing the voice of the disenfranchised in decision making, removing barriers to civic participation and addressing the imbalances of power created by our free enterprise system, institutional grantmaking can make important contributions to advancing equity for all Americans.

While recognizing the disempowering potential of the phrase "marginalized communities,"[5] the latter part of this chapter provides the rationale for why foundations should prioritize economic and racial justice as two important mechanisms for maximizing the public benefit from philanthropy. In the words of Dr. Martin Luther King Jr., "Philanthropy is commendable, but it must not cause the philanthropist to overlook the circumstances of economic injustice that make the philanthropy necessary."[6]

## PRECEDENTS AND RATIONALES FOR PHILANTHROPY THAT BENEFITS MARGINALIZED COMMUNITIES

Historical, religious, philosophical and economic precedents have motivated many American grantmakers to prioritize vulnerable populations in institutional philanthropy.

### The roots of American philanthropy: from Carnegie to Gates

Andrew Carnegie, the Scottish immigrant and steel magnate, often is cited as one of the first American philanthropists. In 1901, Carnegie established major philanthropic institutions and was engaged in charitable giving until his death in 1911. In his seminal 1889 text, *The Gospel of Wealth*, Carnegie addressed capitalism and its impact on the distribution of

> I believe that with great wealth comes great responsibility, a responsibility to give back to society, a responsibility to see that those resources are put to work in the best possible way to help those most in need.
>
> – Bill Gates, Founder, Bill and Melinda Gates Foundation[7]

NCRP strongly believes that philanthropy and the charitable sector are not a substitute for public programs; the government has many obligations to pro-

wealth and resources. His awareness of the inequities of wealth created by this system guided his philanthropic giving later on. Carnegie believed that capitalism promotes the "best interests of the race … but … inevitably gives wealth to the few." Carnegie saw the millionaire as the "trustee for the poor, intrusted [sic] for a season with a great part of the increased wealth of the community."[8] Despite the paternalistic tone of much of his writing in *Gospel*, Carnegie recognized that the wealthy owed their largesse, in no small part, to the poor people who worked for them and helped create their wealth. Thus, he prioritized improving the community and gave precedence in his charitable work to those who suffered from deep wealth inequality.

The Gates Foundation's focus on improving global health by tackling HIV/AIDS and malaria provides one example of modern day philanthropy that reflects Carnegie's values. Gates, like Carnegie, sees a moral obligation to prioritize the needs of disadvantaged communities because the free enterprise system has worked tremendously to his benefit. Gates wants his foundation, which now accounts for one of every ten foundation dollars provided to nonprofits, to focus on the economically disadvantaged.[9]

In fact, Gates reiterated his rationale for prioritizing marginalized groups in his first annual letter about the Gates Foundation posted on its website in January 2009. Gates said, "Foundations provide something unique when they work on behalf of the poor, who have no market power, or when they work in areas like health or education, where the market doesn't naturally work toward the right goals and where the innovation requires long-term investments. These investments are high-risk and high-reward. But the reward isn't measured by financial gain, it's measured by the number of lives saved or people lifted out of poverty."[10]

Hundreds of other large and small grantmaking institutions of all types, independent, family, community and corporate, also elevate the economically disadvantaged or other marginalized communities in their work. These foundations, while too few in number, are too numerous to name here and are an important part of the American philanthropic tradition.

## The religious grounding of Western philanthropy

Institutional philanthropy in the West is premised on ethical values articulated in the Judeo-Christian traditions.[11] The faith-based motivations of early and modern day philanthropists are part of the rationale for why foundations should prioritize those with the least wealth and opportunity. Importantly, philan-

thropy and acts of charitable giving to help the needy and the poor are not the exclusive realm of western religious traditions. Islam, Buddhism, Hinduism, Sikhism and the Greco-Roman "pagan" religions each prioritize the needs of those who are most marginalized and provide guidance on how individual charity and institutional philanthropy can work to improve the lot of those who are most in need. The ethics and values that ground philanthropy and charity across the world draw extensively from the native religious traditions from which each evolved. A common theme across faiths is the appropriate redistribution of excess wealth by redistributing resources to those who are marginalized or lack opportunity. It is on the basis of these moral principles that exemplary philanthropy defensibly can be argued, by necessity and definition, to focus on those with the least wealth, opportunity and power.

## Philosophical arguments for prioritizing marginalized communities

Harvard political philosopher John Rawls, among the most prominent 20th century American thinkers, is perhaps best known for his contribution regarding how a just and fair welfare state ought to be designed. In *A Theory of Justice*, Rawls articulated his now famous and often cited principles of distributive justice. The first principle calls for all people to have "equal rights to the most extensive system of basic civil liberties." The second principle, also called the "distributive justice principle," states that the socio-economic inequalities inherent in the free market system are morally justifiable if they "work to the benefit of the least advantaged"[12] in our society. Rawls sought to ensure justice and fairness, with an emphasis on redistributive justice in the welfare state. Rawls asserted that all wealth in society is made by the cooperation of all the members of society in the context of the arrangements of basic institutions. He stated that there are two types of societies: a capitalist welfare society and a democratic property owning society. The first is concerned with order and will support welfare for the purpose of maintaining order and serving capital. The latter will arrange institutions and norms to support democracy and welfare to secure membership. Capital will be arranged to support democracy and people.[13] In 1999, President Bill Clinton acknowledged Rawls' important contributions by awarding him the National Medal of the Arts and the National

Humanities Medal. Clinton described Rawls as "perhaps the greatest political philosopher of the 20th century. In 1971, when Hillary and I were in law school, we were among the millions moved by a remarkable book he wrote, *A Theory of Justice*, that placed our rights to liberty and justice upon a strong and brilliant new foundation of reason."[14]

Unlike Michael Walzer, who calls for "simple equality,"[15] Rawls believed that inequality must be arranged to serve larger societal goals. In other words, recognizing the implicit power imbalances inherent in the free market system, he argued that inequality could be justified only if the needs of the most disadvantaged are prioritized in the welfare state. Rawls's principles of distributive justice easily are adaptable to philanthropy, with the caveat that charitable organizations are supplementing or complementing, not substituting for, public services. As NCRP's previous work on using Rawls's principles to increase philanthropy's impact stated, "There is a simple elegance in resting social justice philanthropy on these two Rawlsian principles. It requires philanthropy … to direct its attention to those populations that are most disadvantaged."[16] Foundations can play a critical role in democracy by engaging in grantmaking to support membership in society. Philanthropy can increase its impact substantially by directing a significant portion of its resources to those with the least wealth, opportunity and power, to mitigate differences created by our normalized free enterprise socio-economic system that is predicated on inequality.

Great levels of disparity undermine human dignity and our democracy, disallowing the economically marginalized from fully engaging in participatory democracy or realizing their human capabilities and freedoms.

### Social inclusion and human development

As Nobel-laureate economist Amartya Sen highlights, poverty is more than the lack of income or wealth. Poverty is the deprivation of basic human freedoms and capabilities. Emphasizing the historical concern of the social sciences with empowering the lives and capabilities of ordinary citizens, Sen cites the work of free market economists and the Greek philosophers to describe wealth as a means to accomplish something else. "We have to judge the success of a society, including its economy, not just in terms of national wealth or the ubiquitous GNP [Gross National Product], but in terms of the freedoms and capabilities that people enjoy to live as they would value living."[17]

The concept of human development is attributable to Mahbub ul Haq, former finance minister of Pakistan and a pioneering economist of the 20th century. He contended that human progress indicators in developing countries were deficient: they did not present an accurate representation of the real purpose of development, i.e., to improve peoples' lives. Working with Sen and other economists, in 1990, Dr. Haq oversaw production of the first United Nations (U.N.) *Human Development Report*; more than 500 regional and national reports produced since then have sparked important public debates and political engagement.[18] Sen defines human development as "concerned with what I take to be the basic development idea: namely, advancing the richness of human life, rather than the richness of the economy in which human beings live, which is only a part of it." His focus on human development and individuals' ability to exercise their freedoms and capabilities bolsters economic arguments in support of increasing philanthropic resources to benefit the poor.[19]

Sen posits that economic theory lends credence to addressing the needs of those most disadvantaged by the inequities generated by the free enterprise system. Linking human development in the context of economic mobility and an understanding of the connectivity between the two provides institutional grantmaking with a salient rationale to work toward an inclusive poverty paradigm that looks beyond the base measures of economic inequality. In the United States, this leads to an analysis of structural barriers that work to exclude vulnerable populations from equally enjoying the socio-political freedoms and benefits of democratic participation. The United States, however, never had applied a human development approach to well-being in assessing the country's health until 2008.

Rigorous research informed by lessons learned from international development work led to the American Human Development Report, *The Measure of America*. Researchers developed a first-ever American Human Development Index (HDI) that combines human-focused indicators into a single measure of progress and well-being.[20] An important feature of the HDI is that it addresses explicitly human capabilities or the potential for what individuals are or could become. The U.S. HDI was built by analyzing society, which determines the extent to which capabilities can be exercised. Next, three dimensions of capabilities that can be measured—

longevity, access to knowledge and a decent standard of living—were added. Researchers then used geography, gender and race/ethnicity to assess variations among groups resulting in three indices (health, education and income), which then culminate in a composite American HDI. While the dimensions are the same as those used in the U.N.'s standard HDI, the American HDI uses different indicators.[21] Linking human development with social inclusion provides a unique opportunity to advance American well-being on multiple dimensions: economic, social, political, religious, environmental and more.

Inequality is associated with negative outcomes for all society and base measures such as the income gap fail to capture these ripple effects. Contextualizing poverty as both an outcome and root cause of social exclusion is the fundamental premise of moving to social inclusion. Heather Boushey et al. explain social inclusion as "based on the belief that we all fare better when no one is left to fall too far behind and the economy works for everyone."[22]

Similar to the HDI, indicators in a social inclusion paradigm would "assess the extent to which low-paid workers fall behind the rest of the workforce, not only in terms of wages and income, but in a variety of dimensions, including health, education, housing, skills, advancement, and opportunity."[23] For example, in the United Kingdom and Europe, poverty is viewed in this multifaceted way. Poverty is not measured simply as the lack of adequate income; rather, it reflects measures of economic mobility, life opportunities—access to housing, financial and health services—and inclusion. Just as poverty has the potential to divide us, social inclusion offers the opportunity to unite us, with broad society-wide understanding of the reasons for inequality and how improving conditions for the most marginal benefits us all.[24]

Human development and social inclusion provide compelling reasons for institutional grantmakers to contribute to the public good by supporting policies that seek to create a more level playing field. By prioritizing the marginalized communities in grantmaking, philanthropy has the opportunity to maximize the impact of its giving by looking beyond economic indicators to assess the health of people and society on multiple dimensions of well-being. Human development, the capabilities approach and social inclusion provide three tangible ways to reshape how our society conceives of poverty, with better outcomes seen by all communities nationwide.

## INCOME AND WEALTH INEQUALITY

Research demonstrates consistently that the gap between the rich and the poor is the most significant predictor of the health of a country.[26] An analysis of data from the Census Bureau and the Federal Reserve Bank shows that between 1975 and 2005, U.S. households in the bottom 80 percent of the income

> Although we Americans strive to provide equality of economic opportunity, we do not guarantee equality of economic outcomes, nor should we. That said, we also believe that no one should be allowed to slip too far down the economic ladder.
>
> – Ben Bernanke, Chairman, Federal Reserve[25]

distribution saw their proportion of national income decline. Similarly, households in the bottom 40 percent of the income bracket witnessed a drop in income when adjusted for inflation, while the top 20 percent of households in the U.S. saw an increase in their income share, with the lion's share of the increases going to the top 5 percent of households measured by income. Households in the top one-fifth of the income bracket earned about half of the country's income and controlled more than 80 percent of national wealth.[27]

Income inequality in the United States remains a significant barrier to improving one's quality of life and data suggest that income inequality has been exacerbated in recent years. As noted in *The Measure of America*, while real mean income is more than twice what it was in 1947, the income distribution shows extreme concentration among the top quintile of the population. For example, the richest 20 percent of U.S. households earned 50.5 percent of total income in 2006, compared to 3.4 percent earned by the bottom 20 percent.[29] Income inequality in the United

## TABLE 1.1 INCOME INEQUALITY OVER TIME: SHARE OF HOUSEHOLD INCOME[28]

| Year | Highest Quintile | Middle Quintile | Lowest Quintile |
|------|------|------|------|
| 1975 | 43.6 | 17.0 | 4.3 |
| 1985 | 45.6 | 16.2 | 3.9 |
| 1995 | 48.7 | 15.2 | 3.7 |
| 2005 | 50.4 | 14.6 | 3.4 |

## TABLE 1.2 INCOME INEQUALITY: GINI INDEX OVER TIME[33]

| Year | Gini Index |
|------|------|
| 1975 | 0.397 |
| 1985 | 0.419 |
| 1995 | 0.450 |
| 2005 | 0.469 |

## TABLE 1.3 CONCENTRATED POVERTY RATES IN URBAN AREAS[35]

| City | Percent |
|------|------|
| Fresno, CA | 43.5 |
| New Orleans, LA | 37.7 |
| Louisville, KY | 36.7 |
| Miami, FL | 36.4 |
| Atlanta, GA | 35.8 |
| Long Beach, CA | 30.7 |
| Cleveland, OH | 29.8 |
| Philadelphia, PA | 27.9 |
| Milwaukee, WI | 27.0 |
| New York, NY | 25.9 |

## TABLE 1.4 POVERTY RATES IN RURAL AREAS[36]

| Area | Percent |
|------|------|
| McKinley County, NM | 45.6 |
| Holmes County, MS | 41.1 |
| McDowell County, WV | 37.7 |
| Martin County, KY | 37.0 |
| Blackfeet Reservation, MT | 33.8 |

States is similar to the levels observed in developing countries, as seen in Table 1.2.[30] According to the Census Bureau's 2007 American Community Survey (ACS), the Gini index for the United States stood at 0.464, ranging from a high value of 0.537 in the District of Columbia to a low of 0.410 in Utah; most developed countries have Gini indices ranging from 0.23 to well-below that of the United States.[31] The ACS notes that based on 2006 income data, fully 13.3 percent of the U.S. population was living in poverty. Moreover, as several economists and policymakers have noted, the current federal poverty measure depresses the actual level of poverty because it fails to account, for example, for regional variation in the cost of living. According to the Department of Health and Human Services, in 2006, the federal poverty level (FPL) was $9,800 for an individual and $20,000 for family of four.[32] Proposed alternate poverty measures account for basic costs of living such as shelter and food. In contrast, the FPL was established in 1969 and is based primarily on a household's pre-tax income that is spent on food consumption. Rethinking how poverty is measured and defined in the context of human development and capabilities provides a more comprehensive measure of economic well-being. As noted earlier, in the United Kingdom, poverty measures account for access to quality health and education services. Poverty thus is both a root cause and an outcome of social exclusion.

### Urban and rural poverty

Concentrated poverty refers to areas in which the poverty rate exceeds 40 percent for residents of these communities. In 2005, 10.3 percent of the United States population in the 50 largest cities lived in these impoverished, often racially segregated, neighborhoods.[34] Disaggregated data show disproportionately high levels of concentrated poverty in urban areas.

Rural areas also are disproportionately poor. Lack of infrastructure in rural communities often is attributed to disinvestment by public and private entities in these marginal areas. However, private and government investment in rural areas does not always serve the public interest or advance the economic well-being of these communities. As the ACS notes, Utah's Gini is not statistically different than the indices for Alaska, New Hampshire, Vermont or Wyoming. Table 1.4 demonstrates recent trends in rural poverty.

These data demonstrate how rural and inner city populations remain economically marginalized and the lack of voice afforded these communities in decision making that directly impacts their lives and the state of their communities. States such as California, for example, demonstrate how aggregated income data often obscure the variation within states that, on a cursory look, appear to be doing well. Median income in California was close to $56,000, placing it among the ten richest states; yet, the concentrated poverty statistics from Fresno and Long Beach show the persistence of high intra-state income inequality.

It is particularly important for foundations that want to prioritize the economically disadvantaged in grantmaking to analyze disaggregated data to maximize the impact of their grantmaking. A foundation should thus adopt nuanced lenses to determine which communities are historically and persistently denied economic gains seen by neighboring communities within and across states. Importantly, income data provide only a partial representation of poverty in the United States; when analyses of wealth are added to income, the gap between the rich and the poor increases significantly.

### Wealth versus income as a gauge of economic well-being

Since the 1990s, many analyses of economic well-being have shifted their focus from income inequality to wealth inequality. Numerous advantages are correlated with wealth acquisition, including the potential to break the intergenerational transmission of poverty by investing in human capital.[37] These advantages cannot be capitalized on by gains in income alone. The potential to accumulate private wealth reflects institutional arrangements; thus, such analyses speak directly to the role of public policies in fostering and perpetuating how these arrangements work. Moreover, the correlation between income and wealth holdings is surprisingly weak.[38] As Supreme Court Justice Louis Brandeis said, "We can have a democratic society or we can have great concentration of wealth in the hands of a few. We cannot have both."[39]

Wealth provides a more comprehensive understanding of economic disparities for four reasons: liquid assets that can be converted into money are a source of consumption funds independent of current income; homeownership provides more fiscal options to the owner; times of economic crisis can be managed more easily by households with access to liquid assets; and there is a relationship between the distribution of power and wealth distribution.[40] Moreover,

deep wealth inequality leads to macroeconomic conditions that take a serious toll on all Americans of limited financial means. The 2004 Survey of Consumer Finances shows that the wealthiest 5 percent of the population had a median net worth of $924,100 compared to $7,500 for the bottom 20 percent of the population.[41] Graph 1.1 below demonstrates wealth inequality over time measured in 2004 dollars; these data show that wealth inequality has increased. The top 5 percent in particular show a consistent upward trend while wealth for the lowest quintile remains stagnant and extremely low.

Income and wealth inequality negatively affect the entire U.S. economy. Highly concentrated wealth is correlated with concentrated power; this power directly influences the macroeconomic environment, health outcomes, civic engagement and democratic participation. As Chuck Collins notes, high levels of inequality undermine the economic health and well-being of the entire country because as wages fail to keep up with the rising costs of living, the average household's purchasing power is diminished, despite having to work more and often accumulating additional debt simply to stay afloat. Because these trends are not sustainable in the long term, they destabilize the entire economy.[42] Moreover, wealth inequality has a disproportionate negative impact on several special population groups. For example, female-headed households with children had a mean net

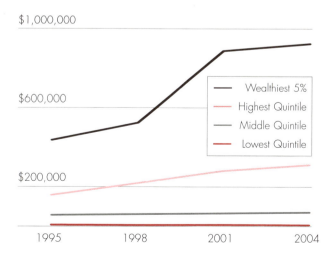

SOURCE: Brian K. Bucks et al., "Recent Changes in U.S. Family Finances: Evidence from the 2001 and 2004 Survey of Consumer Finances," Federal Reserve Bulletin (2006): A8

worth of $61,200 compared to married couple-headed households, which had $370,300, placing female single-parents at a severe disadvantage in being able to deal with financial crises or unforeseen economic hardship.[43] Quantitative analysis further demonstrates the alarming levels of inequality: the richest 1 percent of the U.S. population holds close to one-third of all private wealth.[44] In contrast, the bottom 90 percent of the population accounts for nearly 75 percent of all debts and liabilities.[45] NCRP's analysis of Foundation Center data on special population groups indicates that in the aggregate, just above 20 percent of grant dollars is given for the intended benefit of the economically disadvantaged.[46] This figure is disappointingly low in light of the preceding analysis.

### A socially inclusive poverty paradigm

A reconception of poverty offers a powerful framework to change the economic policy paradigm. The lenses of human development and social inclusion shift the focus from individual poverty to a model of

> To be clear, our grantmaking has never been, and will never become, a welfare program. And because we will not turn away from the reality that structural and institutional racism continue to undermine our effectiveness, it does not mean that we intend to become a civil rights advocacy organization. [...] To move the Kellogg Foundation forward, to move from "better to best" as we "Connect our Legacy to the Future," we are committed to dealing head-on with the truth that racial inequality is a root problem that must be eliminated if we value the potential in all of our children and their families.
>
> – Joseph Stewart, Chair, Board of Trustees, W.K. Kellogg Foundation[50]

social inclusion. Because Americans tend to view poverty as failure at the individual level, economic mobility must be reframed in a community-based model, one in which poverty is seen as the outcome of structures and policy.[47] Connecting the theoretical model of social inclusion approach to poverty accomplishes several objectives. First, it recognizes implicitly the historical impact of structural barriers to wealth accumulation today, addressing the complexities of quantifying its impact.[48] Second, by moving away from traditional conceptions of poverty as failures at the individual level, it provides a more inclusive means to reposition poverty as an issue of concern for

all communities. Third, and perhaps most importantly for philanthropy to elevate marginalized groups in grantmaking, social inclusion posits a discursive and paradigmatic shift in how poverty is viewed, one that is consistent with deep-seated moral values that aim to empower and improve the life opportunities for all individuals and communities. As Boushey et al. note, "From a *values* perspective, a poverty framework is counterproductive because Americans attribute poverty to individual characteristics—such as a lack of a work ethic. The concept of social inclusion has the advantage of situating individuals in a social and relational context. Moreover, the experience of exclusion of some sort, unlike the experience of poverty or discrimination, is nearly universal."[49]

## RACIAL INEQUALITY AND STRUCTURAL RACIALIZATION

Race persists as a significant barrier to social inclusion and to realizing the American Dream. As with income and wealth inequality, philanthropic interventions to address explicitly the unequal playing field because of race provides philanthropy with an opportunity to improve the overall health of American democracy and to directly confront this country's history of racial discrimination. The analysis presents a transformative approach to identifying and discussing race. The benefit of philanthropy that addresses race-based exclusion can generate positive outcomes that extend far beyond the beneficiaries of grants that work toward racial justice.

### Income, wealth inequality and race

Income inequality is a substantial barrier to economic justice; when the data are disaggregated by race, it is clear that racialized poverty persists as a problem today. Census data suggest that racial income inequality has remained at consistent levels over time, with white households clearly earning more than black or Hispanic households.

## TABLE 1.5: INCOME INEQUALITY BY RACE: MEDIAN HOUSEHOLD INCOME[51]

| Year | White | Black | Hispanic |
|------|-------|-------|----------|
| 2005 | $53,937 | $32,774 | $38,200 |
| 1995 | $50,225 | $30,251 | $30,882 |
| 1985 | $46,801 | $27,232 | $32,095 |
| 1975 | $43,566 | $25,958 | $31,063 |

Data suggest that wealth remains highly concentrated in the hands of a disproportionately small percentage of the population. Recent statistics on wealth and race drawn from the 2004 Survey of Consumer Finances by the Federal Reserve paint a bleak picture of the racial distribution of U.S. wealth.

The ratio of wealth holdings by race has remained relatively constant, despite absolute gains in wealth for all. More than 24 percent of white households received an inheritance with the average transfer amount equaling $115,000. In contrast, only 11 percent of black households reported receiving inheritance monies and the mean value of the inheritance was $32,000.[52] This analysis highlights the disadvantaged position of African Americans in the intergenerational transmission of wealth. It also identifies the biggest inheritance deficit among African Americans in the bottom quintile of wealth distribution in the United States.[53] Analysis of old-age poverty and race based on data from the 2004 Health and Retirement Study shows that while less than 10 percent of adults over the age of 65 live in poverty, the rates are double for elderly Hispanics and triple for older African Americans. Adding wealth measures to this analysis reveals greater resource deficiency for elder communities of color. African Americans were 6.4 times more likely than their white counterparts to be asset-poor while older Hispanics were 8.1 times more likely to be poor.[54] The relevant question to ask then is: *why* do racialized wealth disparities persist?

Complementing the rationale for philanthropy that benefits those with the least opportunity leads naturally to a frank discussion of race in the United States. NCRP sees inclusive racial equity efforts as extremely important: emphasizing racial justice is the entry point for foundations to address broader issues of equity for special population groups including but not limited to the elderly, the disabled, immigrants, crime or abuse victims, offenders and ex-offenders, LGBTQ populations, refugees and women and girls. Just as income and wealth inequality have negative spillover effects on the broader society, racial inequality and injustice negatively impacts all of us. Shifting how we view race creates positive opportunities to advance our diverse and pluralistic society by addressing structural barriers to social inclusion.

### Structural barriers to race, gender and class equality

Despite progress, exclusion caused by discrimination persists as a barrier toward realizing social inclusion. An analysis of metropolitan housing markets conducted by the U.S. Department of Housing and Urban Development (HUD) using 2000 data from the Urban Institute found persistent racial discrimination in both the rental and homeownership markets. The baseline data are drawn from 1977 and 1989 when HUD and Urban conducted two similar matched-pairs testing studies to determine whether racial bias is evident in the housing market. In both studies, two individuals, one white and one non-white, with identical socio-economic backgrounds, credit histories and other financial characteristics approach real estate or rental agencies to explore their options. Differential treatment can be attributed to racial discrimination because other factors that would influence outcomes, such as income and age, are controlled for. Overall, the findings of the 2000 analysis indicated persistent housing discrimination against Hispanics and African Americans compared to whites, despite progress in some areas.[55]

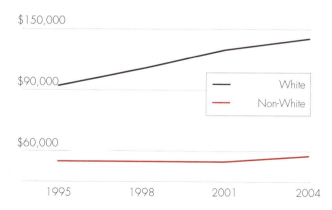

### GRAPH 1.2 WEALTH INEQUALITY BY RACE: MEDIAN NET WORTH 1995–2004

SOURCE: Brian K. Bucks, Arthur B. Kennickell, and Kevin B. Moore, "Recent Changes in U.S. Family Finances: Evidence from the 2001 and 2004 Survey of Consumer Finances," Federal Reserve Bulletin (2006) A8

The dominant diversity framework focuses on individual level racism; it presumes an individual actor, a racist, and an individual act, racism. While racism undeniably persists in the United States, the diversity frame often obscures deeper and more entrenched structures or barriers to achieving racial justice. For philanthropy to benefit most effectively those who are most disadvantaged requires a shift toward a more racially inclusive paradigm. This paradigm explicitly identifies the dominant power of race in determining life chances and outcomes. Once we identify the numerous ways in which race works to exclude groups, we can identify positive spaces created to have honest dialogue about race. Social inclusion, systems thinking and a transformational approach to discussions of race provide important tools to advance philanthropy's impact.

In philanthropy, and American society as a whole, diversity is frequently a euphemism for race and gender differences. Moreover, class seemingly is a verboten term that cannot even enter the discussion. Thus, foundations, and our public discourse, often use proxy terms such as "at-risk youth" or provide grants to tackle poverty that really seek to benefit communities of color. The problem with this use of "diversity" is that it often is decontextualized. Because diversity discourse tends to focus on individual-level racism, it adheres to or reifies existing norms of institutions and power relations. Institutional grant-making can contribute to strengthening democracy by rethinking race in this way.

Many would contend that since the eradication of Jim Crow laws and the passage of the Civil Rights Act, all Americans have equal access to the same life opportunities. It is incontrovertible that the United States has made significant progress in addressing race and racial inequality as exemplified by the fact that we are a more racially and ethnically diverse society than we ever have been. Indeed, the Census Bureau projects non-white populations will become the racial majority in the coming decades. Moreover, women and members of traditionally marginalized racial groups have made notable advances in various professions, with the most prominent recent example being the election of the United States' first African American president, Barack Obama. But the presumption of race neutrality allows the perpetuation of implicitly racialized systems and structures that impact groups differently based on race.

The decontextualization of race and power leads to what Dr. john a. powell terms a distributive or transactional model. As in economics, people are presumed to be rational actors, making logical choices that best suit their individual preferences subject to their budget constraints. However, as in economics, this approach has several limitations. It assumes equal access to knowledge, shared or mutual understanding of power and privilege, and a neutral set of systems and institutions. In the transactional model, the assumption is that the institutions themselves are appropriately established; disparate outcomes are the result of how an individual fares while negotiating those systems and institutions. In short, success or failure is ascribed to an individual's ability to negotiate a presumed race-neutral system that provides equal opportunities to improve one's life.

## Structural racism and structural racialization

Institutional racism identifies the norms in institutions that lead to racialized outcomes. As Andrew Grant-

---

### THE PERSISTENCE OF RACE AS A BARRIER TO SOCIAL INCLUSION IN THE UNITED STATES

> Native American women experience infant mortality rates 20 percent higher than those in other races in the U.S.[56]

> African American infants in the U.S. are two and a half times as likely as white infants to die before the age of one.[57]

> It will take 1,664 years or 55 generations for African American homeownership to equate to white home ownership in America.[58]

> Children of color living in just 10 of New York's neighborhoods have 90 percent of all lead poisoning in all of New York.[59]

> Minority children are clustered in major urban public school systems that are more educationally segregated today than two decades ago: Detroit, with 96 percent black and Latino; Baltimore with 89 percent black and Latino; Washington, D.C., with 94 percent black and Latino.[60]

Thomas and john a. powell note, "The institutional racism framework reflects a broader recognition of the forms through which racialized power is deployed, dispersed, and entrenched."[62] A fundamental distinction between institutional and structural racism is identifying the inter-institutional power dynamics and identifying the fundamental root causes of why normative hierarchies exist. The focus is on the *relationships* among the various institutions and practices. These relationships can produce results not captured by analyzing a single institution. These dynamics also can help shape the practices in a single institution. When engaging institutions or structures, practices can be either transactional or transformative. The problem with an institution is that unlike an individual, it lacks a personality; does one bring people in to transform an institution or to adhere to its established normative and cultural values? For example, simply increasing the number of female lawyers or attorneys of color does not transform the norms or culture at the institution of a law firm. The institution is assumed to be neutral but this never is the case. Structures reflect and promote norms and values that benefit some and burden others. This is the power of structural racialization: it identifies substantive power relations that are embedded in the institution and disallows racial, gender and other forms of marginalization to continue by addressing the deeper values it conveys.[63]

The structural racism framework easily is extended and applied to other marginalized communities. The Center for Social Inclusion underscores the importance of adopting a structural racism lens in addressing social problems: higher rates of poverty and worse health and education outcomes for communities of color "are the symptoms of our collective illness – structural racism. Whether its [sic] education reform, the environment, the workplace, urban planning and development, affordable housing or health care, we must make the role of race visible and understand the structures our institutions construct so that we may rebuild them to create opportunities for us all."[64] Structural racism addresses the cumulative impact of multiple institutions and structures working together to reify racialized power.

Positive externalities generated by programs that target race and gender bias explicitly in systems or structures are shared by the broader public as well. Philanthropy should adopt a long-term vision of raising awareness among the American public about the

## TABLE 1.6 PROJECTED DEMOGRAPHIC CHANGES IN THE UNITED STATES[61]

| YEAR | WHITE | BLACK | HISPANIC | ASIAN | OTHER |
|------|-------|-------|----------|-------|-------|
| 2000 | 69.4 | 12.7 | 12.6 | 3.8 | 2.5 |
| 2010 | 65.1 | 13.1 | 15.5 | 4.6 | 3 |
| 2020 | 61.3 | 13.5 | 17.8 | 5.4 | 3.5 |
| 2030 | 57.5 | 13.9 | 20.1 | 6.2 | 4.1 |
| 2040 | 53.7 | 14.3 | 22.3 | 7.1 | 4.7 |
| 2050 | 50.1 | 14.6 | 24.4 | 8 | 5.3 |

persistence of barriers to race and gender equality and, thus, enhance support for overtly race- and gender-conscious work. Without this intentional identification of race, sexual orientation, immigrant status, class or any of the other categories included in NCRP's definition of marginalized groups, foundations risk perpetuating a system in which advantaged individuals, through no mal-intent, are unable to see the need to explicitly identify barriers to full democratic participation. Discussions about "the un-discussable," such as class, must be framed by local context and positioned as beneficial for society as a whole. This will help move the United States to a more socially inclusive space where demographics do not dictate life opportunities.

Racial justice and equity work provide some concrete examples to understand better this new approach to improve philanthropy. The role of historical precedents and cross-cutting policies[65] demonstrates the limitations of working to address problems in isolation. For example, many African Americans initially were denied access to the New Deal era programs ranging from government subsidized mortgages provided via the Homeowners Loan Corporation and the Federal Housing Administration to Social Security benefits. Another example of the limitations of not adopting an approach that sees the interconnectivity of issues comes directly from the actions of the Supreme Court. With the *Brown* decision, the court mandated integrating previously all-white schools, ostensibly opening up educational opportunities for children of color. However, because the court took a singular approach to its analysis, it was unable to see the *connections* of school policy with housing and transportation policies, and with the disinvestment of private resources in impoverished neighborhoods.

## Structural racialization and choice

The distinction between structural racialization and structural racism is subtle but important. The term "racialization" describes a more comprehensive process than racism. As noted, a limitation of the word racism is that it is strongly associated with conscious individual acts. This is not merely a case of semantics: if foundations and the people working in them unconsciously associate the term "racism" with discriminatory behavior, it is likely that they will miss the role of inter-institutional relationships that work to keep certain groups marginalized. Structural racialization posits that racial hierarchy is perpetuated by institutions, the values and norms that are embedded in them, their relationship to each other and their dynamic role.

An important element of working in this framework is recognizing that choice always is structural, relational, socially constrained and influenced. Racial meaning itself is socially produced and constrained. In light of racial progress, many would argue that the roles of individual choice and personal responsibility account for why communities of color remain marginalized. If communities of color are not fully integrated in the suburbs, if non-white children have theoretical access to good public schools, then any failure to achieve or realize progress is viewed as an individual failure. Choice is constrained by our social relations and institutions regardless of socio-economic status or class. For example, although a wealthy person can afford health care, there are a limited number of doctors and hospitals to select from. For a poor person, the initial constraint is economic, but constraints extend beyond the economic realm to social phenomena that create life opportunities for people. When they do so in a racialized way that works better for some and not for others in a cumulative fashion, it is a manifestation of structural racialization.[68]

The fact that institutions are in relationships with each other and are themselves constantly changing and adapting leads to the applicability of a systems approach that addresses racial inequality in an inclusive and transformative way. We all live in structures but in different locations within these structures. A society where structures are racialized affects all of us. It is not just people of color who feel the effects of housing, school and credit segregation. These arrangements define all of us and often depress the outcomes for the entire society.

## FOUNDATIONS AND RACIAL EQUITY – APPLYING LESSONS LEARNED TO ADVANCE A FAIRER SOCIETY

Some grantmakers have recognized the historical legacy of policies and practice that continue to perpetuate racial inequality and lead to disparate life opportunities because of race for communities of color. Several foundations, including the Charles Stewart Mott, Ford and Tides foundations, recognize the problems of structural racism and provide funds for important work to groups, including the Applied Research Center, the Center for Social Inclusion and the Philanthropic Initiative for Racial Equality, that use the structural racism framework to inform their programs. The Kirwan Institute convened a Structural Racism Caucus that seeks to "unite policymakers, advocates, academics and grassroots organizations to define structural racism, understand the ways in which it operates, and ultimately to dismantle it."

Deborah Harrington, current president of the Woods Fund of Chicago, identifies the problem succinctly with implicit versus explicit racial justice language: "[racial justice is] implicit in our guidelines and mission statement, [however] the lens is poverty, not race, and by addressing poverty, we are generally looking at people of color but not saying it directly."[66] Indeed, applying a racial justice lens to grantmaking allows foundations to make sustainable long-term differences that benefit all Americans. "Racial equity is shaped by multiple issues; the intent ... [is] to highlight racial equity as a starting point for addressing widespread equity."[67] This quote captures concisely the potential systems-wide impact that adopting a racial equity lens can have on broader issues of social equity. It is the starting point for foundations to begin identifying areas of overlap in programs to address them more systemically and increase foundation impact on the public good.

## SYSTEMS THINKING

Systems theory is viewed better as a set of principles that help us understand how complex structures and systems work in relationship to each other. It involves a better understanding of mutual causation. If cause and effect are not easily separated out in a linear form, philanthropic interventions that function in a linear model will fail to address the dynamics that perpetuate racial inequality. Diagram 1.1 helps elucidate the differences between the two approaches.

Moreover, just as individuals struggle to make sense of a world in which linearity is challenged, foundations inevitably will encounter the same issues when they employ a systems approach in their grantmaking. Changing the actual interactions of our institutions is no small task, but neither is change impossible. In fact, a systems approach supports the idea that the only constant is change. There is an inherent element of uncertainty in the systems approach: because an intervention does not necessarily lead to a predetermined outcome, it is impossible to predict accurately the outcome of a given philanthropic initiative. Different elements of the systems are in a state of constant flux so isolating cause and effect is nearly impossible. Foundations working in relationship with each other see the collective *impact* of their funds rather than seeking to connect program outcomes causally with their individual grants.

Because we live in an increasingly interconnected world, what happens in one part of the world has an unanticipated ripple effect in another. Systems thinking challenges mechanical Newtonian models of thought and acknowledges the role of influence and power in everything.[71]

Systems and policies are interactive and mutually constitutive, and there often is a time delay after an intervention before its effect is manifested fully.

Feedback loops emerge: negative feedback comprises interventions that get absorbed by the system without really changing it, keeping the status quo, while positive feedback affects change at the systemic level by affecting the institutions and structures themselves. In the framework of a systems approach, when a small

> Our dominant mode of thinking is Newtonian: we think that there is a single cause and a predictable effect that is mechanical and unidirectional. So A causes B, and B causes C. The knower, the observer, is largely unaffected by this so, in a sense, seems inert or neutral to these systems. There was a period of time where people thought that we eventually would know everything about the universe because it was a mechanical system. It also was based on the notion that if you see something really complex, you could break it down into its constituent parts and understand it, that the whole and the sum of its parts are exactly the same. This paradigm implied certainty. The uncertainty in a systems approach challenges this notion of causation. It's not linear or additive but mutual and cumulative.[69]
>
> — Dr. john a. powell, Executive Director
> Kirwan Institute for the Study of Race and Ethnicity
> at The Ohio State University

event or intervention has a large impact that transforms the system, it is a "catalytic change." This approach recognizes the relationships among institutions and structures, allowing philanthropic initiatives to positively influence a seemingly unrelated component of the system because of their connectivity.

## DIAGRAM 1.1 NEWTONIAN PERSPECTIVE VS. SYSTEMS THINKING

The Newtonian Perspective

Systems Thinking

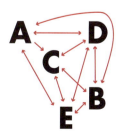

Social phenomena may be understood by breaking down the sum of the constituent parts.

Causation is reciprocal, mutual, and cumulative.

## Philanthropy and transformative change

Transformative change is understood best by contrasting it with transactional or distributive change. The transactional approach to change focuses on the individual and continues seeking change in a linear fashion while leaving the institutional arrangement undisturbed. In institutional philanthropy focused on a single issue such as health care, grant A will result in better outcomes for group A, while grant B will result in better health outcomes for group B. As Dr. powell states, "Small problems hurt us by enticing us to see things as separate, while big problems are more likely to be seen relationally. … It is important for foundations and communities not only to do multi-issue work, but to see issues in relationship."[72]

Foundations that adopt a transformative change approach in their grantmaking are more comfortable with the possibility of a time delay to see the impact of a philanthropic intervention. They do not expect a logical series of interventions and outputs as defined linearly. They enhance equity for all marginalized groups by addressing the issues in a holistic way. Philanthropy also should identify clearly those grants intended for social justice work. In a systems approach, intentional identification of structural barriers allows grantmakers and their grantees to start the process of transformative change. It also is important for grantmakers that adopt a systems approach to support grantees that work in relationship with each other.

There is rich literature and analysis of cognitive framing, inter- and intra-group identity, self-identity and other issues salient to a transformational agenda. A transformative agenda that moves us closer to the end goal of a more inclusive and equitable society must be informed by a relational analysis. Drew Westen recently posited that at a societal level, unconscious racist attitudes will persist unless "strategically framed messages on race that appeal to the conscious mental process" are adopted.[73] Foundations that adopt systems theory and tools to implement transformational grantmaking to address inequality will benefit from acknowledging the role of individual frames and cognitive schemas. Each person, grantee organization and foundation brings personal frames[74] to the table, and this will affect how information is processed and applied.

## Applying lessons from social justice grantmaking to adopt transformational change

As NCRP has noted previously, conservative and progressive philanthropy have contributed actively to social change efforts.[75] In fact, the Foundation Center and Independent Sector's 2005 report on Social Justice Grantmaking adapted NCRP's definition of social justice funding for its analysis of foundation giving trends. Noting that organizations ranging from the Heritage Foundation to the Mexican American Legal Defense and Educational Fund were established during the 1960s, funded primarily by philanthropic monies, NCRP provided a concise definition of social justice philanthropy:

> Social justice philanthropy is the practice of making contributions to nonprofit organizations that work for structural change and increase the opportunity of those who are less well off politically, economically and socially.[76]

Importantly, NCRP, the Foundation Center and Independent Sector emphasize that this definition is not intended to convey or support any specific ideological or political position. Rather, it is a strategy for philanthropy to address root causes of systemic political and socio-economic divisions. More than a decade of research by NCRP has documented the strategic philanthropy of conservative foundations and their success at moving public policies by funding think tanks, impacting education curricula and providing flexible funds to grantees, enabling them to be more effective.[77] NCRP does not believe that "progressive" funders should mirror the behavior of "conservative" counterparts. The emphasis is on learning lessons for holistic change, regardless of ideological leaning.

Several studies of seemingly neutral universalist programs conclude that without an explicit recognition of barriers to equality in grantmaking, such initiatives can serve to reify deeply entrenched structures of privilege and hierarchy, no matter how well-intentioned. Universalist programs can and do result in gains for targeted beneficiaries;[78] but the unconscious reifying of existing racialized structures that lead to disparate outcomes are a cause for concern. Grantmaking that presumes systemic neutrality would achieve their objectives more effectively if they respond to who benefits and apply "targeted universalism," an approach that is targeted to benefit the most marginal, but benefits all in the long run.[79]

## ADVOCACY, ORGANIZING, AND CIVIC ENGAGEMENT: PRACTICAL STRATEGIES FOR A SYSTEMS APPROACH

Advocacy, organizing and civic engagement have played essential roles in the development of our society. Moreover, they are among the most effective strategies for implementing a systems approach and for achieving significant impact on a variety of issues. As stated by the Aspen Institute's Nonprofit Sector Strategy Group, "Nonprofit organizations have long had a special role to play in keeping American democracy vibrant and responsive. Most of the major social movements of the past century have taken shape within this sector and this set of institutions has been a seedbed as well for major policy changes."[81]

Historically, the right of nonprofit groups to organize and advocate was exercised to protest the relocation of Native Americans, seek the abolition of slavery, and secure civil rights for women and African Americans. Today, nonprofit organizations have made groundbreaking strides to develop policies and programs that continue this role, exemplified by efforts to advance the living wage movement, community-driven school reform and faith-based community organizing. In 2000, the Aspen Institute formed the Nonprofit Sector Strategy Group to explore the role of nonprofits in civic participation and advocacy. Stating that "nonprofit participation in the policy process takes advantage of the special insights, competencies, and perspectives that nonprofit organizations have by virtue of their involvement with important societal issues and their ties to a wide range of different social groups,"[82] the ideologically diverse Strategy Group unanimously agreed that advocacy is a fundamental function of the nonprofit sector and one that must be encouraged in the future.

One of the principal reasons indicated by foundation practice to invest in advocacy is the fact that many foundations' missions are meant to support structural or systemic change. As Emmett D. Carson notes, any foundation that has a change-oriented mission must fund public policy work. Failure to do so is a disservice to the founding members' vision of that foundation's contribution to society.[83] Advocacy and organizing are the most effective strategies that allow such goals to be met and have significant measurable impacts.

A growing number of nonprofits and grantmakers are becoming more aware of the measurable impacts of these strategies and the longer time-horizon needed for this work to culminate in the original stated goals. Moreover, funders are seeing the potential for broader sustainable changes over time by adopting multi-strategy approaches in their programs. Human rights is one of the lenses through which this systemic

> Funding advocacy and advocates is the most direct route to supporting enduring social change for the poor, the disenfranchised and the most vulnerable among us, including the youngest and oldest in our communities.
>
> – Gara LaMarche, President, the Atlantic Philanthropies[80]

change has been observed. According to the Ford Foundation, human rights "places the affirmation of human dignity and equality at the center of domestic and foreign policy and counters unilateral tendencies with multilateral commitments, shared with other countries, to promote social and economic justice on a global scale."[84] Among foundations that have added a human rights lens to their decision making are the JEHT Foundation, the Atlantic Philanthropies, the Ford Foundation, the Shaler Adams Foundation and the California Women's Foundation.[85]

Civic engagement and social capital have made important contributions to enhanced participatory democracy and policy innovations. Historically, nonprofit organizations and other voluntary associations built bridges across race, class and religion, and were highly effective at fostering public discussion and mobilizing millions of people to achieve significant national policy outcomes. Social capital appears to have declined over the last quarter century, and many researchers have blamed this decline on a shift away from grassroots mobilization and advocacy strategies intended for the most marginalized groups of society. Researchers such as Theda Skocpol describe a shift from voluntary associations to agile, professional advocacy organizations during the social movements of the 1960s and 1970s that came to rely more on "inside the beltway" lobbying and media work than on mobilizing a membership base to achieve their goals. She argues that the new civic landscape became "oligarchic" because foundation grants favored professional groups over grassroots ones. Advocacy groups had no impetus to appeal to or mobilize a mass base, and there was little bridge-building across class. As a result, bottom-up policies benefiting working-class and poor constituencies were drowned out in the legislatures. Yet, Skocpol notes that nonprofits and foundations that continue to work with these strategies have resurrected social capital and seen positive outcomes through sustained, long-term initiatives. She states, "Taking longer and asking for a greater commitment may result in greater payoff. … It takes time to connect leaders and members to one another across places and institutions, yet, this is the only way to draw large numbers of people into a movement and the best way to generate sustained leverage to make a difference beyond one issue, battle or election."[86]

Skocpol's work is important for understanding civic engagement and participatory democracy, but her analysis merits an important caveat. While advocacy and organizing work informed by communities is integral to advancing the needs and voices of those marginalized by our institutions and structures, centralized advocacy work informed by the needs of local communities also is effective. Systemic change in any form that challenges existing power structures and arrangements that lead to inequality are important to achieving long-term, sustainable improvements in a holistic socio-economic paradigm. As Gara LaMarche notes, "In the interdependent ecosystem of advocacy and social change, elite voices play an important part, too, and they always have."[87]

There are several resources available to foundations that either want to begin or increase their funding of advocacy and organizing, specifically, policy work. Many foundations do not fund these vital areas of work because they lack the in-house knowledge or capacity to understand what role community organizing and advocacy can play in advancing their mission and promoting sustainable, participatory democracy. Some foundations might have knowledgeable staff that can help educate their boards but the majority of foundations do not employ staff. "Policy experts"[88] outside of the foundation world can offer important guidance and tools for developing a legally sound (process-related) and well-informed (substance-relat-

ed) public policy strategy. Often, the best advice can come from informed but neutral third-party experts who have a better understanding of the policy process. These experts should be used as appropriate and necessary by foundations to build their knowledge and understanding of the world of policy advocacy, and the important role that this, together with organizing and civic engagement, plays in moving policy agendas. Grantees can benefit from policy advice as well; many nonprofits do not engage in advocacy or lobbying because they do not have the right information or appropriate human resources to devote to this work. It is, thus, important for foundations to invest in the capacity of their grantees to engage substantively in policymaking on Capitol Hill and in local communities.

## Investing in advocacy, community organizing and civic engagement: contributing to our pluralistic democracy

When a grantmaking institution adopts a socially inclusive systems approach that includes advocacy, organizing and building multi-issue alliances, it has the potential to increase and unite the voices of those who historically are marginalized and improve their lives. Indeed, the Center for Social Inclusion identified *funders* as a crucial component of successful multiracial coalition work in rebuilding the City of New Orleans. As the center noted, the key is finding the appropriate balance between the paradigms of racialism and inclusiveness. With more funders adopting inclusion in their grantmaking, there is hope for advancing a more level playing field for all.

Andrew Friedman, co-director of Make the Road by Walking, an African American and Latino-led community organization in Brooklyn, summarized the importance and expanded impact of using a racial justice approach to the organization's language discrimination work: "[A] civil rights framework has been important. If we had just framed our work as poor people's issues, we would not have gotten the support from the broader civil rights, African American, and Latino communities."[89] Friedman's movement building was strengthened by building alliances using civil rights as the framework. This example demonstrates that sustainable, long-term impact is best achieved when foundations and groups take a holistic rather than a single-issue approach to their work.

The recognition of multi-issue and integrated approaches to address persistent discrimination is evident in the work of several foundations and non-profits. For example, the National Funders for Lesbian and Gay issues adopted a racial equity lens in 2008 following recognition of the fact that the experience of discrimination as an LGBTQ person of color synthesizes sexual orientation and racial dimensions. Similarly, acknowledging the crossover of environmental protection with workers rights informed by race and gender discrimination is a more powerful movement building strategy that allows single-issue focused groups to develop integrated approaches across organizations by identifying areas of common interest. Several legal practitioners have begun to realize the power of international law and rights. Groups working in the environmental justice movement, civil rights and prisoners rights find the broad and binding nature of U.N. human rights law as less subject to interpretation and thus more useful in highlighting U.S. exceptionalism exemplified by disparities in our criminal justice system. The United States accounts for 5 percent of the world's population but 24 percent of the world's prisoners and, as a nation, we incarcerate people at a significantly higher rate than our peer countries, resulting in 7 of every 1,000 of our residents in prisons.[90]

## Why foundations should support advocacy, public policy and community organizing

Organizations working on policy advocacy, organizing and civic engagement offer a powerful real-world example of systems thinking and theory in action. This work enhances our pluralistic democracy, provides voice to communities that would otherwise not be heard, demonstrates an understanding of systemic reform and results in tremendous impact.

With several notable exceptions, civic engagement, advocacy and organizing are under-funded by foundations, and community groups struggle to raise the resources needed to engage in this important work. Many foundations avoid advocacy funding for a variety of reasons, including several misperceptions: that funding advocacy and organizing might be "risky"; that outcome measurement is transferable more easily to direct services; and that lobbying is the same as advocacy or organizing. Research indicates that advocacy across the nonprofit sector is inconsistent, focuses on crisis situations, and does not sustain ongoing, consistent efforts. Some of the barriers to advocacy include limited resources, restricted and inconsistent funding by foundations, and a misunderstanding of tax regulations.[91]

Michael Edwards[92] posits that foundation boards find it difficult to calculate the "social rate of return" from investments in citizen action, leaving them to

## ADVOCACY AND ORGANIZING IN ACTION: LIVING WAGES

Economic security and the fight for living wages are persistent issues addressed by advocates and community organizers nationwide, often with notable success. In 1994, Baltimoreans United in Leadership Development (BUILD) led a coalition that secured passage of the first living wage ordinance in the country, triggering a national movement. Since then, organizing and advocacy groups have formed coalitions and succeeded in passing at least 123 living wage ordinances that provide more than 250,000 workers with $750 million in additional wages annually. Studies of living wage ordinances find that they benefit primarily lower-income adults working full time and positively impact communities of color. They also benefit employers by reducing turnover rates and improving productivity.[112] Coalitions also secured local and state minimum wage boosts benefiting millions of workers. Economists estimate that minimum wage increases enacted in Massachusetts, San Francisco, Illinois, Florida and New York between 2001 and 2005 benefit more than 3.2 million workers and resulted in more than $2.5 billion in new annual wages.[113] In 2007, this movement finally compelled Congress to increase the federal minimum wage to $7.25 an hour in three phases, after it stagnated for 10 years at $5.15 an hour. Significantly, the living wage movement has marshaled a broad base of support for the idea that people who work full time should be able to earn enough to meet their basic needs and those of their families.

rely on "business metrics and measures of success, privilege, size, growth and market share as opposed to the quality of interactions between people in civil society." Arguing that quantifiable outcomes are not the exclusive or best metrics for structural change, he states that "in civil society processes of engagement with other institutions and constituencies may be more important as a measure of impact than tangible outputs. … Social transformation requires humility and patience, a mirror image of the impatience and short-term thinking that drives most markets and entrepreneurs."

Similarly, Prudence Brown notes that "foundations' quest for greater impact is not usually accompanied by an increased tolerance for conflict or risk."[93] Many foundations display risk-aversion in their grantmaking, funding "safe" direct services or practicing "patronage" philanthropy in support of elite interests. Funders that support advocacy grants tend to do so with timeframes too abbreviated to demonstrate measurable, community-level impact. A survey conducted by the Johns Hopkins University found that while nearly three-quarters of nonprofits engage in advocacy and lobbying work, 85 percent of respondents devoted minimal resources to either type of activity. Citing lack of human and financial resources, 68 percent of respondents said that they

could do more advocacy work if they had funds to hire a policy specialist, while 65 percent identified unrestricted funding as essential to being able to expand their work in this area. Nonprofits that received private support from foundations and individuals are significantly less likely to engage in advocacy than those groups that receive government funding. Advocacy and policy work are integral to the country's nonprofits' role of providing a "voice to the voiceless,"[94] making this work all the more resonant for many institutional grantmakers that seek to impact the structures and systems that can move American society closer to equality of achievement.

### Quantifying the impact of a foundation's support of advocacy, organizing and civic engagement and measuring and evaluating outcomes

Foundations that support organizing have sought to quantify the impact of their grantees' work. Some have estimated a return on investment to demonstrate impact by analyzing the foundation's contributions. The Jewish Funds for Justice (JFJ), the Needmor Fund, and the Solidago Fund all undertook analyses that aggregated the quantifiable successes of a set of grantees and then calculated a return on investment based on their support of those grantees. JFJ estimated conservatively that 5 million people benefited

## ADVOCACY AND LOBBYING: A CRITICAL DISTINCTION

A persistent barrier to funding and engaging in policy advocacy is the flawed perception that advocacy and lobbying are synonymous. This is a cause of concern in the nonprofit sector because the word "lobbying" has undeservedly taken on negative connotations among some charitable organizations. Many nonprofit leaders believe that receiving government money precludes lobbying; in fact, an analysis of nonprofit advocacy found that nonprofits that receive government funding are significantly more likely than those that receive

only private funding to conduct advocacy work.[104] Although lobbying can be utilized as an advocacy strategy, advocacy does not necessarily have to involve lobbying. This is a critical distinction. Federal law governs how much lobbying a nonprofit organization can undertake, but there are no limits on how much a nonprofit can engage in other types of advocacy. Neglecting advocacy ultimately has a negative impact on society because advocacy allows the nonprofit sector to share its valuable knowledge with key decision makers and ultimate-

ly advance the public interest. Nonprofit policy participation is in the public interest, regardless of whether it is in the pursuit of conservative, liberal or non-ideological objectives.[105] As Hodding Carter III, former president and CEO of the John S. and James L. Knight Foundation, said, "All voices, all points of view should be heard. A full, unfiltered and unfettered debate is the prerequisite for good policy. Those who are most affected by policy decisions should have at least as much opportunity to influence them as everyone else."[106]

from all of its grantees' victories and that its distribution of $5 million in grants over five years contributed to $2 billion in benefits, or a ratio of $1 to $500. When outliers were removed, the return on investment was more modest but still impressive— $1 to $50.[95] The aggregate dollar amount of 18 Needmor grantees' wins totaled more than $1.37 billion. Needmor's investment generated a return on investment of $1 to $512—very close to the figure calculated independently by JFJ.[96] Solidago refined the methodology to discount the value of the grantee victories based on whether the group deserved full or shared credit for the win and to discount the foundation's contribution based on what proportion of the group's budget Solidago's grant represented. The Solidago return on investment was $1 to $59—close to the more conservative return on investment that JFJ calculated.[97] All three foundations provide demonstrable examples of impact resulting from investments in organizing and advocacy.

Recent multi-year efforts by funders to invest in and evaluate the impacts of community organizing also have helped to demonstrate the effectiveness of this strategy in creating significant change. The Ford Foundation commissioned an evaluation of its Community Organizing Initiative, which provided resources to local community organizing groups through local and regional funders in five communities.[98] The Charles Stewart Mott Foundation commissioned a six-year study to measure the impact of community organizing for school reform on student outcomes in seven sites.[99] The Cross City Campaign for Urban School Reform also showed the value of organizing for school reform in its study of five organizing groups.[100] All of these evaluation efforts documented significant returns. Notably, organizing for school reform was found to be critical to improving student performance and developing youth and parent leadership.

Recent research has demonstrated the tremendous strides made in the field of advocacy evaluation. There has been a proliferation of reports, guides and tools to help funders understand what advocacy is, what their grantees legally can do to engage in and support advocacy, and how to evaluate its success. Under its Grantmaking for Community Impact Project,[101] NCRP is producing a series of reports, *Strengthening Communities, Increasing Opportunities*, that documents the positive impacts of advocacy, organizing and civic engagement work in different

parts of the United States. The first report conducted in New Mexico found a high return on philanthropic investments that funded this work: every dollar dedicated to advocacy and organizing yielded $157 in community-wide benefits.

The Association of Community Organizations for Reform Now (ACORN) sought to demonstrate its impact by quantifying in dollars as many of its campaign victories as possible over a ten-year period. The cumulative impacts were impressive—more than $15 billion in benefits to lower and moderate income residents between 1995 and 2004.[102]

Whatever the benchmarks or methods of measurement, researchers agree that the context for engaging in organizing and advocacy must be considered when gauging success. In assessing impact, it is crucial that funders and advocacy groups seek to understand their contribution to policy change, rather than try to make a causal link between one grant or one group's work and the policy outcome. Increasing flexible grant dollars for advocacy and organizing is an important and practical tool for grantmakers working in a systems approach. The W.K. Kellogg Foundation has developed a tool to help its program staff and evaluators assess social change efforts guided by a systems approach, contributing an important resource for foundations that adopt this approach.[103] In short, although evaluation of social change initiatives in a systems approach appears challenging because it is non-linear, there are tools available to help institutional philanthropy make this important paradigm change in their approach to grantmaking.

### Resources for grantmakers to support advocacy, organizing and civic engagement

In 2004, the Alliance for Justice published a guide for funders interested in supporting advocacy. The alliance states that "advocacy" encompasses a broad range of activities that can influence public policy, including research, policy analysis, public education, lobbying, and voter engagement.[107] The guidebook also includes detailed benchmarks for evaluating the success of advocacy efforts. It makes the important point that even if a policy goal is not achieved, there are many outcomes that are important to measure, such as increased knowledge of the political process, awareness-raising around an issue, and leadership development. These outcomes build the capacity of organizations and increase their likelihood of suc-

## ADVOCACY AND ORGANIZING IN ACTION: AFFORDABLE HOUSING

Affordable housing is an important priority for many community organizing and advocacy groups. The Housing Trust Fund movement has been especially effective. A housing trust fund is an innovative policy solution to address the limited resources for affordable housing. These funds are established at the state or local level, usually with a dedicated public revenue source. Local decision makers have the discretion to decide how the funds can best serve diverse housing needs. As federal housing budgets have been reduced over the last few decades, the number of housing trust funds has grown dramatically, from less than 25 in 1985 to nearly 600 in at least 43 states today. As of 2006, local and state housing trust funds were generating $1.6 billion annually for affordable housing across the country—more than double the amount produced by funds just five years earlier.[114] The vast majority of funds or the legislation that enables them was secured through organizing and advocacy. Many of them depend on these strategies to maintain and increase revenue for affordable housing. For example, in 2008, the George Gund Foundation partnered with The Coalition on Homelessness and Housing in Ohio to increase resources for the Ohio Housing Trust Fund, which serves more than 87,000 families each year.[115]

ceeding in the next advocacy effort. Thus, losing an advocacy campaign the first time should not be viewed narrowly as a "failure." The alliance groups advocacy evaluation benchmarks as follows: outcome benchmarks (a policy result achieved and improvements made in programs or services); progress benchmarks (key activities accomplished and incremental results obtained); and capacity-building benchmarks (activities that strengthen an organization's ability to advocate).

The ensuing years have seen some positive collaborations between foundations and advocacy and organizing groups, such as Blueprint R&D, the California Endowment, GrantCraft, the Ford Foundation, the Harvard Family Research Project, the James Irvine Foundation, the Annie E. Casey Foundation, Innovation Network, and Continuous Progress. This growing literature offers several innovative methods for evaluating advocacy. More recently, GrantCraft and the Center for Community Change's Linchpin Campaign published a useful guide for funders on community organizing.[108] Many experts agree that funders and grantees each should have a theory of change or logic model that lays out what they hope to accomplish and how to get there. There is a clear consensus around the value of tracking outcomes and interim and capacity-building benchmarks. There is a range of models for developing outcome measures related to the stages of a policy campaign. The number and types of stages vary by model but typically include things such as public awareness, base- and alliance-building, policy change and implementation, and the direct impact of policy on individuals and communities.[109]

Recent efforts to measure leadership development and the skills gained by citizens who participate in community organizing are important as well, bringing rigor to an area that is often viewed as intangible. For People Improving Communities through Organizing (PICO), a faith-based network, Paul Speer devised and implemented a methodology to measure the public policy leadership skills of PICO leaders in California. Speer found a statistically significant difference in policy skills, knowledge and experience between PICO leaders and ordinary residents.[110] Heidi Swarts measured leadership capacity and political efficacy for her comparative study of faith-based and secular organizing groups. She found that leaders had developed specific skills such as chairing meetings, conducting research and public speaking. Groups had a greater sense of empowerment after becoming involved in the organization.[111]

Advocacy, community organizing and civic engagement are effective strategies with demonstrable impact that promote social inclusion and build social capital, especially for marginalized populations. Some funders are growing increasingly comfortable with supporting this work because they do have measurable impact, especially when considered over a longer time horizon. These strategies are tools to promote long-term systemic changes that challenge the norms and values carried by our institutions. As more funders take on this work, there are numerous existing resources for them to build their understanding of the critical role this work plays in advancing participatory democracy.

## SETTING THE BAR FOR PHILANTHROPY AT ITS BEST

To ensure that our *Criteria for Philanthropy at Its Best* are informed by current practice, NCRP worked with the Foundation Center to produce a custom dataset on marginalized communities. The dataset reported disaggregated foundation giving by eleven intended beneficiary groups for a three-year period from 2004–2006. NCRP used the three-year mean to avoid the potential influence of high or low outliers that can sometimes be generated in a single year by unusual grants. The resulting data present a reasonably reliable picture of the percentage of grants or grant dollars each foundation gave based on the eleven intended beneficiary groups NCRP identified as marginalized or vulnerable.[116]

There were 809 large foundations in Foundation Center's database[117] with sufficient data to be included in NCRP's analysis of intended beneficiaries. While there now are approximately 1,200 foundations in the database, some could not be included in the analysis because they did not provide data for all three years. Total average grant dollars awarded by these 809 grantmakers was $14,926,350,872 for the time period analyzed.[118] Although some grants are coded for multiple intended beneficiary groups, the total amounts of grantmaking intended to benefit specific populations are not double-counted in the total giving numbers. NCRP also used aggregate statistics from the Foundation Center's annual reports for 1998–2006 as a broader frame in which to analyze our custom dataset. NCRP believes that the three year combined dataset provides the best indicator of current trends in the field.

Within the 2004–2006 time period from which the NCRP dataset was drawn, in the aggregate, 33.2 percent of all grant dollars were provided for all 11 intended beneficiary groups.[119] That means that approximately $1 out of every $3 granted by larger foundations was intended to benefit communities with the least wealth, opportunity or power and that $2 out of every $3 granted could not be classified as benefiting those communities. The median for the proportion of grant dollars intended to benefit vulnerable communities was 20.9 percent for all 794 foundations that made at least one such grant. To set a standard metric for Philanthropy at Its Best, NCRP examined individual foundation grantmaking intended to benefit marginalized communities. The 80 foundations that provided the highest proportion of their grant dollars gave at least 56 percent of their grant dollars to benefit vulner-

able groups. These grantmakers comprise approximately 10 percent of the total NCRP sample. There likely are many more foundations that prioritize special populations in their grantmaking but either do not provide data to the Foundation Center or might not have done so consistently in the timeframe from which the NCRP sample was drawn. In other words, being excluded from this sample does not imply that an individual grantmaking institution is not providing this important type of support.

A quartile analysis of the data shows that the top 25 percent of our sample provided between 36–100 percent of all grant dollars to benefit disadvantaged communities; the second quartile had a range of 20.3–35.6; the third quartile had a range of 8.5–20.2, and; the bottom quartile's range was 0.0–8.5 percent. As the quartile ranges show, an exceptionally large proportion of our sample for grantmaking intended to benefit marginalized communities does so at disappointingly low levels: 71.32 percent of foundations in our sample provided less than $1 out of every $3 granted for the intended benefit of marginalized communities. Dropping the threshold to 20 percent of grant dollars intended to benefit marginalized groups, or $1 out of every $5 granted, 49.44 percent of foundations fell below that mark; 50.56 percent of the sample provided at least that much or more in such grants.

These figures are even more disturbing when taking into account that the data analysis includes only large foundations. Previous NCRP research has suggested that smaller foundations provide significantly lower percentages of their grant dollars for the intended benefit of vulnerable communities than do larger foundations.[120] **Leading the field, 108 foundations, or about 13.35 percent of our sample, provided at least 50**

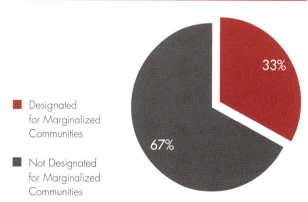

## GRAPH 1.3 FOUNDATION SUPPORT FOR MARGINALIZED COMMUNITIES, BROADLY DEFINED

33%

67%

■ Designated for Marginalized Communities

■ Not Designated for Marginalized Communities

percent of their grant dollars for the intended benefit of marginalized communities. This is the benchmark for Philanthropy at Its Best. A list of all 108 foundations that currently meet or exceed this benchmark can be found in the Data Appendix.

In a 2005 report, the Independent Sector and the Foundation Center found that grantmaking for structural change efforts (using "social justice philanthropy" as proxy) comprised a meager 11.8 percent of total grants in 1998 and fell to 11 percent in 2002.[121] This quantitative analysis was the first attempt to establish a consistent benchmark and provide insight into the state of social justice philanthropy. In the 2009 report, which analyzed grants made in 2006, this figure rose by a muted 1 percent to 12 percent.[122] Michael Edwards advocates that foundations demonstrate their commitment to addressing systemic and structural change by allocating at least 50 percent of their annual payout for social justice initiatives.[123]

To look more closely at current giving in this arena, NCRP analyzed disaggregated data in social justice grantmaking. Grants that meet the social justice definition described in this chapter and in the Foundation Center's publications on social justice grantmaking are included. Because the Center tracks only larger foundations, there very likely are many more foundations—such as the Woods Fund of Chicago and the Liberty Hill Foundation of Los Angeles—that fund social justice work that are not included in our sample. The list drew the leading social justice grantmakers from the Foundation Center's database[124] with sufficient data to be included in our analysis of systems or structural change grants. Some foundations could not be included in the analysis because they did not provide data for all three years.

NCRP's analysis of social justice grantmaking as a share of overall grantmaking demonstrates great variability among the leading U.S. social justice grantmakers. In the aggregate, 682 of our total sample of 809 foundations, or 84 percent of the sample, made at least one social justice-related grant during the three-year time period; average giving over three years was $1,549,135,953 comprising 11,958 grants.

In spite of 84 percent of the sample having made at least one social justice grant in the time period analyzed, many did so at very low levels. There is high variability even among the top 25 social justice grantmakers; the range is 43–81 percent of this type of grantmaking as a share of overall giving.[125]

**Leading the field, 56 foundations, or about 6.9** percent of our sample, provided at least 25 percent of their grant dollars for social justice. This is the benchmark for Philanthropy at Its Best.[126] A list of all 56 foundations that currently meet or exceed this benchmark can be found in the Data Appendix.

## CONCLUSION

All foundations should prioritize those with the least wealth, opportunity and power in their grantmaking. Regardless of a foundation's mission, investing in organizations and programs that focus on special population groups benefits our pluralistic society. It also advances substantive democracy and moves the United States closer to a truly inclusive society with equal opportunities for life achievements for all its residents.

A significant body of research demonstrates the effectiveness of advocacy, organizing and civic engagement as sophisticated strategies to promote long-term change. Funding for these strategies remains limited because of misperceptions of the risks and rewards. As the snapshots of advocacy and organizing groups, and the legal definitions and resources provided in this chapter demonstrate, some exemplary institutional grantmakers are currently funding this important work and are able to see returns on their investments.

NCRP acknowledges that certain foundations have missions that make it implausible for them to prioritize marginalized communities at the 50 percent level. But all grantmakers, regardless of mission, can see benefits from prioritizing the most vulnerable in their grantmaking. For example, a foundation that focuses on the arts might find benefit from directing some of its funding to special population groups such as the disabled, single parents, and people with HIV/AIDS. Arts organizations sometimes have difficulty securing support from policy makers because they are perceived as serving only elite interests. A strategic effort by arts funders to intentionally include marginalized communities could yield important community and public policy benefits. Premised on philanthropy's special role to nurture our pluralistic democracy, NCRP advocates that all grantmakers make marginalized communities a high priority in their giving. Just over half of all foundations analyzed meet or exceed a 20 percent threshold for giving to benefit marginalized communities. NCRP views this as a bare minimum standard for exemplary philanthropy. We challenge grantmakers whose missions seem on the surface to be unrelated to these issues to reexamine those assumptions in light of the arguments presented in this chapter.

# Criterion I: Values

A grantmaker practicing Philanthropy at Its Best serves the public good by contributing to a strong, participatory democracy that engages all communities.

a) Provides at least 50 percent of its grant dollars to benefit lower-income communities, communities of color and other marginalized groups, broadly defined

b) Provides at least 25 percent of its grant dollars for advocacy, organizing and civic engagement to promote equity, opportunity and justice in our society

## DISCUSSION QUESTIONS

NCRP encourages staff and trustees of foundations and other grantmakers to engage in serious discussions about each criterion and the chapter that elaborates on the criterion. Sample discussion questions are provided here to help get you started.

> Which parts of the chapter did you like the most? Why?

> Which parts did you like the least? Why?

> Do you agree that it's important to contribute to a strong, participatory democracy and to support marginalized communities? Why or why not?

> How do we define marginalized communities in the context of our mission? Have we ever thought about how increasing our giving to marginalized communities might align with our mission?

> What percentage of our foundation's grant dollars do we estimate are intended to benefit marginalized communities, broadly defined? Are we satisfied with that percentage? Why or why not? How did we establish our current position?

> How is advocacy, community organizing and civic engagement relevant to our current grantmaking or programmatic work? Have we ever considered how these strategies might align with our mission?

> What percentage of our foundation's grant dollars do we estimate are for advocacy, community organizing and civic engagement? Are we satisfied with that percentage? Why or why not? How did we establish our current position?

> What else from this chapter should inform our current grantmaking priorities?

> If we want to make any changes based on this discussion, what will need to happen in order to make those changes? What are the next steps?

# NOTES FOR CHAPTER I: VALUES

1.  The eleven groups are: economically disadvantaged; racial or ethnic minorities; women and girls; people with AIDS; people with disabilities; aging, elderly, and senior citizens; immigrants and refugees; crime/abuse victims; offenders and ex-offenders; single parents; and LGBTQ citizens.

2.  Heather Boushey, Shawn Fremstad, Rachel Gragg and Margy Waller. *Social Inclusion for the United States*, (Washington, D.C.: Center for Economic and Policy Research & Inclusion, April, 2007) http://www.inclusionist.org/files/socialinclusionusa.pdf.

3.  Alexis de Tocqueville. *Democracy in America and Two Essays on America,* translated by Gerald E. Bevan (London, U.K.: Penguin Books, 2003; original publication of *Democracy in America,* 1835).

4.  Ibid.

5.  The term "marginalized communities" is used interchangeably with "special populations," "disadvantaged groups," "underserved communities," "underrepresented" or "vulnerable communities" in this chapter.

6.  Martin Luther King Jr. *Strength to Love* (New York, NY: Harper & Row, 1963).

7.  Bill Gates. "A New Era of Technical Leadership at Microsoft" (remarks at news conference Redmond, WA, June 15, 2006), http://www.microsoft.com/presspass/exec/billg/speeches/2006/06-15transition.mspx.

8.  Andrew Carnegie. *The Gospel of Wealth*, (Indianapolis, IN: Indiana University Center on Philanthropy, 1993; Original publication: *North American Review*, CXLVIII, June, 1889), p. 4, p. 10.

9.  Marcia Stepanek and Cristina Maldonado. "Rockefeller 2.0: Gates Relaunches Philanthropy," *MSNBC* June 24, 2008. http://www.msnbc.msn.com/id/25332025/.

10. Bill Gates. *2009 Annual Letter from Bill Gates: The Economic Crisis*, January, 2009, p. 8, http://www.gatesfoundation.org/annual-letter/Pages/2009-economic-crisis.aspx.

11. Birger A. Pearson. *Ancient Roots of Western Philanthropy* (Indianapolis, IN: Indiana University Center on Philanthropy, 1997).

12. John Rawls. *A Theory of Justice* (Cambridge, MA: Harvard University Press 1971).

13. john a. powell. "The Needs of Members in a Legitimate Democratic State," *Santa Monica Law Review* 44 (2004).

14. Bill Clinton. "Remarks by the President at Presentation of the National Medal of the Arts and the National Humanities Medal" (Speech, Washington D.C.: September 29,1999), http://clinton4.nara.gov/WH/New/html/19990929.html.

15. Michael Walzer. *Spheres of Justice: A Defense of Pluralism and Equality* (New York, NY: Perseus Publishing, 1983).

16. Rick Cohen. *Building Solid Foundations: New Approaches to Substantive Philanthropic Accountability* (Washington, D.C.: National Committee for Responsive Philanthropy, December, 2006), p. 16.

17. Amartya Sen. foreword to *The Measure of America: American Human Development Report 2008–2009*, by Sarah Burd-Sharps, Kristen Lewis, and Eduardo Borges Martins (New York, NY: Columbia University Press, 2008), xi.

18. Burd-Sharps, Lewis and Martins , Op. cit. p 10.

19. For a more detailed discussion, see Amartya Sen, *Development as Freedom* (New York, NY: Knopf, 1999); Burd-Sharps, Lewis and Martins, Op. cit.

20. Ibid.

21. Burd-Sharps, Lewis and Martins, 2009, Op. cit: p. 14–15. It is beyond the scope of this writing to do justice to the extant literature and research on human development and capabilities. For additional resources, please see the works of Amartya Sen and Martha Nussbaum.

22. Boushey et al., Op cit.

23. Boushey et al., Op. cit.: p. 2.

24. Ibid., p. 3.

25. Sue Kirchhoff. "Bernanke: Fixing income gap will take education," *USA Today,* February 7, 2007, http://www.usatoday.com/money/economy/fed/2007-02-06-bernanke-education_x.htm.

26. Cecile Andrews, "What's it Going to Take? Challenging Our Faith in Wealth," United for a Fair Economy, http://www.faireconomy.org/news/challenging_our_faith_in_wealth; United Nations Habitat, "American cities as unequal as African and Latin American cities according to UN-HABITAT's new *State of the World's Cities Report 2008/9: Harmonious Cities*," (Press release, 2008), http://www.unhabitat.org/downloads/docs/presskitsowc2008/PR%201.pdf; Burd-Sharps, Lewis and Martins, Op. cit.

27. Uri Berliner. "Haves and Have-Nots: Income Inequality in America," *NPR.org,* February 5, 2007, http://www.npr.org/templates/story/story.php?storyId=7180618.

28. "Table A-3: Selected Measures of Household Income Dispersion: 1967 to 2005," U. S. Census Bureau, http://www.census.gov/hhes/www/income/histinc/p60no231_tablea3.pdf.

29. Burd-Sharps, Lewis and Martins, Op. cit., p. 133.

30. Bruce H. Webster Jr., and Alemayehu Beshaw. *Income, Earnings and Poverty Data from the 2006 American Community Survey,* (Washington, D.C.: U.S. Census Bureau, August 2007). The Gini index provides a summary measure of inequality. It ranges from 0 to 1, with numbers closer to 1 indicating deep levels of inequality.

31. "Table H-4. Gini Ratios for Households, by Race and Hispanic Origin of Householder: 1967 to 2007." U.S. Census Bureau, http://www.census.gov/hhes/www/income/histinc/h04.html; Field Listing - Distribution of Family Income - Gini Index," U.S. Central Intelligence Agency, https://www.cia.gov/library/publications/the-world-factbook/fields/2172.html.

32. Excluding Alaska and Hawaii; figures apply to the 48 contiguous states and the District of Columbia.

33. "Table H-4. Gini Ratios for Households, by Race and Hispanic Origin of Householder: 1967 to 2007." U.S. Census Bureau, http://www.census.gov/hhes/www/income/histinc/h04.html.

34. Alan Berube and Bruce Katz. *Katrina's Window: Confronting Concentrated Poverty Across America* (Washington, D.C.: The Brookings Institution, October 2005).

35. Berube and Katz, Op. cit.

36. Berube and Katz, Op. Cit.; "The Enduring Challenge of Concentrated Poverty in America: Case Studies from Communities Across the U.S.," Community Affairs Offices of the Federal Reserve System & The Metropolitan Policy Program at The Brookings Institution, http://www.frbsf.org/cpreport/.

37. H.S. Terrell. "Wealth accumulation of black and white families: the empirical evidence," *The Journal of Finance,* 26 (May 1971): 363.

38. L.A. Keister and S. Moller. "Wealth inequality in the United States," *American Review of Sociology,* 26 (2000): 63.

39. Chuck Collins. "A Problem of Riches," *Sojourners Magazine* (September/October 2008), http://www.ips-dc.org/articles/694.

40. Edward N. Wolff. *Recent Trends in Wealth Ownership, 1983-1998 , Working paper No. 300,* (New York, NY: Bard College and Jerome Levy Economics Institute, 2000).

41. Brian K. Bucks et al. "Recent Changes in U.S. Family Finances: Evidence from the 2001 and 2004 Survey of Consumer Finances," *Federal Reserve Bulletin* (2006): A4.

42. Collins, Op. cit.; Burd-Sharps et al., Op. cit.

43. Edward N. Wolff. *Changes in Household Wealth in the 1980s and 1990s in the U.S. Working paper No. 407,* (New York, NY: New York University and Jerome Levy Economics Institute, 2004), http://www.levy.org/pubs/wp407.pdf.

44. Burd-Sharps, Lewis and Martins, Op. cit., p. 134.

45. Wolff 2004, Op. cit. Table 6.

46. Based on NCRP data analysis of Foundation Center data giving by special population groups. The search set is based on the Foundation Center's grants sample database, which includes all of the grants of $10,000 or more awarded to organizations by a sample of 1,172 larger foundations for circa 2004, 1,154 for circa 2005, and 1,263 for circa 2006. For community foundations, only discretionary grants are included. Grants to individuals are not included in the file. In-depth data analysis is included later in this chapter.

47. Boushey et al., Op. cit.

48. Dalton Conley. *Being Black, Living in the Red* (Berkeley, CA: University of California Press, 1999); Shehnaz Niki Jagpal, *Racial Inequality in the United States: Analyzing the Wealth Gap,* (Master's thesis, Georgetown University, 2007); Melvin L. Oliver and Thomas M. Shapiro. *Black Wealth/White Wealth: A new perspective on racial inequality*, (New York, NY: Routledge, 1997, 2006).

49. Boushey et al., Op. cit. p 4. Emphasis added.

50. Joseph Stewart. "Making the Case for Racial Equity" (remarks at Building the Dream community dialogue, Battle Creek, MI, March 17, 2008).

51. Measured in 2007 constant dollars. "Table H-5. Race and Hispanic Origin of Householder—Households by Median and Mean Income: 1967 to 2007," U.S. Census Bureau, http://www.census.gov/hhes/www/income/histinc/h05.html.

52. Wolff 2000, Op. cit.

53. Ling Xin Hao. "Immigration and wealth inequality in the U.S." (paper presented at the Population Association of America annual meeting, Boston, MA, April 1–3, 2004.

54. Barbara A. Butrica. *Do Assets Change the Racial Profile of Poverty among Older Adults? Opportunity and Ownership Facts No. 8* (Washington, D.C.: The Urban Institute, March, 2008), http://www.urban.org/UploadedPDF/411620_racial _poverty.pdf.

55. As the report states: "Significant discrimination remains, raising the cost of housing searches for African Americans and Hispanics, creating barriers to homeownership and housing choice, and helping to perpetuate racial and ethnic segregation." Margery Austin Turner, Stephen L. Ross, George Galster and John Yinger. *Discrimination in Metropolitan Housing Markets: National Results from Phase I of HDS2000* (Washington, D.C.: The Urban Institute, 2002), http://www.urban.org/UploadedPDF/410821_Phase1_Report.pdf.

56. Statement by Charles W. Grim. D.D.S., M.H.S.A, Assistant Surgeon General Director, Indian Health Service at the 17th Annual IHS Research Conference and the International Meeting on Inuit and Native American Child Health. (Seattle, WA, April 29, 2005). Infant mortality rates are reported as a proportion of 1,000 live births.

57. Joseph Stewart. "Diversity and Leadership in Philanthropy" (session at the Council of Michigan Foundations 35th annual conference, Dearborn, MI, October 23, 2007), http://www.michiganfoundations.org/s_cmf/bin.asp?CID=577 4&DID=12691&DOC=FILE.PDF.

58. Ibid.

59. Ibid.

60. Ibid.

61. "U.S. Interim Projections by Age, Sex, Race and Hispanic Origin," U.S. Census Bureau, http://www.census.gov/population/www/projections/usinterimproj/natprojtab01a.pdf.

62. Andrew Grant-Thomas & john a. powell. "Toward a Structural Racism Framework," *Poverty & Race* (November/December 2006), http://www.prrac.org/full_text.php?text_id=1095&item _id=10188&newsletter_id=90&header=Symposium:%20Stru ctural%20Racism.

63. Personal communication with john a. powell, 2008.

64. "Definition: Structural Racism," Center for Social Inclusion, http://www.centerforsocialinclusion.org/struct_racism.html.

65. Conley, Op. cit.; Jagpal, Op. cit.; Oliver and Shapiro, Op. cit.

66. Will Pittz and Rinku Sen. *Short Changed: Foundation Giving and Communities of Color* (Oakland, CA: Applied Research Center, 2004), 10.

67. Robert Espinoza. *LGBTQ Grantmakers 2008 Report Card on Racial Equity,* (New York, NY: Enterprise Press, Funders for Lesbian and Gay Issues, 2008).

68. Interview with john a. powell, July, 2008. For a fuller discussion of this interview and corresponding analysis, please see: Niki Jagpal. "Changing the World for All: A New Approach" *Responsive Philanthropy*, (Fall 2008): 6.

69. Adapted from interview and discussion by Niki Jagpal with Dr. john a. powell, July 9, 2008.

70. john a. powell. "Structural Approaches to Produce Schools that Work for Everyone" (presentation, Grantmakers for Education annual conference, Baltimore, MD, October 20, 2008).

71. For a fuller discussion of this interview and corresponding analysis, please see Jagpal 2008, Op. cit.

72. Jagpal 2008, Op. cit.

73. Drew Westen. *The Political Brain; The Role of Emotion in Deciding The Face of the Nation* (New York, NY: Public Affairs, 2007); john a. powell. "Addressing 21st Century Poverty: Transformational strategies for talking, thinking and acting on issues of poverty," (presentation at Northwest Area Foundation Public Policy Roundtable, St. Paul, MN, July, 2008).

74. A simple way to think of cognitive frames is as a mental "filing system" that we all use to make sense of the world.

75. The National Committee for Responsive Philanthropy. *Social Justice Philanthropy: The latest Trend or a lasting lens for grantmaking?* (Washington, D.C.: The National Committee for Responsive Philanthropy, 2005).

76. For a fuller definition, see Ibid. or Steven Lawrence, ed. *Social Justice Grantmaking: A report on Foundation Trends,* (New York, NY: Independent Sector & The Foundation Center, 2005).

77. Sally Covington. *Moving a Public Policy Agenda: The strategic philanthropy of conservative foundations.* (Washington, D.C.: The National Committee for Responsive Philanthropy, 1997, 2004); Jeff Krehely et al. *Axis of Ideology: Conservative foundations and Public Policy.* (Washington, D.C.: The National Committee for Responsive Philanthropy, 2004).

78. Medicare and Social Security are two such prominently noted programs.

79. powell July 2008, Op. cit.

80. The Atlantic Philanthropies. *Why Supporting Advocacy Makes Sense for Foundations - Atlantic Reports: Investing in Change* (New York, NY: The Atlantic Philanthropies, 2008).

81. Nonprofit Sector Strategy Group. *The Nonprofit Contribution to Civic Participation and Advocacy*, (Washington, D.C.: The Aspen Institute, Fall 2000), 12,.http://www.nonprofitresearch.org/usr_doc/Advocacy.pdf.

82. Ibid., p. 5.

83. Emmett D. Carson. "On Foundations and Public Policy: Why the Words Don't Match the Behavior," in *Power in Policy: A Funder's Guide to Advocacy and Civic Participation*, ed. David F. Arons (St. Paul, MN: Fieldstone Alliance, 2007), 14.

84. Larry Cox and Dorothy Q. Thomas, ed. *Close to Home: Case Studies of Human Rights Work in the United States* (New York, NY: Ford Foundation, 2004), 6.

85. Cox and Thomas, Op. cit.

86. Theda Skocpol. *Diminished Democracy: From Membership to Management in American Civic Life* (Norman, OK: University of Oklahoma Press, 2003) 273–274.

87. Gara LaMarche. "When Foundations Should Lead – and When They Should Get Out of the Way," in *Power in Policy: A Funder's Guide to Advocacy and Civic Participation*, ed. David F. Arons (St. Paul, MN: Fieldstone Alliance, 2007).

88. E.g., The Center for Lobbying in the Public Interest, the Alliance for Justice. For additional resources, please see NCRP's *Resource List for Funding Advocacy, Organizing and Civic Engagement,* http://www.ncrp.org/campaigns-research-policy/communities/gcip/gcip-resources.

89. Quoted in Pittz and Sen, Op. cit., p. 13.

90. Burd-Sharps, Lewis and Martins, Op. cit, p. 142

91. Gary D. Bass et al. *Seen but not Heard: Strengthening Nonprofit Advocacy* (Washington, D.C.: The Aspen Institute, 2007).

92. Michael Edwards. *Just Another Emperor? The Myths and Realities of Philanthrocapitalism* (New York, NY: Demos: A Network for Ideas & Action, 2008).

93. Prudence Brown, et al. *Toward Greater Effectiveness in Community Change: Challenges and Responses for Philanthropy,* (New York, NY: The Foundation Center, September 2003), 20.

94. Lester M. Salamon & Stephanie Lessans Geller 2008. *Nonprofit America: A Force for Democracy?* (Johns Hopkins University Listening Post Project, Communiqué #9: Nonprofit Advocacy and Lobbying, 2008), http://www.jhu.edu/listening-post/news/pdf/advocacy9.pdf.

95. See *Report on Outcomes of JFJ Grantmaking 1996–2001,* (unpublished report, Jewish Funds for Justice, May 2003).

96. See Lisa Ranghelli. *Program Assessment Executive Summary* (Toledo, OH: Needmor Fund, 2004), http://www.needmor-fund.org/special_report.htm.

97. See *Community Benefits Report Brief* (Northampton, MA: Solidago Foundation, 2008), http://www.solidago.org/.

98. Marilyn Gittell, Barbara Ferman, and Charles Price. *Assessing Community: An Evaluation of the Ford Foundation's Community Organizing Initiative, Volume II (2004–2007)* (New York, NY: Howard Samuels Center, 2007).

99. Kavitha Mediratta et al. *Organized Communities, Stronger Schools: a Preview of Research Findings.* (Providence, RI: Annenberg Institute for School Reform, Brown University, March 2008).

100. Eva Gold, Elaine Simon and Chris Brown. *Successful Community Organizing for School Reform Strong Neighborhoods, Strong Schools: The Indicators Project on Education Organizing* (Chicago, IL: Cross City Campaign for Urban School Reform, March 2002).

101. The Grantmaking for Community Impact Project analyzes advocacy and organizing wins through the lens of the groups sampled to deconstruct the persistent myth that funding such work does not provide donors with quantifiable returns.

102. Lisa Ranghelli. *The Monetary Impact of ACORN Campaigns: A Ten Year Retrospective, 1995–2004* (New Orleans, LA: Association of Community Organizations for Reform Now, November 2006).

103. The W.K. Kellogg Foundation. *Designing Initiative Evaluation: A Systems Oriented framework for Evaluating Social Change Efforts.* (The W.K. Kellogg Foundation, September, 2007), http://www.wkkf.org/DesktopModules/WKF.00_DmaSupport/ViewDoc.aspx?fld=PDFFile&CID=281&ListID=28&ItemID=5000521&LanguageID=0.

104. Salamon & Lessans Gellar, Op. cit.

105. Adapted from Bass et al., Op. cit.

106. Hodding Carter III. foreword to *Power in Policy: A Funder's Guide to Advocacy and Civic Participation*, ed. David F. Arons (St. Paul, MN: Fieldstone Alliance, 2007).

107. Alliance for Justice. *Investing in Change: A Funder's Guide to Supporting Advocacy.* (Washington, D.C.: Alliance for Justice, 2004).

108. Craig McGarvey and Anne Mackinnon. *Funding Community Organizing: Social Change Through Civic Participation,* (New York, NY: GrantCraft and the Linchpin Campaign, 2009).

109. For additional resources, please see NCRP's *Resource List for Funding Advocacy, Organizing and Civic Engagement,* http://www.ncrp.org/GCIPresources.asp.

110. Paul W. Speer. *Evaluation Report – People Making Public Policy in California: The PICO California Project.* (Human and Organizational Development, Peabody College, Vanderbilt University, May 2002).

111. Heidi J. Swarts. *Organizing Urban America: Secular and Faith-Based Progressive Movements* (Minneapolis, MN: University of Minnesota Press, 2008).

112. Jeff Thompson and Jeff Chapman. *The economic impact of local living wages,* briefing paper 170 (Economic Policy Institute, February 16, 2006), http://www.epi.org/content.cfm/bp170.

113. Ranghelli November 2006, Op. cit.

114. *Housing Trust Fund Progress Report 2002* and Mary E. Brooks *Housing Trust Fund Progress Report 2007* (Frazier Park, CA: Housing Trust Fund Project, Center for Community Change 2002 & 2007). Examples of campaigns can be found in the *Housing Trust Fund Project News*, a newsletter of the Center for Community Change.

115. The Atlantic Philanthropies, Op. cit.

116. The eleven groups are: economically disadvantaged, racial or ethnic minorities, women and girls, people with AIDS, people with disabilities, aging, elderly, and senior citizens, immigrants and refugees, crime/abuse victims, offenders and ex-offenders, single parents, and LGBTQ citizens.

117. The search set is based on the Foundation Center's grants sample database, which includes all of the grants of $10,000 or more awarded to organizations by a sample of 1,172 larger foundations for circa 2004, 1,154 for circa 2005, and 1,263 for circa 2006. For community foundations, only discretionary grants are included. Grants to individuals are not included in the file.

118. This figure is the denominator used in NCRP's calculations; if analyzed within giving sub-samples, these figures would be higher and likely overstate the current giving trends. Using the full samples average total giving provides a more comprehensive framework for analyzing the different types of grants.

119. Please see the data appendix for further details.

120. NCRP compared 2005 giving for the intended benefit of economically disadvantaged groups and for racial minorities by larger and smaller Minnesota foundations using data from the Foundation Center and from the MN Council on Foundations and found that the larger foundations provided support for vulnerable populations at much higher levels than the smaller foundations did. The methodologies used to create the data sets are extremely similar but not identical, resulting in our statement that there is a strong indication, but not proof, that smaller foundations are less supportive of vulnerable communities than are larger foundations.

121. Lawrence, Op. Cit. 9, Table 2.

122. Foundation Center. *Social Justice Grantmaking II* (New York, NY: Foundation Center, 2009).

123. Edwards 2008, Op. Cit. p. 88-89.

124. The search set is based on the Foundation Center's grants sample database, which includes all of the grants of $10,000 or more awarded to organizations by a sample of 1,172 larger foundations for circa 2004, 1,154 for circa 2005, and 1,263 for circa 2006. For community foundations, only discretionary grants are included. Grants to individuals are not included in the file.

125. Please see the data appendix for a list of the top 25 social justice grantmakers and the proportion of each foundation's overall giving that this type of grant comprised.

126. The two metrics described in this criterion are not additive. It is assumed that the 25 percent of grant dollars going for advocacy and organizing work will be a subset of the 50 percent of grant dollars going for the intended benefit of marginalized communities.

# Chapter II: Effectiveness

# Criterion II: Effectiveness — At A Glance

A grantmaker practicing Philanthropy at Its Best serves the public good by investing in the health, growth and effectiveness of its nonprofit partners.

a) Provides at least 50 percent of its grant dollars for general operating support

b) Provides at least 50 percent of its grant dollars as multi-year grants

c) Ensures that the time to apply for and report on the grant is commensurate with grant size

> The ability of nonprofits and grantmakers to be effective—to have impact on the issues, causes and communities they care about—is of paramount importance.

> General operating support is fundamental to enhancing grantee impact; it provides organizations with the flexible funding they need to achieve their missions effectively. In the aggregate, only 16 percent of grant dollars is provided for general operating support. But 125 exemplary foundations (15.5 percent of our sample) provided at least 50 percent of their grant dollars for general operating support, meeting the benchmark for Philanthropy at Its Best.

> Multi-year funding also is crucial for the health, growth and effectiveness of nonprofits. This funding allows grantees to respond to crises and opportunities, maintain staff continuity and organizational leadership, overcome unforeseeable challenges and improve planning. Disappointingly, more than 40 percent of foundations in our sample did not provide *any* multi-year grants. Leading the field, however, 132 foundations (16.3 percent) provided 50 percent or more of their grant dollars as multi-year grants. This is the benchmark for Philanthropy at Its Best.

> Applying for and reporting on grants primarily facilitate accountability, but these activities also can help grantees clarify their thinking and improve their work. However, too often, applications are needlessly complicated and evaluations are not used appropriately, creating significant burdens for grantees. Exemplary grantmakers understand the important concept of the net grant and ensure their application and reporting requirements are proportional to the grant size and useful for all parties.

> Because grantmakers rely primarily on grantees to carry out their charitable purposes, exceptional funders engage nonprofits in meaningful partnerships, which help both parties advance their missions and contribute to the public good. This creates an environment of trust and maximizes the social benefit of philanthropy. Grantmakers committed to true partnership provide sufficient overhead in project grants, fund capacity building and leadership development, and interact with grantees in respectful and responsive ways as part of enhancing effectiveness.

# Chapter II: Effectiveness

Long-term and unrestricted funding supports the learning and innovation needed to have an impact. If foundations are serious about leadership development and supporting their nonprofits, start with giving leaders what they say they most need – multiyear, unrestricted, general operating support.

– John Esterle, Executive Director
The Whitman Institute[127]

Institutional grantmakers rely primarily on non-grant-making nonprofits to carry out their charitable purposes and maintain their tax exempt status. Considerable attention has been paid in recent years to increasing the social value and public benefit of philanthropy, with a special emphasis on efficacy. There are many compelling reasons for foundations to invest in their grantees' effectiveness; unfortunately, too few grantmakers provide the types of support needed most by grantees. In addition, a majority of grantmakers overburden their grantees with excessive administrative requirements, diminishing sector-wide impact.

Research consistently suggests that when grantmakers provide general operating support and multi-year funding, the civil society sector is able to maximize impact. Making application and reporting requirements commensurate with grant size is another way in which exemplary grantmakers can enhance the sector's effectiveness. Investing in the long-term sustainability of a strong, diverse and enabled nonprofit civil society sector by engaging grantees as true partners is an important corollary to help foundations achieve their own missions.

Many contend that there is an insurmountable power differential between grantmakers and grantees because of the "power of the purse." This dynamic creates an imbalance in the important relationship of the supply and demand sides of the nonprofit sector. Re-conceiving the power asymmetry as a relationship that reflects true partnerships offers funders one way to help grantees understand that they are working toward the same goals. A grantmaker's *reliance* on its grantees to carry out its charitable purpose places an impetus on the funder community to identify ways that engage grantees on a level playing field. When grantmakers treat their grantees as true partners, they can work toward building a relationship premised on mutual trust. By providing generous grant dollars for true general operating support, making commitments of two or more years in multi-year grants, and demonstrating trust in its grantees by making administrative requirements commensurate with grant size, a foundation displays exemplary philanthropy in practice.

## GENERAL OPERATING SUPPORT

Improving the effectiveness and impact of the civil society sector remains a salient and increasingly researched issue. NCRP, Grantmakers for Effective Organizations, the Center for Effective Philanthropy, CompassPoint, researchers at the Center on Philanthropy at Indiana University and many foundations and grantees have highlighted the importance of the types of grants or the resources needed to bolster the infrastructure and internal capacity of nonprofits as important to the health and impact of grantee organizations. As the Center for Effective Philanthropy (CEP) states, "Ultimately, the beneficiaries of better

> We know enough about the field and organizations and their behavior to know that organizations need patient financial support. We know these organizations are most in need of general operating support and most in need of the assurance and the confidence that our support will be there.
>
> —Gregg Behr, Executive Director, the Grable Foundation[128]

foundation–grantee relationships are not just grantees and foundations, but the people and issues they seek to affect through their work. By working more productively together, foundations and grantees can create more positive social impact. This, after all, is the ultimate goal of both parties."[129]

General operating support is fundamental to enhancing grantee effectiveness and impact. Yet, institutional philanthropy has a history of preferring project or program support over general operating support. A 2002 board briefing document developed by the Council on Foundations notes that the debate about which type of support is a better strategy dates back about a century, nearly as old as institutional grantmaking itself.[130] NCRP historically has advocated that grantmakers increase significantly the proportion of grant dollars allocated as core, unrestricted support.[131] Table 2.1 summarizes key highlights of NCRP's recent research and work on this issue.

General operating support[132] is unrestricted funding that an organization may use as it best sees fit to achieve its mission. The unencumbered nature of true core support offers myriad benefits to grantmakers

and grantees alike. It eases administrative burdens on both and allows funders to invest in an entire organization and mission. As Carol Watson, program officer at the Rockwell Fund, notes, "The strategy should be to invest in organizations that are successful and to trust them to do the social engineering."[133] Unlike program support with predetermined metrics and outcome measures, general operating support provides both parties with the needed flexibility to increase the impact of the democratic civil society sector. Moreover, such support does not imply a lack of accountability. In its 2007 Action Guide for funders, Grantmakers for Effective Organizations (GEO) debunks several common misperceptions about providing core support. Among these is the issue of a perceived lack of accountability in this type of support compared to restricted program support. GEO counters this, noting that "there is very little difference in accountability between project and general operating support. In both cases, the grantmaker needs to work with the grantee to design evaluation questions that clarify the *impact* of the grantee's work."[134]

Some foundation leaders also recognize the importance of core support. Paul Brest, president of the William and Flora Hewlett Foundation, raises several salient issues in his 2003 discussion of strategic philanthropy in the *Stanford Social Innovation Review*. Notably, he links the importance of providing operating support with maximizing impact in his framework of "strategic philanthropy."[135] Kathleen Buechel and Esther Handy highlight the F.B. Heron Foundation and the Whitman Institute's approaches to successful core support funding. Both foundations emphasize attribution or collective impact: Heron uses a performance scorecard to assess overall organizational success and Whitman states that "the direct role our funding plays is less important to us than the overall success of the organization"[136] when assessing operating support initiatives.

In addition to research done by NCRP, GEO, CEP and others, Jeanne Bell et al.'s survey of nearly 2,000 nonprofit executives and program managers also demonstrates the value that grantees place on flexible general operating support. The analysis found that "respondents ranked providing more unrestricted and multiyear support as the two funder actions that would most help them in their work."[137] These findings are reinforced by a recent series of focus groups done by GEO that found that executives from foundations and grantee organizations alike believe that providing more general operating support would be one of the most beneficial ways grantmakers can support nonprofit success.[138] As noted in the *Harvard Business Review,* "by helping grantees to improve their own capabilities, foundations can affect the social productivity of more resources than just their slice of the whole."[139]

## Credit: contribution and attribution

In an important 2008 supplement to its *Action Guide,* GEO returned to the issues of accountability and presumed ceding of control. As the supplement notes, "Compared with grants for specific programs or projects, general operating support requires grantmakers to give up some control over where the money goes. This does not mean, however, that grantmakers have to give up on the expectation that their investments will yield demonstrable results. Rather, grantmakers need to think about assessment in a different way. *This means changing the focus from program-level outcomes to the social impact of the organization as a whole.*"[140] This returns institutional philanthropy's focus to its bottom line—to maximize the social benefit and impact of its contributions by investing in the long-term effectiveness of its grantees. By demonstrating trust in their nonprofit partners in this way, and looking at alternate metrics and accountability models for core support, the lack of control or the perceived inability to measure success is defrayed.

As GEO notes in debunking the perceived myth of a funder's loss of influence and impact in developing programs to solve problems, "increased general operating support can lead to greater impact for both parties. General operating support also can strengthen the relationship, leading to more influence for the grantmaker and a more productive partnership. Instead of supporting part of a program, the grantmaker is contributing to the organization as a whole."[141]

NCRP, GEO, researchers at Harvard University and grantmakers that provide substantial core support are among those that emphasize the importance of re-conceiving the grantmaker's role in terms of credit: it

| TABLE 2.1 RECENT NCRP WORK ON CORE SUPPORT | |
|---|---|
| 2002 | *State of Philanthropy.* Biennial publication included several analyses and commentary that highlighted the need for increased core support. |
| 2003 | *The Core of the Matter.* Findings summarized conclusions from NCRP's convening of nonprofit leaders that 50 percent of grant dollars should be provided in this way. |
| 2003 | *Axis of Ideology: Conservative Foundations and Public Policy.* Research demonstrated impact of long-term core support among conservative foundations, noting that mainstream foundations were less likely to provide support in this way. |
| 2004 | *Standards for Foundation and Corporate Grantmaking.* Publication called for 50 percent of grant dollars for unrestricted support. NCRP presented testimony to the Senate Finance Committee advocating for significant increases in core support by grantmakers. |
| 2005 | *Not All Grants Are Created Equal.* Report demonstrated that conservative foundations were more likely than mainstream ones to provide core support. |
| 2007 | *A Call to Action: Organizing to Increase the Effectiveness and Impact of Foundation Grantmaking.* Report summarized findings from nonprofit leaders' focus group discussions convened by NCRP in 2005 and 2006 from urban and rural areas. |

is the foundation's *contribution* to the organization as a whole that is important, not the *attribution* of certain outcomes to a particular funder. As Brest states, "Providing general operating support is no different from any other activity that depends on many people's contributions … where no individual makes a difference, but where aggregate contributions are critical."[142] Similarly, Chuck Hamilton, executive director of the Clark Foundation, notes the important role that core support plays in addressing community needs and states, "Knowing where the money is going can be overly seductive. Some foundations make the mistake of looking at the number served vs. the number actually helped. We have to get comfortable with evaluating operating support — looking at financials and other paperwork, trusting the organization by talking with them"[143] Even the Council on Foundations noted this needed paradigm shift to rethink institutional philanthropy's approach to how it perceives credit. The 2002 board briefing document includes quotes from prominent grantmakers of varying types in support of operating support. The "collective glory" of grantees' overall work, "trust," and investments in capacity building and infrastructure are among the benefits highlighted by the Pew Charitable Trusts, the Albert Kunstadter Family Foundation and J.P. Morgan Chase.[144]

Buechel and Handy address the challenge of measuring the impact of general operating support based on funder perspectives articulated at the 2007 *Capital Ideas* symposium cosponsored by Harvard's Hauser Center for Nonprofit Organizations and the Nonprofit Finance Fund. They encourage funders and grantees to engage in deliberate conversations about the effectiveness of core support, to share metrics tied to organizational health and outcome measurement, and to suggest identifying appropriate ways for grantmakers to get credit for their core support contributions to grantees. As Hank Beukema of the McCune Foundation notes in addressing the perceived loss of credit, "We need to encourage these funders to share the stage with others and to take a longer term view." This statement echoes CEP's findings that core support alone is insufficient; rather, core support provided with a sufficient time frame is what grantees value most in their funders.

### Accountability

Despite the findings about the benefits of general operating support, some grantmakers still believe that core support diminishes accountability compared to project-specific support with predetermined metrics of success. To address this perceived "accountability gap," some foundations have taken steps toward trying to build accountability mechanisms into core sup-

port grants. One prominent example comes from the William and Flora Hewlett Foundation. Paul Brest advocates providing more grant dollars to "negotiated general operating support," grants that allocate funding toward core operations with caveats and restrictions to preserve accountability. Such support is defined as a grant in which "the funder engages in a due diligence process, which culminates in an agreement about what outcomes the organization plans to achieve, how it plans to achieve them, and how progress will be assessed and reported."[145]

The California Wellness Foundation uses a similar but more flexible approach to core support grants, clarifying the impact of the grantee's work and designing an evaluation mechanism in partnership with the grantee. In its 1999 annual report, this funder noted the demands of fundraising and project-specific grants as placing "contrived requirements" that negatively impact grantee effectiveness. The report succinctly summarized the benefits of core support: "Nonprofit organizations are given the opportunity to assess and address internal needs. …With the aid of unrestricted grants, nonprofit organizations can strengthen their infrastructures, reevaluate missions and otherwise set themselves on a strategic course for long-term success. Above all, core operating support can serve as a catalyst, opening the door to discussions of 'big picture' topics and investing in the vision and ideas of nonprofit leaders."[146] Gary Yates, president and CEO of the foundation, explained its decision to begin providing half of its grants in the form of core support. Noting that other funders remained "ambivalent" about core support, he said that the change could be one of the most strategic ways for the foundation to support its grantees. Addressing the value that core support adds, he said, "While project funding tends to stretch and even weaken nonprofits, core-operating dollars can have the opposite effect: strengthening organizations and helping them stay focused on their mission. Now that's adding value!"[147] The California Wellness Foundation's grantmaking demonstrates how core support and program support grants are complementary. When the foundation announced its decision to provide half of its grants as core operating support, it remained committed to providing the balance of its grants as program support to ongoing health initiatives.

The Sobrato Family Foundation, which provides exclusively general operating support grants to nonprofits in Silicon Valley, places even fewer restrictions on grantees, Sobrato's executive director Diane Ford says, "Our bottom line is to build robust, healthy local organizations to serve local public needs. It makes sense to give them the money and let them put it where they need to put it to fulfill their missions. They know best where that is."[148] Another example is the Hawaii Community Foundation, which was struggling with how to measure impact and then realized how much of the qualitative information it had was, in fact, rife with metrics. This funder's impact metrics evolved from the stories that their organizations shared with them. The experiences of the Hawaii Community Foundation are especially relevant for rethinking impact and assessment of core support grants.[149]

The 2002 Council on Foundations (COF) board briefing document lists six reasons that some funders prefer general operating support over program support:

1. Helps grantees build and sustain their capacity and infrastructure. "An organization cannot be effective without efficient operations and strong management."
2. Contributes positively to grantee sustainability.
3. Keeps grantees focused on mission.
4. Core support creates a more level playing field because it builds trust and improves the relationship between the funder and the grantee. "Limited or short-term project funds can lead to less than successful endeavors and frustration on both the part of the funder and grantee."
5. By giving grantees more control, they are enabled to generate innovative solutions. "It is a grantee-centered approach instead of an approach powered by a funder's agenda."
6. General support grants align with the long-term interest of the foundation's board. "The board can become engaged in thinking about the big-picture needs of the community."[150]

Grantee organizations ultimately are accountable to their communities and constituents. This is the non-profit sector's *raison d'être:* social impact. Accountability from a grantee to a grantmaker also is important for numerous reasons, the most obvious being disclosure of how grant dollars were used. True general operating support and accountability are not, however, mutually exclusive.

### Flexibility

Institutional grantmakers can find that providing core support helps them meet their own interests. For example, NCRP's *A Call to Action* highlights the work of Woods Bowman, Elizabeth Keating and Mark Hager in the section on "organizational slack," a concept very familiar to many in the private sector who link it with organizational effectiveness. "Slack" is a buffer of resources that allows an organization to adapt to changes in the environment, respond to new opportunities and adjust programmatic priorities based on on-the-ground realities. As Rick Cohen, for-

## CORE SUPPORT AND MEASURABLE IMPACT[154]

The Blue Shield of California Foundation provides one example of a grantmaker that found ways to quantify the impact of its core support grants. The foundation sponsored the Core Support Initiative, providing more than $12 million in flexible financing to nearly 200 community health clinics in California "to cover whatever [the clinics] need most, from utility bills to hiring new staff to expanding services." Survey results following completion of the initiative in 2006 found that fully 98 percent of respondents singled out the substantial role core support played in their ability to cover operating expenses, sustain service levels, and cover uncompensated costs. Beyond maintaining the infrastructure of these clinics, "respondents cited how core support funding helped them to augment their visibility, credibility and legitimacy. In addition, half the clinics leveraged Blue Shield of California Foundation grants to raise additional public or private funds." One clinic even described how flexible funding allowed for new hires to relieve overtaxed clinical care personnel, increase training and correspondingly boost the morale of staff members. This foundation identified the measurable impact of its grantees and attributed impact to the type of support it provided that allowed for this impact: core support.

mer executive director of NCRP and author of the report, states in discussing organizational slack, "Because they don't have to be immediately and restrictively pumped into program operations, unrestricted resources can be used for important organizational slack purposes that enhance effectiveness and impact. In their view, investment income is a particularly appropriate source of revenue but the proportion that will be able to generate large sums for this purpose is slim."[151] Grantees, particularly smaller organizations, often lack investment income and thus unrestricted core support serves as the organizational slack instead, allowing grantees the flexibility to adapt to ever-changing environments and to respond to program opportunities and crises.

Dennis Derryck and Rikki Abzug highlighted the "shock absorption" that core support provides grantees and note that insufficient flexibility can leave a grantee vulnerable, especially in the wake of pressing needs. In the words of an urban nonprofit participant in NCRP's focus group discussions, "Core money gives you time for relationship-building, for forward-thinking."[152] NCRP and Bell et al.'s interviews and focus group discussions with grantee staff, particularly executive leaders, consistently reflect increased trust in the grantmaker–grantee relationship as an important outcome of providing general operating support as well.[153]

### MULTI-YEAR FUNDING

Providing multi-year grants is crucially important for the health, growth and effectiveness of nonprofits. A significant portion of the literature on multi-year funding links this type of support with overall foundation investments to build and strengthen nonprofit infrastructure.[156] A report from the Center for Effective Philanthropy (CEP) found that the type, duration and size of grants all are intimately connected with nonprofit perceptions of the impact of the grant on effectiveness. CEP found that general operating support grants of sufficient size and duration generated the highest ratings.[157] But, as the CEP report states, core support alone is insufficient to ensure a grantee organization is enabled to succeed and increase its impact. Core support must be provided with a long enough timeframe for the grant recipient to demonstrate its impact. As CEP states, "Most grants are simply too small and short term for it to matter much to grantees whether they are for program or operating support. … It is not operating support alone that generates higher ratings of impact on the grantee organization, but rather operating support of sufficient size and duration."[158] Additionally, policymakers and business gurus, including Hillary Rodham Clinton, Bill Bradley and Jim Collins, also have noted the inefficiencies generated in the nonprofit sector from the lack of multi-year funding and core support.[158]

Taken together, lack of sufficient flexible core support funds with unrealistically short timeframes negatively influence the civil society sector's effectiveness and decrease grantee impact. As a rural youth nonprofit organization's representative stated during an NCRP focus group, "Being a model program and having all these national replications … a five-year grant initially … allowed us time to implement the program and evaluate it over a period of time that really showed results…. [With] a one to three year grant, you don't have the time to do that, and it's just like continually starting over again when you have those short term grants. So that the fact that somebody had the foresight to offer a five-year grant really made the difference for us. It was the thing that helped us to be successful and nationally recognized."[160]

Multi-year funding, much like general operating support, provides nonprofits with the needed flexibility to

> In recent years, however, funders have become increasingly conscious of their grantees' need for long-term, multi-year funding commitments to support organizational growth and sound infrastructure. General operating support and longer-term grants naturally align with the more forward-looking and performance-centered evaluations…
>
> — Kramer et al., FSG Social Impact Advisors[155]

respond to both crises and opportunities. This funding allows grantees to maintain staff continuity and organizational leadership, overcome unforeseeable challenges and improve planning. Multi-year grants generally reduce the administrative burden for grantmakers and grantees. Similar to core support, once the goals and objectives of the grantee organization are agreed upon, both parties are free to make more strategic use of their time. Multi-year funding is distinct from continuing support; multi-year grants offer grantees a firm commitment of funding for more than one year, while continuing support grants are a series of renewable one-year grants from a foundation to the same grantee. Continuing grants are important, but exemplary grantmakers provide multi-year grants.[161]

There appears to be emerging consensus across the civil society sector that multi-year funds are as fundamental to impact and effectiveness as core support grants. GEO's *Change Agent Project* included focus group discussions with nonprofit executives who articulated increasing the amount of multi-year funding as integral to grantee success. Bell et al.'s survey of nonprofit executives found that more multi-year support ranked second only to more general operating support among the types of support that funders could provide to help leaders of grantee organizations better implement their work.[162] Case studies conducted as part of an overhead study by Indiana University's Center on Philanthropy solicited feedback from grantee CEOs as well. The findings were similar to those seen in Bell et al.'s research. The short timeframe of most foundation grants was associated with grantee leadership burnout and frustration. Previous NCRP and GEO focus group discussions with nonprofit CEOs found similar results.[163]

Kevin Bolduc et al. of CEP addressed the length of funding in assessing foundation practices that improve grantee satisfaction. While the survey analysis did not find an association between multi-year funding and grantee perceptions of foundations, it notes that this may be attributable to the fact that very few of the grantees surveyed actually received multi-year funding (60 percent were one-year grants and 19 percent were three years or longer in duration). Moreover, CEP's analysis found that close to 80 percent of respondents had received grants from the same foundation and many reported receiving continuous funding. As CEP concludes, "The transactional nature of this relationship, while not detrimental to

| TABLE 2.2 FOUNDATION AWARDED MULTI-YEAR GRANTS OF TWO OR MORE YEARS SOMETIMES, OFTEN OR ALWAYS*** | |
| --- | --- |
| RESPONDENT | PERCENT |
| All respondents | 60 |
| $10 million or less | 47 |
| $10–$50 million | 57 |
| $50–$100 million | 62 |
| $100–$400 million | 73 |
| More than $400 million | 81 |

***p≤0.001[169]

grantee satisfaction, does tend to increase the administrative burden on the grantee and the foundation."[164] In short, it is possible that grantees simply do not receive adequate long-term funding and, thus, are less inclined to link the duration of the grant with what they need when assessing their funders. Moreover, the administrative burden noted by CEP echoes the frustrations of constant fundraising discussed in this section. Although continuous funding is beneficial, NCRP sees such grants as necessary but insufficient. Thus, exemplary grantmakers provide multi-year grants of at least two years or more.

Multi-year grants make it easier for nonprofits to overcome the challenges identified by Bell et al.'s survey of nonprofit CEOs; notably, these challenges are exacerbated by the paucity of real core support.[165] As with unrestricted support, multi-year grants make it easier to maintain staff continuity and foster organizational leadership. Confirmed multi-year support allows for better planning and reasonable compensation.

Participants in NCRP focus group discussions raised frustrations about the lack of multi-year funds as an impediment to their ability to meet their missions. As a staff member of a rural youth nonprofit stated, "Giving us two- or even three-year grants, because that way the issue of training staff, you know that you're going to have the money over time, the investment is not going to be lost … *Grants over a two- to three-year period would really be helpful to organizations for stability*."[166] Coupled with the longer timeframe needed to achieve specific organizational outcomes raised in these discussions, the stability and flexibility provided to grantees allows them to make better use of their resources and time, depending on organizational needs.

A 2008 GEO survey, *Grantmaking Practices that Support Grantee Success: Survey Report*,[167] asked respondents questions about multi-year funding, i.e., grants with a duration of two or more years. GEO's analysis of the data suggests a positive association between foundation size and the likelihood of providing multi-year support. Respondents from larger foundations were substantially more likely to report providing multi-year grants; the smallest foundations reported providing the least number of such grants (47 percent) compared to the largest foundations (81 percent).[168] These figures represent the low and high bounds observed in GEO's analysis. A comparable proportion of the smallest foundations surveyed stated that they renewed one-year grants. Table 2.2 is adapted from GEO's report and shows the association between foundation asset size and provision of multi-year support.

cally link this work with impact and effectiveness. NCRP encourages those engaged in and supporting exemplary philanthropic practice within the sector to conduct additional research on this issue. Moreover, because the Foundation Center tracks this type of support, NCRP's preliminary analysis of multi-year grants, discussed in depth later in this chapter, makes a needed contribution to the sector to begin collecting data for future longitudinal comparisons and time-series data.

## ADMINISTRATIVE REQUIREMENTS

Grantees encounter considerable variability about what is needed for a grant application to be considered by a funder and spend significant time producing unique grant proposals, reports and evaluations, customized by individual funder. To avoid this counterproductive scenario, a grantmaker that practices exemplary philanthropy seeks to simplify application and reporting requirements and makes reasonable administrative requirements of its grantees.

The concept of the "net grant"[173] is particularly relevant to grantmakers in determining what defines "reasonable" application requirements. The Nonprofit Finance Fund led by Clara Miller has made an important contribution to the field by introducing this idea. The "net grant" is the total grant with the grantee's fundraising, reporting and other administrative costs subtracted from the overall amount. Minimizing the transaction costs of fundraising for grantees has immediate benefits for both funders and grantees.[174] For example, shifting away from cumbersome customized grant applications to simple letters of inquiry, making funding guidelines readily available on a foundation's web site and reducing the turnaround time for grant proposals are some generally agreed upon good grantmaking practices to rethink the grant application process.[175]

> Our sector faces an effectiveness paradox. Funders, striving to be strategic and diligent, adopt what seem like sensible application and reporting requirements. But these practices—multiplied by thousands of grantmakers—place a heavy burden on organizations seeking funding, hampering their ability to be efficient with their time and effective in their missions.
>
> —Jessica Bearman, Project Streamline[172]

The type of foundation also influences whether or not the funder is likely to provide multi-year support. The GEO survey compared the type of foundation with the likelihood of providing this support and found that corporate (73 percent) and private foundations (67 percent) were much more likely than community foundations (36 percent) to report making multi-year grants.[170] This finding is in keeping with community foundations' provision of general operating support. These foundations are less likely than their corporate and independent counterparts to provide general support. However, community foundations reported providing a higher proportion of their grant dollars as core support relative to three years ago.[171]

Beyond the works discussed above, there is a scarcity of research on multi-year grants that specifi-

A recent report by Project Streamline identified ten ways in which current practices by foundations create significant burdens on the time, energy and effectiveness of nonprofits. It is a thorough and compelling report that gives collective voice to what nonprofits have been saying for years. The report was commissioned by several grantmaking associations, funder affinity and collaborative groups, and the National Council of Nonprofits.[176] This collaboration is a positive example of donors and grantees working together to identify the areas in most need to improve the civil society sector. NCRP is encouraged that this project will continue dialogue with funders and grantees to identify and overcome impediments to effectiveness.

Among the ten key areas identified by Project Streamline as "flaws in the system," several relate directly to making administrative requirements more reasonable. The research surveyed 858 foundations, held focus group discussions and conducted interviews with foundations, nonprofits and intermediaries. Project partners worked with the Center for Effective Philanthropy (CEP) to review findings from a set of CEP Grantee Perception Reports. CEP used data from perception reports of 170 foundations and coded 540 grantee recommendations; the center also conducted regression analyses to determine statistical significance and the predictive power of four variables related to administrative requirements.[177] Project Streamline's report demonstrated that administrative requirements were identified by grantees as a signal of lack of trust between the funder and the grantee, something clearly detrimental to moving toward a more level playing field or engaging in a partnership model. Further, the report found that fully 13 percent of all foundation dollars is spent on administration,[178] suggesting that current administrative requirements create inefficiencies among funders as well.

### Evaluation requirements and efficiency: A philanthropic paradox

Evaluations in particular have the potential to be a drain on the time of nonprofits and foundations alike. According to Alana Conner Snibbe, senior editor of the Stanford Social Innovation Review, "Boards and funders don't misuse evaluations because they are dumb or lazy, or even because they are ornery. Instead, their misuses and abuses reflect the fact that good evaluation is extremely difficult."[179] These findings are similar to those identified by both Project Streamline and GEO's research. Project Streamline's research found that very few foundations actually use grant reports in a meaningful way: they do not inform future grant making and many are "shelved" and never read.

## GRANTMAKER PRACTICES THAT NEGATIVELY IMPACT SECTOR EFFECTIVENESS

1. Significant variability in grant application and reporting requirements
2. Singular approach to requirements regardless of grant size
3. High costs of grant applications that might not be worth the effort
4. Transferring grantmaker administrative requirements onto grantees
5. Diminished grantee trust from overly burdensome administrative requirements
6. "Reports on a [grantmaker's] shelf" sometimes never are read
7. Grantees engage in "fundraising gymnastics" to satisfy administrative requirements
8. Funders overemphasis on due diligence, negatively impacts grantee effectiveness
9. Counterproductive attempts to streamline strategies such as e-filing
10. Self-imposed funder inefficiencies – 13 percent of foundation dollars spent on administration of grants

Adapted from *Drowning in Paperwork, Distracted from Purpose: Challenges and Opportunities in Grant Application and Reporting* by Project Streamline (2008).

General operating and multi-year support require a different set of metrics than project-specific grants. GEO notes, "As grantmakers consider how to assess the impact of general operating support, they should make sure their assessments do not stand in the way of the broader goal of improving the capacity of nonprofits to deliver meaningful results. This means using assessment as a platform for promoting learning and continuous improvement among grantees. It also means using assessment as a platform for a stronger grantmaker-grantee relationship and ensuring that assessment does not become an added burden for grantees."[180]

Institutional grantmakers also should recognize that qualitative data are just as meaningful as quantitative data. NCRP and Bell et al.'s survey and focus group discussions with nonprofit CEOs found that these two types of support ranked higher than any other grantmaking practice among nonprofit leaders.

CEP's research also found that core support of sufficient duration ranked highest among surveyed grantees. Especially when considering long-term sustainability of philanthropic interventions, patience is essential—results may not be measurable using any metrics for several years. There are, however, interim and continuous progress indicators that can serve the intermediate role of demonstrating that impact is in its nascent forms.[181]

## Foundation theory and practice – a disconnect that impedes impact

Many foundations believe that evaluation should be useful for informing future grantmaking decisions and for improving program design or making mid-course corrections. This is especially relevant for core and multi-year grant reporting requirements. Although these types of support often require a grant report, the form of the report is similar to an evaluation because a) it often looks for demonstrable organizational impact; b) of the longer timeframe of these types of support; and c) of the different measures and metrics used to assess impact. Of course, to get evaluations of sufficient quality to produce these benefits foundations need to allow nonprofits to invest in the capacity to conduct meaningful evaluation. Core support can be used for a variety of ways that build evaluative capacity, such as staff training in monitoring outcomes or funds for external consultants who can conduct evaluations more rigorously without additional upfront investments. Yet, despite the rationale for evaluations of long-term unrestricted grants to serve this purpose, studies comparing foundation theory with practice find a consistent gap in this area.

In 2004, the Urban Institute partnered with GEO to produce an important report authored by Francie Ostrower. *Attitudes and Practices Concerning Effective Philanthropy*[182] remains a seminal publication; it is the first large-scale survey of the U.S. foundation world's own perceptions of its variable attitudes and practices. The report found several areas in which foundation self-reported grantmaking practices differed greatly from actual grantmaking practices. The 2008 GEO survey discussed in this chapter was conducted as a follow-up survey to the 2004 report, and repeated many, though not all, of the same questions. The 2008 GEO survey thus allows for some longitudinal comparisons, though with cautions and caveats about drawing conclusions for some areas.

Ostrower's analysis found that final reports were the most common way that foundations monitor whether their funds were spent in accordance with the grant parameters. However, a survey of 300 nonprofit CEOs and executive directors in Ohio and New York shows that there are insufficient resources for evaluation. Fully 75 percent said they do not feel they have enough time for evaluation, 61 percent felt they lacked the staff capacity for it, and 45 percent voiced a sense of a lack of funding for evaluation.[183] This suggests that grantmakers often make high demands of their grantees to demonstrate impact without providing sufficient funds for their grantees to conduct formal evaluations. Foundations ought to: a) make evaluations more meaningful in terms of self-evaluations and grantee evaluations; b) provide funds that allow grantees to invest in their evaluative capacity if the funder demands rigorous evaluations; and c) not try to emulate the private sector in terms of evaluation.

## YOU CAN'T MEASURE EVERYTHING THAT MATTERS

"Climate change" or global warming is a pertinent example for the effectiveness paradox created by the "tyranny of measurement." The environment is a pure public good because it meets the two criteria of being non-rival and non-exclusive. Non-rival means that once the "good" is provided, the resource's availability is not impacted by another individual's consumption of it, while non-exclusive means that nobody can be kept from consuming the good once it has been provided. But how does one quantify or evaluate the impact that environmental justice groups working to address global warming may have on future generations? The impact will take time to materialize, and the benefits likely will be time-delayed or qualitative. Can we really quantify the positive impact of clean air for the future? Does not having a metric tied to this crucial work diminish today's investment when it ensures future security? This is the kind of nuance of the depth and breadth of work undertaken by our vibrant nonprofit sector that should inform all evaluations.

This final point is crucial: much has been written about the professionalization of the nonprofit sector or holding the civil society sector to metrics established in the private sector. Not only is there a significant difference in the core reason for evaluation (profit maximization versus social impact or benefit), but private sector evaluations are not immune to problems any substantial evaluation presents. It is arduous work to conduct a rigorous evaluation, and making measurement more meaningful means learning from "failures," which can serve as learning opportunities for funders and grantees. Identifying issues or barriers as they arise also provides the chance for midcourse corrections, allowing more effective use of human and financial resources for the balance of a grant period, including a core support grant or multi-year funding. And a program that looks like a "failure" in the short-term may in fact yield high returns in the long-term. This is especially so for grants made with an eye toward long-term sustainable change. Institutional philanthropy and the nonprofit sector's approach to evaluations must be informed by these issues, compelling grantmakers to rethink what the real purpose of evaluation is and how to make it more useful for both parties.

### Grant dollars per hour of administrative requirement

In its 2008 follow-up survey to Ostrower's report, GEO found that only 12 percent of foundations surveyed reported collecting data on the length of time a grantee needs to meet administrative requirements.[184] The GEO survey notes that larger foundations are twice as likely as smaller counterparts to have collected this information. Yet, there remains a significant knowledge gap that results in foundations underestimating the amount of time it takes grantees to meet administrative requirements.[185] Foundations with a median grant size of $50,000 reported that grantees spent a median of eight hours for reports and evaluations and a median of ten hours for administrative requirements related to fundraising. In contrast to these estimates, the Center for Effective Philanthropy's survey of grantees reported that respondents spent a

median of ten hours on evaluation and reporting and a median 20 hours on development-related administrative requirements.[186] Because the GEO and CEP surveys analyzed grantmakers and grantees with similar funding parameters and found such different results, this example highlights the importance of actively soliciting grantee feedback.

The 2008 GEO survey asked respondents to estimate the amount of time a grantee spends on meeting its administrative requirements along with an estimate of median grant from the funder. GEO members provided a median of $2,500 in grant dollars per hour of administrative requirements compared to $1,500 provided by non-members. As the analysts note, the $2,500 aggregate median grant dollars per administrative hour aligns with figures reported by CEP in its survey of grantees that gauged more than 100 foundations of variable types and sizes. These analyses suggest that the $2,500 figure is a relatively accurate estimate of current practice trends in the sector. As with all the metrics established by NCRP in this book, current giving trends inform where exemplary philanthropy begins but Philanthropy at Its Best must aspire to improve current trends. A more reliable way to establish reasonable administrative benchmarks is found in GEO's in-depth analysis of these data, discussed in detail in the *Setting the Bar for Philanthropy at Its Best* section later in this chapter. GEO's quartile analysis shows that some exemplary grantmakers provide more than $3,500 in grants per administrative hour.[187]

All of the above point to the need for a paradigm shift that moves the asymmetric power relationship between grantmakers and grantees to one of true partnership and mutual trust. Fundamental to this paradigm shift is ensuring that a foundation's administrative requirements are reasonable and commensurate with grant size.

> A program that looks like a "failure" in the short-term may in fact yield high returns in the long-term. This is especially so for grants made with an eye toward long-term sustainable change. Institutional philanthropy and the nonprofit sector's approach to evaluations must be informed by these issues …

## PARTNERSHIPS

Grantmakers rely on their grantees to carry out their charitable purpose, compelling institutional philanthropy to reconsider seriously the nature of the relationship it has with its non-grantmaking partners. In a true partnership, the funder that controls the supply side (the funds) and the grantees that identify and address the demand side (social and community

> It's the difference between coming up with an idea yourself for how you think social outcomes should be achieved and funding people that do that versus looking for the best organizations out there that are already doing it and asking how to help them do it better. We are not at odds with the grantee. We are getting behind their plans and the set of results that their board is focused on to begin with. We provide the "glue money" that is hard to raise and helps you build the capacity you need to grow and enhance your programs.
>
> —Nancy Roob, President, the Edna McConnell Clark Foundation[188]

needs) do not confront an insurmountable power differential. Rather, exemplary grantmakers engage grantees in a meaningful partnership that helps both parties advance their mission and contributes to the public good. Not only does this maximize the social benefit of philanthropy, it creates an environment of trust in which problems can be identified and resolved more efficiently and learning opportunities on several fronts are enhanced. Recently, Arthur Schmidt, founder of GuideStar, suggested nine strategies to implement his proposed core doctrine of augmenting institutional philanthropy's social value. For the purposes of the grantmaker-grantee relationship, one recommendation stands out: "shattering the benefactor/supplicant condition endemic in grantmaker/grantee relationships…"[189] Asked by Bell et al. what executive directors at grantee organizations liked the least about their jobs, one responded, "I hate the power dynamics with funders," while another stated, "I hate having to prove to funders what we do all the time. I hate the bureaucracy around money and the sort of prejudice of it, the irrationality of it and the competition around it. I think the system is broken."[190]

Some foundations find significant value from the funder perspective in leveling the playing field by providing core support. For example, in 2002, Melanie

Beene of the William and Flora Hewlett Foundation stated, "From the funder's perspective, it gives us greater leverage for organizational change. Because the grant is so highly prized, people are willing to take seriously our concerns about what they're doing or not doing, and I think it's much more of a partnership relationship. We also have a really broad sense of the whole organization. For both of us, I think the dialogue is more realistic and more targeted and more honest."[191]

Clara Miller of the Nonprofit Finance Fund notes, "Deeply ingrained 'best practices' frequently add cost and reduce management flexibility in already difficult operating conditions. We end up hurting organizations we mean to help." Highlighting that much capacity building is intended to strengthen nonprofit management, she states that "much greater leverage resides in improvement of funding practices, where both funders and nonprofits create broader and more powerful system change."[192]

There are several ways that grantees who receive exemplary core and multi-year funding can use their funds to demonstrate the effectiveness of these grants. For example, many nonprofits will use these funds to diversify their funding base by shoring up their income development infrastructure. This is crucially important for grantmakers to understand as it allays a perennial concern about creating funder dependency if a grantee relies exclusively on a short list of foundations for these grants.

Nonprofit partners that receive sufficient levels of flexible unrestricted funds can also exercise care and judgment in determining what best meets their needs to fulfill their charitable purpose. Enabled with these grant dollars, they can use their discretion to invest in capacity building and leadership development, two increasingly researched and effective strategies that ensure the long-term health of the U.S. democratic civic sector.

### Capacity building and leadership development
Capacity building helps nonprofits improve their operations, infrastructure and effectiveness. Capacity

building grants are more restrictive than core operating support, but are valuable because they recognize that strong organizations are needed to create impact. If an organization receives a sufficient amount of true general operating support as defined in this chapter, the need for capacity building and leadership development grants decreases.

Investing in capacity is not a new concept; in the 1970s, the *Harvard Business Review* included an article coauthored by Richard Mittenthal, president of the TCC group, which highlighted the extant underfunding of nonprofit capacity. As he noted then, "The majority of large national foundations continue to limit funding to special programs and short-term projects, creating disincentives to good management, rather than supporting the organizational capacity building that nonprofits need."[193]

Investing in leadership development can be an incredibly beneficial form of capacity building that accomplishes two objectives. First, it addresses the staff continuity issues raised by grantees and, second, it advances opportunities to transition leadership to the next generation of civil society leaders. The Center for Creative Leadership distinguishes between leader development as "the expansion of a person's capacity to be effective in leadership roles and processes" and leadership development as "the expansion of the organization's capacity to enact the basic leadership tasks needed for collective work: setting direction, creating alignment, and maintaining commitment."[194]

Grantees that receive sufficient core support can use these funds to enhance both leader and leadership abilities. Moreover, because shared objectives between a grantmaker and grantee discussed earlier lead to positive social impact, nurturing leadership at the community level is yet another dimension to consider in the ways grantmakers provide funds to nonprofits.

Building community-level leadership is an example of "collective leadership," also known as inclusive, relational, participatory, cooperative and shared leadership.[195] Because of these characteristics, collective leadership lends itself naturally to the nonprofit sector, which seeks to enhance the public good, and especially to groups that work in relationship with each other to provide human services and work toward social change.[196] "The collective leadership model … raises questions about the utility of leadership development programs that are focused exclusively on the executive director. Rather, the idea is to create holistic, vertically integrated programs that reap rewards from the entire organization and, often, for the broader community."[197]

An important issue that emerges in GEO's research on leadership development is coupling it with capacity building: leadership development is a type of capacity building and capacity building is a form of leadership development.[198] NCRP extends this argument further: providing long-term unrestricted core support in the form of true general operating support and multi-year grants enables grantees to use their discretion in determining individual organizational needs, be they for capacity building or leadership development. Moreover, because these types of grants have demonstrated measurable impact and display an important level of trust between the grantee and grantmaker, they reinforce the need to shift to meaningful partnerships that lead to a potentially higher net benefit for the entire U.S. nonprofit sector. NCRP's position is reinforced by the findings in Bell et al.'s survey of nonprofit CEOs regarding what changes institutional grantmakers could make to facilitate survey respondents' jobs and make them more effective. General operating support ranked first and multi-year funding ranked second, while investments in executive leadership, specifically coaching and professional development, ranked last.[199] As the report notes, this does not mean that leadership development is irrelevant; rather, it indicates that nonprofit CEOs would be more effective if they had flexible funds that they could use at their discretion.

## The role of the program officer – competing demands

The role of the program officer, usually the exclusive point of contact between grantmakers and grantees, emerges here as crucial. Because the majority of interactions with the foundation happen through the program officer, she or he plays a critical role in establishing a sense of trust and partnership between a foundation and its grantees. A program officer can take simple steps—such as returning phone calls in a timely manner—that demonstrate responsiveness to the grantee. Additionally, being honest with grantees about the prospects of securing funding results in immediate efficiency gains, showing respect for the time of overworked nonprofit leaders. Some particularly helpful program officers take the additional step of referring applicants to other potential funders. In sum, the program officer's central role in mediating and building the important relationship with grantees can be made more meaningful by adopting simple mechanisms that demonstrate responsiveness.

Some program officers want authentic feedback from grantees, but honesty is hindered by the threat that grantees feel in sharing negative experiences. This highlights the importance of seeking anonymous feedback from grantees. Third-party or neutral external actors can often help foundations elicit the needed anonymous feedback on their performance. Independent consultants present funders with an opportunity to get authentic feedback that is not euphemized because of the threat of lost funding.

### Overhead in project grants – providing sufficient funds to cover indirect costs

It may not always be appropriate to make a general support grant; some situations require project grants. In such a scenario, true partnership means ensuring that grantees receive sufficient funding for overhead. Unlike general operating support, program support or project support is designated to cover the expenses of a particular project and frequently is subject to strict monitoring and evaluation Although program support may cover some overhead costs, the funding is restricted to "carry out specific activities"[200] and cannot support general operating expenses unassociated with the project. Moreover, research demonstrates consistently that the overhead provided in project support grants is insufficient.[201] Ensuring that an appropriate level of overhead is included in restricted project funding is essential to good grantmaking.

An Urban Institute study found that restricted program support without sufficient overhead actually undermines grantee capacity. Ken Wing and Mark Hager's research found that smaller nonprofit organizations with the most restricted program support had the greatest difficulty in paying for overhead expenses, leading to diminished capacity and inconsistent outcomes. As they note, "Small size combined with restricted funding is a double whammy that appears to almost guarantee inadequate organizational infrastructure."[202] Wing and Hager advocate increasing overhead support because of the positive association between such grantmaking and grantee impact.[203]

Patrick Rooney et al. found that 69 percent of foundations supported overhead expenses and nearly half made grants for general operating support. Their foundation survey results are in direct contrast to the perceptions of grantee organizations they surveyed. Fully two-thirds of surveyed health and education service organizations said they lacked adequate support to cover administrative and core operating costs. "Over half, 53.4 percent, reported the cause of their inadequate overhead funding was foundations desiring to support programs and not administrative expenses."[204] The survey's findings suggest that foundations may be more willing to cover overhead expenses in project grants than grantees generally believe. Yet, the lack of core support articulated by grantees in this research as well as previous NCRP interviews[205] with nonprofit leaders underscores why real general support grants are needed to maintain a robust nonprofit sector, enabled to respond to crises and opportunities alike.

### Long-term sustainability

Exemplary grantmakers recognize that true partnerships extend beyond supporting individual organizations. Instead, these funders acknowledge the importance of ensuring the long-term sustainability of the entire U.S. civil society sector. The Nonprofit Finance Fund and Harvard University's Hauser Center for Nonprofit Organizations convened a diverse group of nonprofit stakeholders in 2007. As the title of the convening, *Capital Ideas: Moving from Short-Term Engagement to Long-Term Sustainability*, suggests, this group sought to develop recommendations to address the persistent undercapitalization of the nonprofit sector, to elicit a paradigm shift in the way that funders view their investments in their grantees and to identify appropriate tools that would enhance the U.S. nonprofit sector as a whole. The issue of nonprofit sustainability is a salient lens for reviewing the financial mechanisms funders can use to increase their impact. Yet, foundation impact does not increase in isolation. Rather, by providing support in the form of core grants with a minimum of a two-year commitment, funders can create an enabled civil society sector that makes these organizations more effective and sustainable in the long term. As the report from the convening concluded, "Although business techniques are necessary, they are not sufficient. Market discipline is crucial in some areas, but social problems addressed by nonprofits exist often because markets are not working effectively. There also is an issue of perspective. When financial incentives are given to middle- and upper-class people, it is called *policy*, when funds are given to low-income and low-wealth people, it is called *subsidy*. Funders should make more policies for the communities we care about."[206]

When institutional philanthropy engages grantee

organizations in a relationship that reflects true partnerships premised on trust, it enhances the long-term sustainability of the civil society sector. GEO's research presents several case studies that highlight foundations such as the Grable Foundation, the Forbes Fund, the Bruner Foundation and the Charles Stewart Mott Foundation, among others that engage in different practices to include grantees in more substantive and meaningful ways. These foundations focus on improving grantee effectiveness by working towards true partnerships. A few exemplary foundations take partnerships to a higher level and include the grantee voice in decision-making processes of the foundation. Others include nonprofit partners in the grants process while some include constituent representatives on the board of trustees. NCRP supports all these exemplary practices; many of them are addressed more extensively in Chapter 3 of this book.

The need for more core support grant dollars of sufficient duration is even more pronounced when looking at the issue of partnerships and sustainability. Renowned former Stanford business school professor and current-day business management consultant Jim Collins concisely stated the importance of general operating support: "Restricted giving misses a fundamental point: To make the greatest impact on society requires first and foremost a great organization, not a single great program."[207] A grantmaker can demonstrate its trust in its grantees by disengaging from the day-to-day operations of the organization, knowing that long-term accountability is ensured. Gara LaMarche, president and CEO of the Atlantic Philanthropies, highlights the importance of general support and multi-year funding as a sign of trust, stating that "trusting [grantees], in a supportive relationship, to set their own course and make their own decisions about programmatic priorities … is best done with general support that gives organizations the flexibility they need and multi-year grants that provide room to plan and give some relief from the endless cycle of fundraising and the paperwork that most foundations seem to generate."[208]

In 2005, the New Hampshire Charitable Foundation revised its grantmaking guidelines to include multi-year and general operating support grants; it also increased the size of individual grants. As noted by Jennifer Hopkins, director of programs, "It frees [grantees] from crafting a project to fit our guidelines … and it helps with the problem of being grant-rich but cash-poor because every grant is restricted to a specific project or, even worse, every

grant does not cover real overhead costs."[209] This exemplary grantmaker assesses its grantees' long-term impact using the organization's strategic plan, an efficient use of already existing resources and an example of a reasonable administrative requirement.

## SETTING THE BAR FOR PHILANTHROPY AT ITS BEST

To ensure that our *Criteria for Philanthropy at Its Best* are informed by current practice, NCRP worked with the Foundation Center to produce a custom dataset on general operating support and multi-year funding. The dataset reported disaggregated foundation giving by types of support for a three-year period from circa 2004-2006. NCRP used the three-year mean to avoid the potential influence of high or low outliers that can sometimes be generated in a single year by unusual grants.. The resulting data present a reasonably reliable picture of the percentage of grants or grant dollars each foundation gave based on the two types of support NCRP identified as associated with positive investments in the health, growth and effectiveness of its grantee partners.

There were 809 large foundations in Foundation Center's database[210] with sufficient data to be included in NCRP's analysis of types of support. While there now are approximately 1,200 foundations in the database, some foundations could not be included in the analysis because they did not provide data for all three years. Total average grant dollars awarded by

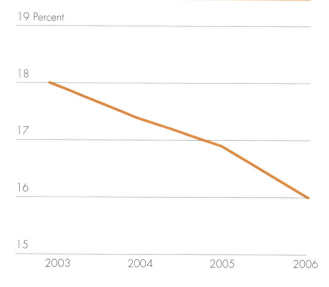

**GRAPH 2.1 AGGREGATED GENERAL OPERATING SUPPORT AS A PERCENT OF TOTAL GIVING, 2003–2006**

19 Percent

18

17

16

15

2003    2004    2005    2006

## GRAPH 2.2 PERCENT OF FOUNDATIONS MEETING NCRP'S CRITERIA FOR GENERAL OPERATING SUPPORT

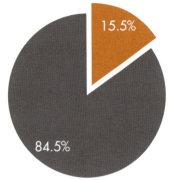

- Foundations Designating 50% or More of Grant Dollars for General Operating Support

- Foundations Designating Less Than 50% of Grant Dollars for General Operating Support

15.5%

84.5%

## GRAPH 2.3 PERCENT OF FOUNDATIONS MEETING NCRP'S CRITERIA FOR MULTI-YEAR FUNDING

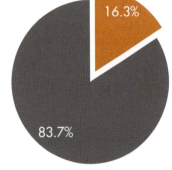

- Foundations Designating 50% or More of Grant Dollars for Multi-Year Funding

- Foundations Designating Less Than 50% of Grant Dollars for Multi-Year Funding

16.3%

83.7%

## TABLE 2.3 MEDIAN GRANT DOLLARS AWARDED BY RESPONDENTS PER ADMINISTRATIVE HOUR[217]

*Based on Funder Estimates of both Median Grant Size and Hours a Typical Grantee Spends on Meeting their Administrative Requirements*

| PERCENTILES | ALL RESPONDENTS (N=577) | ALL RESPONDENTS TRIMMED* (N=549) |
|---|---|---|
| 10th | $284 | $333 |
| 25th | $625 | $647 |
| 50th | $1,667 | $1,667 |
| 75th | $3,750 | $3,586 |
| 90th | $9,148 | $7,500 |

*Both ends of the distribution were trimmed by 2.5% (the extreme 5% of the data were discarded).*

these 809 grantmakers was $14,926,350,872 for the time period analyzed.[211]

Of the 809 foundations in NCRP's total sample, 617 foundations provided at least some grant dollars for general operating support.[212] In the aggregate, 16.2 percent of grant dollars was provided for general support. To set a standard metric for Philanthropy at Its Best, NCRP examined individual foundation grantmaking. The 50 foundations that provided the highest proportion of their grant dollars for general operating support gave more than 90 percent of their grant dollars over all three years for general support. These grantmakers comprise just over 6 percent (6.18) of the total NCRP sample. Within this sub-sample, 30 foundations provided fully 100 percent of their grant dollars for this type of support. The median was fairly disappointing, at 13 percent of all grant dollars for general operating support.

These findings are in keeping with aggregate statistics on core support compiled by the Foundation Center, which indicate that general operating support has declined continuously since 2003: it comprised 18.0 percent of grant dollars awarded a percentage of overall giving in that year, 17.4 percent in 2004, 16.9 percent in 2005 and 16 percent in 2006.[213]

Given the background on aggregate general operating support and the median of the NCRP sample, it is unsurprising that there was an exceptionally large group of foundations providing disappointingly low levels of operating support. The 370 foundations that account for nearly 46 percent (45.74) of the total NCRP sample provided less than 20 percent of their grant dollars for general operating support, with 268 of those foundations, comprising more than 33 percent (33.13) of the sample providing less than 10 percent of their grant dollars for these purposes.

**Leading the field, 125 foundations or about 15.5 percent of the total NCRP sample provided at least 50 percent of their grant dollars for general operating support. This is the benchmark for Philanthropy at Its Best. A list of all 125 foundations that currently meet or exceed this benchmark can be found in the data appendix.**

For multi-year grants, 483 foundations of our 809 foundation sample (59.7 percent of the total sample) provided at least one multi-year grant during the three-year time period. This number is disturbing considering the stated constraints on smaller foundations' ability to provide this type of support noted in this chapter. Because the Foundation Center tracks only larger foundations, if smaller foundations were included in the sample, the numbers would be even lower. Interestingly, these findings align with self-reported data from the 2008 GEO survey, which found that 60 percent of foundations, regardless of asset size, provided multi-year grants sometimes, often or always.[214] For foundations that made any multi-year grants, the median when measuring multi-year grant dollars as a proportion of overall grantmaking was just below 34 percent (33.7).

**Leading the field, 132 foundations or 16.3 percent of the of the total NCRP sample provided 50 percent or more of their grant dollars as multi-year grants. This is the benchmark for Philanthropy at Its Best.[215] A list of all 132 foundations that currently meet or exceed this benchmark can be found in the data appendix.**

Encouragingly, NCRP identified 38 exceptional field leaders; each of these foundations provided more than 75 percent of its grant dollars as multi-year grants. In contrast, 160 foundations provided less than 25 percent of grant dollars as multi-year grants. Additionally, 326 foundations (more than 40 percent of the total sample) provided no multi-year grants whatsoever.

The data available regarding administrative requirements are less robust but some longitudinal comparisons are possible between the GEO's *Grantmaking Practices that Support Grantee Success: Survey Report* and the 2004 Urban and GEO report, *Attitudes and Practices Concerning Effective Philanthropy*. In their 2008 follow-up analysis, GEO used a combination of foundations' own estimates of the time it would take a grantee to fulfill application and reporting requirements with the same foundations' self-reported median grant size to produce a measure of administrative burden; it is the median grant dollars awarded by foundations per administrative hour. In the aggregate, all foundations granted a median $1,667 per hour of administrative work but GEO's analysis found important differences in analyzing the median amounts granted per administrative hour by foundation type and grant size. For example, when median grant size was $50,000, foundations reported providing $2,639 per administrative hour compared to the full 820 foundation sample.[216]

NCRP is not establishing a metric for dollars granted per administrative hour at this time. There are insufficient publicly-available data, especially longitudinal studies, to measure true partnerships between nonprofits and grantees. This is an especially challenging concept to quantify and establish a corresponding metric. At a future date, NCRP and partners may develop survey mechanisms to capture this important element of good grantmaking. Because GEO's survey was anonymous,

we are not able to report the names of the field leaders for this metric. Still, the quartile analysis of GEO's 2008 data in Table 2.2 shows the top 25 percent of its sample reported awarding more than $3,500 per administrative hour, providing a helpful cut point to draw a possible measure for exemplary philanthropy.

## CONCLUSION

All foundations should focus on the types of support they provide and ensure that a significant proportion of grant dollars is allocated to general operating and multi-year support. Complementing these types of support with minimizing the inefficiencies in current administrative requirements offers great potential to augment the impact and social benefit of institutional philanthropy. Moreover, as this chapter demonstrated, creating a more level playing field by repositioning the power dynamics between foundations and grantees offers significant potential for sector-wide improvements in the U.S. civil society sector. Fundamental components of engagement founded on the values of true partnership include: trusting non-profit grantees, learning to be comfortable with a degree of uncertainty, minimizing the power differential by engaging grantees as true partners, and ensuring that grantees are sufficiently enabled to carry out the work funded by a grantmaker. Reasonable administrative requirements, particularly in terms of application and reporting, would enhance greatly the impact of institutional grantmaking from both the funder and grantee side. A significant body of research demonstrates that there are many already-existing tools for foundations to use to change the dynamics on which their relationships with grantees are based.

Based on the analysis presented in this chapter, NCRP advocates that all institutional grantmakers engage their grantees as true partners by providing sufficient general operating and multi-year support, investments that grantees can use to bolster infrastructure to ensure long-term viability of the civil society sector. By ensuring that application and reporting requirements are commensurate with grant size, both grantmakers and grantees will make more effective use of their time and increase their impact on the communities they serve. As more foundations begin to measure up to the fair and reasonable benchmarks established under this criterion, both grantmakers and grantees will see increased impact and effectiveness, and the vibrant civil society sector of the United States will better-serve the public's most pressing needs.

# Criterion II: Effectiveness

A grantmaker practicing Philanthropy at Its Best serves the public good by investing in the health, growth and effectiveness of its nonprofit partners.

a) Provides at least 50 percent of its grant dollars for general operating support

b) Provides at least 50 percent of its grant dollars as multi-year grants

c) Ensures that the time to apply for and report on the grant is commensurate with grant size

## DISCUSSION QUESTIONS

NCRP encourages staff and trustees of foundations and other grantmakers to engage in serious discussions about each criterion and the chapter that elaborates on the criterion. Sample discussion questions are provided here to help get you started.

> Which parts of the chapter did you like the most? Why?

> Which parts did you like the least? Why?

> Is it important to invest in the health, growth and effectiveness of our grantees? Why or why not? Have we ever held explicit discussions related to this?

> In what ways do you think our foundation currently invests in the health, growth, and effectiveness of our grantees? Are there other examples from our past?

> What percentage of our foundation's grant dollars do we estimate are given as general operating support? As multi-year grants? How did we establish those percentages? Do they satisfy us? Why or why not?

> Considering the mission of our foundation, are there ways we might increase our general operating support and our multi-year grants and still be effective in achieving our goals?

> Do we think our application and reporting requirements are burdensome to nonprofits? How do we know how long it takes grantees to apply for and report on a grant from us?

> Do we think our requirements are reasonable considering the size grants we offer? Do we want to consider altering anything about grant size or requirements? Why or why not?

> Considering the mission of our foundation, are we doing everything we can to promote effectiveness of our grantees?

> What else from this chapter should inform our current grantmaking priorities?

> If we want to make any changes based on this discussion, what will need to happen in order to make those changes? What are the next steps?

# NOTES FOR CHAPTER II: EFFECTIVENESS

127. Grantmakers for Effective Organizations. "Investing in Leadership: Young Leaders 'On the Verge,'" *IMPACT newsletter*, (October 2006), 2, http://www.onthemovebayarea.org/files/GEO%20Article%20on%20OTV.pdf.

128. Quoted in Grantmakers for Effective Organizations. *Imagine, Involve, Implement: Transforming Grantmaker Practices for Improved Nonprofit Results* (Washington, D.C.: Grantmakers for Effective Organizations, January 2008), 38.

129. Kevin Bolduc, Phil Buchanan and Judy Huang. *Listening to Grantees: What Nonprofits Value in Their Foundation Funders* (Cambridge, MA: The Center for Effective Philanthropy, 2004), 3.

130. Council on Foundations. "At Issue: Project vs. Operating Support – Which is the Better Strategy?" Council on Foundations Board Briefing: Type of Funding, December, 2002, http://www.cof.org/files/Documents/Governing_Boards/BBProjectOperating.PDF.

131. See, for example, many articles written by NCRP cofounder and current board member Pablo Eisenberg on the rationale for increasing grant dollars allocated to unrestricted general operating support. See also Table I for recent NCRP work on core support.

132. General operating support often is used interchangeably with the terms core support, core operating support, general support and operating support.

133. Grantmakers for Effective Organizations. *General Operating Support: GEO Action Guide* (Washington, D.C.: Grantmakers for Effective Organizations, July 2007), 31.

134. Ibid., p. 19. Emphasis added.

135. Paul Brest. "Smart Money: General Operating Grants Can Be Strategic – for Nonprofits and Foundations," *Stanford Social Innovation Review* (Winter 2003): 49.

136. Kathleen W. Buechel and Esther Handy. *The Road Less Traveled: Funders' Advice on the Path to Nonprofit Sustainability* (working paper no. 40, Harvard University, The Hauser Center for Nonprofit Organizations, July, 2007), 8.

137. Jeanne Bell, Richard Moyers and Timothy Wolfred. *Daring to Lead: A National Study of Nonprofit Executive Leadership* (Washington, D.C.: CompassPoint Nonprofit Services and The Eugene and Agnes E. Meyer Foundation, 2006), 33.

138. Grantmakers for Effective Organizations. January 2008, Op. Cit., p. 4.

139. Michael E. Porter and Mark Kramer. "Philanthropy's New Agenda: Creating Value," *Harvard Business Review* 77 (November-December 1999): 124. http://www.ncbf.org/Philanthropys_New_Agenda.pdf.

140. Grantmakers for Effective Organizations. *General Operating Support vol. 2: Assessing the Impact* (Washington, D.C.: Grantmakers for Effective Organizations, 2008), 5. Emphasis added. The issue of making evaluations more meaningful and looking at alternative metrics is discussed in detail later in this chapter under administrative requirements.

141. Grantmakers for Effective Organizations, July 2007, Op. Cit., p. 19.

142. Paul Brest., 2004, Op. Cit., p. 50.

143. Quoted in Council on Foundations 2002 Op. Cit. p. 7.

144. Ibid.

145. Paul Brest, Op. Cit., p. 44.

146. The California Wellness Foundation. *Core Operating Support: Annual Report 1999* (Woodland Hills, CA: The California Wellness Foundation, 1999).

147. Gary L. Yates. "Good to the Core," *Foundation News and Commentary* (July/August 2001).

148. Grantmakers for Effective Organizations, July 2007, Op. Cit., p. 7.

149. Buechel and Handy. 2007. Op. Cit. p. 11. The context of these metrics was executive leadership development but easily can be extrapolated to core support grants as well.

150. Adapted from Council on Foundations 2002, Op. Cit. p: 4-5.

151. Cohen, 2007, Op. Cit. p. 12.

152. Cohen 2007, Op. Cit., p. 13.

153. Mark Hager et al. "Paying for Not Paying for Overhead," *Foundation News & Commentary* 46 (2005); Cohen, Op. Cit.; Bell et al., Op. cit.

154. Blue Shield of California Foundation. *Strengthening the Safety Net: Core Support for Community Clinics* (San Francisco, CA: Blue Shield of California Foundation, 2007), 3. http://bscaf.com/assets/files/reports/Core_Support_Evaluation_2007.pdf.

155. Mark Kramer et al. *From Insight to Action: New Directions in Foundation Evaluation* (Boston, MA: FSG Social Impact Advisors, 2007), 13.

156. Kristin A. Grønbjerg and Laney Cheney. *Indiana Nonprofit Capacity Survey Series Report #1: Indiana Capacity Assessment: Indiana Charities, 2007* (Indianapolis, IN: School of Public and Environmental Affairs at Indiana University, May 15, 2007); Grantmakers for Effective Organizations. *Listen, Learn, Lead: Grantmaker practices that Support Nonprofit Results,* (Washington, D.C.: Grantmakers for Effective Organizations, December 2006); Grantmakers for Effective Organizations, January 2008, Op. Cit.; Mark Kramer et al., Op. Cit.

157. Judy Huang, Phil Buchanan and Ellie Buteau. *In Search of Impact: Practices and Perceptions in Foundations' Provision of Program and Operating Grants to Nonprofits* (Cambridge, MA: Center for Effective Philanthropy, December 2006).

158. Ibid., p. 15.

159. Cohen, Op. Cit. p.10; Center for Effective Philanthropy 2004, Op. Cit. p. 15; Grantmakers for Effective Organizations, July 2007, Op. Cit. p. 1.

160. Quoted in Cohen 2007, Op. Cit. p 10-11.

161. NCRP acknowledges that many smaller foundations find it challenging to make multi-year commitments but encourages them to consider real multi-year funding.

162. Bell et al., Op. Cit.

163. Cohen 2007, Op. Cit.; Grantmakers for Effective Organizations, December 2006, Op. Cit.

164. Kevin Bolduc, Phil Buchanan and Judy Huang. *Listening to Grantees: What Nonprofits Value in their Foundation Funders* (Cambridge, MA: Center for Effective Philanthropy, 2004).

165. Bell et al., Op. Cit.; Huang et al., Op. Cit.

166. Cohen, Op. Cit. p. 11. Emphasis added.

167. Grantmakers for Effective Organizations, *Grantmaking Practices that Support Grantee Success: Survey Report* (Washington, D.C.: Grantmakers for Effective Organizations, October 2008).

168. Grantmakers for Effective Organizations. *Is Grantmaking Getting Smarter: A National Study of Philanthropic Practice— Data Highlights* (Washington, D.C.: Grantmakers for Effective Organizations, 2008), 11.

169. Adapted from Ibid. the p-value for this statistic was <0.001 meaning that the probability that these findings do not reflect reality based on self-reported multi-year funding is less than 1 in 1,000.

170. Ibid., p. 10.

171. Ibid., p. 13.

172. Jessica Bearman. *Drowning in Paperwork, Distracted from Purpose: Challenges and Opportunities in Grant Application and Reporting* (Washington, D.C.: Project Streamline, 2008), 5.

173. Kathleen W. Buechel, Elizabeth K. Keating and Clara Miller. *Capital Ideas: Moving from Short-term engagement to Long-Term Sustainability* (Cambridge, MA: Hauser Center for Nonprofit Organizations, Harvard University, and Nonprofit Finance Fund, 2007).

174. Ibid.

175. Bearman, Op. Cit.; NCRP confidential discussions with funders and grantees.

176. Grantmakers for Effective Organizations, Grant Makers Network, Association of Fundraising Professionals, the Association of Small Foundations, the Council on Foundations, the Forum of Regional Associations of Grantmakers and The Foundation Center are the other members of the collaborative. NOTE: the National Council of Nonprofits was called the National Council of Nonprofit Associations at the time that the Project Streamline report was published.

177. The CEP data are available online at www.projectstreamline.org.

178. Bearman, Op. Cit., p. 19.

179. Alana Conner Snibbe. "Drowning in Data," *Stanford Social Innovation Review*, 4 (Fall 2006): 40.

180. Grantmakers for Effective Organizations 2008, Op. Cit., p. 25.

181. Please see NCRP's series of *Grantmaking for Community Impact Project* reports for a comprehensive list of interim progress indicators. http://www.ncrp.org/campaigns-research-policy/communities/gcip.

182. Francie Ostrower. *Attitudes and Practices Concerning Effective Philanthropy: Survey Report* (Washington, D.C.: the Urban Institute, September 2004).

183. J.G. Carman and J.L. Millensen. "Nonprofit Program Evaluation: Organizational Challenges and Resource Needs," *The Journal of Volunteer Administration,* 23 (2005). Cited in Snibbe, Op. Cit.

184. Grantmakers for Effective Organizations 2008, Op. Cit., p. 4.

185. Ibid., p. 35.

186. Center for Effective Philanthropy. *Analysis of Key Predictors of Grantee Ratings of Process Helpfulness and Time Spent* (prepared for Project Streamline). Based on data from over 14,000 grantees of large foundations (a median grant size of $50,000.) Grantmakers for Effective Organizations October 2008, Op. Cit. p. v.

187. Internal GEO communication shared with NCRP.

188. Quoted in Grantmakers for Effective Organizations January 2008, Op. Cit., p. 22.

189. Arthur "Buzz" Schmidt. "Escaping the Perpetuity Mindset," *The Nonprofit Quarterly* (Fall 2008).

190. Bell et al., Op. Cit., p. 13.

191. Quoted in Rick Cohen. "Cutting to the Core," *Responsive Philanthropy* (Fall 2002).

192. Clara Miller. "Risk Minus Cash Equals Crisis: The Flap about General Operating Support," in *State of Philanthropy 2004* (Washington, D.C.: The National Committee for Responsive Philanthropy, 2004), 122.

193. Quoted in Paul Connolly. *Building to Last: A Grantmaker's Guide to Strengthening Nonprofit Organizations* (New York, NY: The TCC Group, March 2001).

194. Ellen Van Velsor and Cynthia D. McCauley. "Our View of Leadership Development," in *The Center for Creative Leadership Handbook of Leadership Development, 2nd edition,* ed. Ellen Van Velsor and Cynthia D. McCauley, (San Francisco, CA: Jossey-Bass, 2004); cited in Betsy Hubbard, *Investing in Leadership, Vol. I: A Grantmaker's Framework for Understanding Nonprofit Leadership Development,* (Washington, D.C.: Grantmakers for Effective Organizations, 2005), 13.

195. K.A. Allen et al. *Leadership in the Twenty-First Century: Rethinking Leadership,* (College Park, MD: Academy of Leadership Press, 1998); cited in Hubbard, Op. Cit.

196. Hubbard, Op. Cit.

197. Kathleen P. Enright. *Investing in Leadership, volume 2: Inspiration and Ideas from Philanthropy's Latest Frontier,* (Washington, D.C.: Grantmakers for Effective Organizations, February 2006), 15.

198. Hubbard, Op. Cit; Enright, Op. Cit.

199. Bell et al., Op. Cit., p. 14.

200. Brest Op. Cit.

201. Grantmakers for Effective Organizations October 2008, Op. Cit.; Grantmakers for Effective Organizations 2008, Op. Cit.; Rooney and Frederick Op. Cit.; Bell et al. Op. Cit.; Bearman Op. Cit.; Please see Pablo Eisenberg's and NCRP's extensive writings on general operating support.

202. Mark Hager et al. *Getting What We Pay For: Low Overhead Limits Nonprofit Effectiveness – Nonprofit Overhead Cost Project Brief No. 3* (Washington, D.C.: Urban Institute & Center on Philanthropy Indiana University, August 1, 2004).

203. Ibid.

204. Rooney and Frederick, Op. Cit., p. 13.

205. Rick Cohen. *A Call to Action: Organizing to Increase the Effectiveness and Impact of Foundation Grantmaking* (Washington, D.C.: National Committee for Responsive Philanthropy, 2007).

206. Kathleen W. Buechel, Elizabeth K. Keating and Clara Miller. *Capital Ideas: Moving from Short-Term Engagement to Long-Term Sustainability* (Cambridge, MA: Hauser Center for Nonprofit Organizations, Harvard University, and Nonprofit Finance Fund, 2007), 27.

207. Jim Collins. *Good to Great and the Social Sectors: A Monograph to Accompany Good to Great* (New York, NY: Harper Collins, November 30, 2005) 24.

208. Gara LaMarche. "When Foundations Should Lead – and When They Should Get Out of the Way," in *Power in Policy: A Funder's Guide to Advocacy and Civic Participation*, ed. David F. Arons (Saint Paul, MN: Fieldstone Alliance, 2007), 34.

209. Grantmakers for Effective Organization July 2007, Op. Cit., p. 36.

210. The search set is based on the Foundation Center's grants sample database, which includes all of the grants of $10,000 or more awarded to organizations by a sample of 1,172 larger foundations for circa 2004, 1,154 for circa 2005, and 1,263 for circa 2006. For community foundations, only discretionary grants are included. Grants to individuals are not included in the file.

211. This figure is the denominator used in NCRP's calculations; if analyzed within giving sub-samples, these figures would be higher and likely overstate the current giving trends. Using the full samples average total giving provides a more comprehensive framework for analyzing the different types of grants.

212. The Foundation Center's grants classification system does not differentiate between unrestricted core support and negotiated core support; both are included in the general operating support category.

213. The Foundation Center provides online access to highlights in annual giving trends on its website and in its *Foundation Giving Trends* series available online at www.foundationcenter.org. These data are only on the proportion of grant dollars classified for general operating support, not general support, which includes other types of giving such as income management.

214. Grantmakers for Effective Organizations 2008, Op. Cit., p. 3.

215. The two metrics described in this criterion are not additive. For example, a grant that is both multi-year and for general support counts towards meeting both measures.

216. Grantmakers for Effective Organizations 2008, Op. Cit., p. 22.

217. Internal GEO communication shared with NCRP.

# Chapter III: Ethics

# Criterion III: Ethics — At A Glance

A grantmaker practicing Philanthropy at Its Best serves the public good by demonstrating accountability and transparency to the public, its grantees and constituents.

a) Maintains an engaged board of at least five people who include among them a diversity of perspectives—including of the communities it serves—and who serve without compensation

b) Maintains policies and practices that support ethical behavior

c) Discloses information freely

> An exemplary grantmaking institution operates as an ethical steward of the partly public dollars with which it is entrusted. Unfortunately, too many individuals continue to abuse philanthropy for personal gain. As the institution's ultimate decision-making authority, trustees have a legal and moral obligation to ensure that their organizations are functioning in ways that ensure ethical stewardship.

> Board composition is critically important to ethical operations. Research indicates that diverse groups make better decisions, and that a minimum of five people is needed to achieve a plurality of perspectives. Many family foundations and other grantmakers have seen tangible value from including the grantee perspective on their boards.

> As a rule, trustees should serve without compensation. Research does not support the contention that compensated boards serve their institutions better. Moreover, every dollar spent on trustee compensation is one that could have gone toward achieving the mission of the foundation. The only exceptions should be if the CEO also is a trustee or if the foundation compensates lower-income board members who otherwise could not afford to serve.

> One of the most important things a grantmaking institution can do to build public trust in its operations is to maintain appropriate policies and practices that make the possibility of abuse less likely and demonstrate substantive accountability. These policies include, but are not limited to: a) maintaining appropriate conflict of interest and whistleblower protection policies; b) establishing reasonable, not excessive, executive compensation; and c) subscribing to any of a number of available codes for ethical conduct and good governance.

> Transparency also is integral to preventing abuses and enhancing meaningful accountability. A grantmaker practicing Philanthropy at Its Best should share freely extensive information regarding its grants, governance, management, investments and operations.

> Because data on the issues covered by the ethics criterion are neither centralized nor easily available, we cannot say what proportion of the nation's grantmakers meet or exceed these benchmarks. But many exemplary grantmakers operate in ways that meet or exceed the measures for this criterion.

# Chapter III: Ethics

Foundation board positions are no longer ceremonial. Board members must be fully engaged in the oversight of their foundations' operations and must actively seek to improve their skills. It is essential that foundations do everything they can to guard against both real and perceived abuses.

—Emmett D. Carson, President and CEO
Silicon Valley Community Foundation[218]

Private foundations and other institutional grantmakers play a vital role in sustaining the U.S. civil society sector, and exemplary foundations operate ethically and with great integrity. Unfortunately, too many grantmakers do not take the necessary steps to demonstrate that they are using their tax subsidies to further their charitable purpose. It is incumbent on a foundation to demonstrate accountability and transparency in its operations so that regulators and the public know that all grantmaking institutions are acting as ethical stewards of the tax-subsidized dollars with which they are entrusted. As the Internal Revenue Service's *Governance and Related Topics* guidelines for nonprofit organizations state: "The public expects a charity to abide by ethical standards that promote the public good. The organization's governing body bears the ultimate responsibility for setting ethical standards and ensuring they permeate the organization and inform its practices."[219] As the ultimate decision-making body of a grantmaking institution, it is incumbent on a foundation board in particular to ensure that the institution it oversees complies with regulatory and legal requirements, public policy and generally-accepted ethical practices.

In 1975, the total number of foundations in the United States was 21,877. The most recent data available show a dramatic increase since then, with a significant surge in the type, number and assets of foundations. Currently, there are 72,477 grantmaking institutions, including independent, community, corporate and operating foundations. According to the Foundation Center, in 2007 the total assets of these foundations grew to $670 billion, the highest level yet recorded.[220] Although the current financial crisis has reduced that figure significantly, foundations continue to control vast wealth. Because institutional grantmakers largely are exempt from taxation, the government foregoes substantial revenue that could be used to expand social safety net programs or provide for the common good in other ways. Steven T. Miller, commissioner of the Tax Exempt and Government Entities division of the Internal Revenue Service (IRS), underscored the purpose of the tax subsidy afforded to charitable organizations when he asserted that "every charity should make responsible and appropriate use of its resources to achieve its charitable purposes. That is what the tax-subsidy is for."[221]

Moreover, researchers estimate that "at least 45 percent of the $500 billion that foundations hold in their coffers belong to the American public … 'When a foundation is created today, the burden of lost tax revenue is borne by citizens today in the form of a tax expenditure,' with the promise that it will be paid out in the future."[222] This partially public nature of foundation dollars means that the public has a vested interest and a right to expect ethical behavior and a reasonable level

Institutional philanthropy historically has shown a preference for self-regulation over government regulation, with foundation trade associations and affinity groups frequently voicing collective opposition to any increase in governmental scrutiny. Even something seemingly as innocuous as mandated information disclosure is viewed with alarm, invoking unsubstantiated rhetoric about the "slippery slope" that leads to increased regulation. But disclosure regulation would not infringe on a foundation's independence or decision-making; it simply would provide grantmakers, policymakers and the public with more robust information about the sector. Given that government regulation of philanthropy currently

> Accountability and transparency have become meaningless buzz words despite some foundations taking steps toward enhancing public trust in philanthropy by voluntarily disclosing relevant information that demonstrates they are meeting their charitable purpose and furthering their missions.

of disclosure about foundation operations. This also is in keeping with the IRS's statement that charitable organizations must be "*organized* and *operated* exclusively for one or more *exempt* purposes."[223] Organizations must ensure that any earnings do not benefit any private individual or shareholder, and do not operate for the benefit of any private interests, including those of the founder, her or his family, its shareholders or any individuals controlled by these interests.[224]

Viewed from a strictly legal perspective, some contend that foundation dollars are private dollars and ought not to be subject to public scrutiny. Yet, seen through a public policy lens, foundations, their grantees and the public are partners in pursuit of the common good. Coupled with the exempt organization's legal obligation to demonstrate that it serves the public good and not private interests, as stated above, this is a compelling and justifiable rationale to expect institutional grantmakers to behave as ethical stewards of the partly public monies with which they are entrusted. Accountability and transparency have become meaningless buzz words despite some foundations taking steps toward enhancing public trust in philanthropy by voluntarily disclosing relevant information that demonstrates they are meeting their charitable purpose and furthering their missions. Too few foundations engage in such disclosure, limiting the information the public needs to know that its tax dollars are being used appropriately.

is so minimal, rigorous self-regulation is all the more important; but without substantive self-regulation further governmental regulation of foundations is likely. Sharing relevant information provides the public with important information from which it is free to draw its own conclusions; vigorous self-regulation is possible only with the right tools.

Independent research and congressional testimony by IRS officials demonstrate that the IRS's tax exempt organizations division is extremely shorthanded and underfunded. State attorneys general lack the capacity to analyze voluminous foundation reports submitted to them each year with limited financial and human resources. Fully 36 states had one or fewer full-time equivalent attorneys dedicated to nonprofit oversight, with 17 states lacking any such legal capacity whatsoever.[225] In other words, oversight capacity has not kept pace with the explosive growth among foundations. The quasi-public nature of foundation assets makes it incumbent on foundations to act ethically and prevent philanthropic abuses.

The information that private foundations must disclose publicly to maintain their tax-exempt status is limited to what is available on the IRS's tax forms for these organizations, the 990 PF form,[226] and annual reports provided on a voluntary and variable basis. Further, media reports indicate that many individuals continue to abuse philanthropy for personal gain. Examples range from political cronyism to extravagant compensation and retirement packages for foundation trustees and executives. Coupled with the limited publicly available data on foundation operations, the public trust in institutional grantmakers has diminished and must be rebuilt. These are compelling reasons for foundations to take robust voluntary steps that demonstrate high levels of transparency and accountability.

There are three things that a foundation can do to make ethical operation more likely:

1. Maintain an engaged board with a minimum of five trustees that brings a plurality of perspectives to its decision-making;
2. Maintain policies and practices in support of ethical behavior; and,
3. Disclose significant amounts of information to the public.

As more foundations take meaningful steps in this direction, the public trust will be rebuilt and grantmakers will maximize the social benefit of their contributions to the American civil society sector.

## Recent regulatory and policy history of philanthropic accountability and sector reform

Issues of foundation accountability and regulation date back to concerns that the early philanthropists such as Andrew Carnegie and John D. Rockefeller were using the charitable tax subsidy to exert undue influence on many dimensions of the public sphere through their giving.[227] Government regulation declined in the early 1980s, following an IRS "examination study," which concluded that private foundations were complying with the dictates of their tax exemption status. Faced with financial and human resource deficiencies, the total number of audits on private foundations decreased dramatically throughout the 1990s, leaving the sector with markedly less oversight and making it increasingly reliant on self-regulation.[228]

The bull market period of the 1990s saw a tremendous surge in the number of foundations and their total assets. As The Robert Wood Johnson Foundation states, "although this boom … suggests that foundations are thriving as never before, it is precisely this rise in numbers, influence and complexity, coupled with reductions in government spending for social services that leaves them vulnerable to claims that they are 'unaccountable.'"[229]

In 2001, rampant scandals reported among corporations, government agencies and churches led to increased public scrutiny and demands for more investigations into foundations and other charitable organizations. The public trust in institutional philanthropy diminished significantly following a series of investigative media reports by the *Washington Post* and *Boston Globe* in 2003. The newspapers ran in-depth articles, demonstrating high levels of financial abuses, particularly among foundation trustees and executives. Financial scandals at Enron, Tyco International, Adelphia and other corporations led to the bipartisan Sarbanes-Oxley Act of 2002. The act established uniform standards for all U.S. public company boards and management because of the impact of the drop in private sector shares on publicly traded securities. In light of the philanthropic abuses documented by the media, policymakers and regulators began to consider the applicability of similar provisions to nonprofit organizations to ensure compliance with the law and justify the lost tax revenue from the charitable exemption.

State attorneys general and members of Congress with oversight of federal tax laws raised concerns about their capacity to ensure that charitable organizations were complying with the law, leading to diminished oversight. In 2004, the Senate Finance Committee chaired by Sen. Charles Grassley (R-Iowa) began a series of hearings to determine the extent of the problem. Among the myriad testimonies presented to the committee, IRS authorities admitted that the nonprofit sector long had been treated as a "compliant area" by tax regulators. Because of limited financial and human resources, the agency audited less than half a percent of the roughly one million charitable organizations it is supposed to oversee. This was in keeping with prior testimony from Marcus Owens, former director of the IRS's Exempt Organization Division during the Clinton Administration, who stated that the IRS could access only 20 percent of the information found on 990 PF forms, and with a budget of $59 million in 1999, the exempt division was incapable of conducting more than 115 audits of the more than 60,000 foundations under its oversight in the same fiscal year.[230] Much of this depletion of staff and resources at the IRS came in the wake of Sen. William Roth's (R-Del.) testimony on IRS abuses in 1997, which led to a massive reorganization of the agency and Congress maintaining tight control over the IRS budget.

Representatives of the National Association of State Charity Officials (NASCO) also underscored the paucity of funds available to support charitable enforcement cases. Mark Pacella, then president of NASCO, testified that financial resources were severely overextended and NASCO offices had insufficient personnel to conduct investigations of charitable organizations. Pacella noted that 990 PF forms frequently were submitted by organizations with inaccuracies and "filed one or more years after the fiscal period for which they relate has passed, making it doubly difficult for regulators to … pursue enforcement actions in a timely manner."[231] William Josephson, assistant attorney general for New York State, offered similar testimony, stating that although fully one-tenth of all 990 PF forms that his office reviewed raised red flags, resource deficiency and a void of legal expertise resulted in these cases often not being investigated. NASCO and several state attorneys general emphasized the need to reform the 990 PF tax form, promote greater communication between IRS and state enforcement agents, and create electronic filing systems that were available readily to both tax authorities and state jurisdictions. Watchdog groups such as NCRP also testified on the need to improve philanthropic accountability. In his June 2004 testimony during the Senate Finance Committee's hearings on reforming charitable sector reform and oversight, Rick Cohen, then executive director of NCRP, noted three guiding principles that informed NCRP's agenda for recommendations to reform accountability:

1. The laws and regulations for addressing the accountability of foundations and correcting the excesses reported in the press need to be strengthened.
2. Notwithstanding improved statutory and regulatory standards, the philanthropic sector itself has to get serious about dealing with the malefactors who sully the good work of organized philanthropy.
3. There should be an increase in the resources devoted to governmental oversight of philanthropy at the federal and state levels—and NCRP several months ago [in 2004] issued a specific proposal for the reuse of the foundation excise tax just for this purpose.[232]

Following the 2004 hearings, the Senate Finance Committee recommended the formation of an independent panel to analyze the state of governance and make recommendations to strengthen accountability and transparency in the nonprofit sector. In response, the Independent Sector convened a coalition of non-profit experts and the Panel on the Nonprofit Sector was created to address concerns articulated by Congress, nonprofits, the public, and federal and state oversight agencies about the illegal and unethical practices of some charitable organizations. The panel produced final and supplemental reports, including recommendations for sector-wide reform, in 2005 and 2006.

The Senate Finance Committee eventually merged these recommendations into legislation passed as the Pension Protection Act of 2006. Provisions of the 2006 act subjected charitable organizations to more rigorous reporting requirements, authorized the IRS to revoke the tax-exempt status of any nonprofit or foundation that failed to file returns within three years, and established harsher penalties to inhibit inappropriate compensation and payout practices at charitable organizations, including foundations. The IRS also developed an electronic 990 form to improve the accuracy of nonprofit data collection and make information more accessible between state and federal enforcement personnel. In October 2007, the Independent Sector and the panel published the *Principles for Good Governance and Ethical Practice: A Guide for Charities and Foundations*, a list of 33 separate principles to strengthen ethical standards through self-regulation within the philanthropic community. Unfortunately, despite these various regulatory reforms and tools for self-regulation, abuses of philanthropy that diminish the public trust continue until today. For example, *Bloomberg News* reported suspicious insider dealing at the Robin Hood Foundation in 2007. An investigation revealed that the foundation maintained an emergency fund that grew from $20 million to $144.5 million in less than a decade and was invested in 19 hedge funds, of which seven were operated by Robin Hood donors and trustees. These board members were paid 2 percent of assets and 20 percent of profit for managing the donations; the charity paid $14 million in fees for hedge-fund management in 2005.[233] These actions demonstrate a direct violation of the IRS's guidelines for maintaining the charitable exemption. As the application guidelines for exempt status state, all 501 (c) (3) organizations "must not operate for the benefit of private interests such as those of … its shareholders or persons controlled by such interests."[234] After congressional scrutiny, Sen. Grassley voiced disapproval of the foundation's trustee fee policies and the Robin Hood Foundation changed its practices. In a letter to foundation supporters, then-Executive Director David Saltzman defended the foundation's policies, noting that none of the seven trustees served on the board's investment committee. Still, because of the media and regulatory concerns, Saltzman's letter announced a change in operations: "Although we are totally comfortable with these procedures, as part of our board's ongoing governance review over the past year, and to avoid even the appearance of any conflict, we have decided that none of Robin Hood's leadership will manage these funds going forward."[235] Such reports underscore the need for substantive reform of the way accountability and transparency are demonstrated in the philanthropic sector. This also ensures legal compliance barring insider dealing.

As NCRP co-founder and long-time commentator on the charitable sector Pablo Eisenberg stated before the Senate Finance Committee in 2004, "Public confidence in our charitable organizations has decreased. … There is a growing perception that the nonprofit sector lacks accountability. We cannot maintain strong and vibrant foundations and nonprofits without public trust. Restoring that trust must be the objective of any attempts to reform what is wrong with the system and to strengthen those practices that have been effective."[236] The partially public nature of foundation dollars, coupled with the significant increase in foundation assets, makes restoring the public trust in institutional philanthropy a practical and a moral imperative.

## BOARD COMPOSITION
Board composition is critically important for any grantmaking institution. Boards need to be large and diverse enough to protect the public trust and to reflect authentically the priorities of communities served by the foundation.

### Board size
Recent research indicates that diverse groups are better at problem-solving. Because a small board restricts the number of perspectives of a foundation's decision-making body, increasing board size is an important corollary to diversifying board composi-

tion. In contrast to the final panel recommendations made to the Senate Finance Committee that boards ought to include a minimum of three people, the tenth principle from the Panel and the Independent Sector's *Principles* to improve governance and ethical behavior suggests that boards should comprise a minimum of five individuals. Similarly, in his 2004 statement to the Senate Finance Committee, Eisenberg noted that neither regulation nor legislation should mandate the maximum size of a board. Highlighting that many grantee organizations have between 20 and 30 board members, he emphasized the benefits of larger boards: "Often, their size is an important asset, enabling them to achieve regional, ethnic, professional and community diversity and capacity."[238] Eisenberg added that while committee staffers recommended a minimum of three board members, maintaining a minimum of five trustees "provides a better guarantee that the organization can have a broad perspective and better understanding of the organization's purpose and programs."[239] The potential negative consequences of a three-person board become clearer when one looks, for example, at the Bill and Melinda Gates Foundation, discussed in the case study of this chapter. Taken together, these perspectives suggest that ensuring at least a five-person board at a foundation increases the likelihood that collective preferences will inform and lead to better decision-making. Improved decision-making is not a panacea for eliminating abuses of philanthropy for personal gain. But, at a minimum, it offers the potential for better judgment to curb the level of abuse and restore the public trust in institutional philanthropy.

The board [of a charitable organization] should have enough members to allow for full deliberation and diversity of thinking on governance and other organizational matters. Except for very small organizations, this generally means that the board should have at least five members … The board of a charitable organization should include members with the diverse background (including but not limited to, ethnic, racial and gender perspectives), experience and organizational and financial skills necessary to advance the organization's mission.

—Panel on the Nonprofit Sector, Principles 10 and 11[237]

Diversifying board composition

Recent studies indicate that foundation staffs, particularly program officers, are becoming more diverse, but the same cannot be said of boards. This means that decision-making remains concentrated in the hands of a homogeneous group at most foundations. Moreover, while staffs are becoming more diverse, progress appears to have slowed in recent years and the majority of staff diversity is attributable to the increase in the number of female program officers. A recent study commissioned by the Rockefeller Philanthropy Advisors on the diversity of foundation staff and boards over the last 25 years found that while there has been much progress, it has been inconsistent.[240] The biggest gains were seen in the first half of the time period, but stagnation set in during the second half. For example, board diversity increased by 127.9 percent from 1982 through 1994; from 1994 to 2006, the gains were only 32.7 percent. Currently, 87 percent of foundation board members are white, and demographic data on socio-economic status of trustees do not exist. Coupled with the small size of many boards, this means that decision-making remains significantly concentrated in the hands of homogeneous groups. These are disturbing trends among foundation decision-makers, especially considering the tremendous increase in foundation assets, which remain largely exempt from taxation, controlled by these groups.

Similarly, CEO diversity increased by 156.3 percent from 1982 to 1994 and then by only 41.5 percent from 1994 to 2006. Foundation CEOs were even less diverse than the boards analyzed; total CEO diversity increased by a mere 5.8 percent in 2006. Regarding program officer diversity, the majority of increases in the proportion of diversity were between 1982 and 1994. Notably, the period from 2002 to 2006 saw a decline in program officer diversity.[241] Neither the report nor this writing seeks to identify causal relationships between the factors related to increases in staff and board diversity and the trends identified. But even for those in the group that has seen the biggest gains in diversity, the statistics are telling: although the percentage of women in philanthropy increased, particularly as a proportion of program officers,[242] these gains were made largely by

## THE BILL AND MELINDA GATES FOUNDATION: IMPLICATIONS OF CONCENTRATED DECISION-MAKING AND A NON-DIVERSE BOARD

The board of the Bill and Melinda Gates Foundation comprises three people: Warren Buffett, Bill Gates and Melinda Gates. Can such a small group of decision-makers bring a plurality of perspectives to the board, especially in the absence of critical feedback? This is a vitally important question considering the mammoth size of the Gates Foundation.

Pablo Eisenberg, Joel Fleishman and Dr. Arata Kochi, the former leader of malaria programs for the World Health Organization (WHO), are among the few voices that have raised concerns about the lack of controls or honest feedback from grantees to ensure that the Gates Foundation is achieving its mission. In fact, Dr. Kochi no longer is with the WHO, although the organization states that he is on leave and that his departure is unrelated to his criticism of the Gates Foundation as a "cartel" that imposed its agenda on the WHO and was unreceptive to critical feedback.[252] Even the former director of the Gates Foundation, Patty Stonesifer, cautioned about the dangers the foundation faces because of its lack of receptivity to critical feedback, stating in the 2007 annual report that "the danger isn't in what people do tell you – it's in what they don't."[253]

While the mission and vision of the Gates Foundation are almost universally accepted as laudable, some like Dr. Kochi raise important issues, for example about the reliance on technological solutions such as the malaria vaccine versus addressing immediate problems such as dire poverty in less developed countries. Indeed, many developing countries that welcome the infusion of monies to improve health find themselves in the awkward position of lacking the needed infrastructure to put those resources to use. Health systems white women. Moreover, even white women remain underrepresented on foundation boards, comprising 31 percent of all board members in 2006.[243]

Diversity is a nuanced, complex and dynamic concept; true and inclusive diversity cannot be reduced to numbers and measures alone.[244] Thus, demographic diversity is not the only important factor in determining how diverse or inclusive a foundation or its board is. As Mary Ellen Capek and Molly Mead note in defining "deep diversity," "Diversity also works to democratize boards and staffs of organizations. More diverse boards and staffs have a better shot at being effective. Understanding gender in the context of other diversities like race, class and culture—which also means understanding the insidious, often subtle and unacknowledged preference for 'normal'—is essential for building healthier institutions. Philanthropic and nonprofit leaders interviewed for our book emphasized the need for new language to capture this understanding, so *throughout our book, we use the term 'deep' diversity to describe an institutionalized understanding of diversity that goes wide as well as deep.*"[245]

University of Michigan professor Scott E. Page's seminal book *The Difference: How the Power of Diversity Creates Better Groups, Firms, Schools and Societies*[246] presents compelling evidence that diversity leads to enhanced effectiveness and gains in efficiency. Drawing on various statistical models, Page contends that diversity should be valued for its positive contributions within a market framework and especially for decision-making and addressing problems. His findings indicate that diverse groups outperform homogeneous groups, even when ability is controlled for. Page argues that diverse backgrounds, perspectives and opinions lead to more accurate collective predictions and better decisions. The link between "diversity" and effectiveness is one that resonates with many funders, particularly given the connections between philanthropy and the private sector. Importantly, Page's work must be contextualized so that "diversity" does not get reduced to simple metrics. Social inclusion and authentic ways to diversify foundation boards suggest including the grantee and community perspectives as two important means to achieve meaningful "deep diversity." As Dr. Robert K.

overwhelmed by large amounts of cash are unable to keep pace with the amount of work that nonprofits now are funded to do because of the Gates Foundation. The effect has been described as the "Bill Chill" specifically because, despite claims to the contrary, many grantees fear incurring the wrath of the Gates Foundation and the possibility of losing grant monies.[254]

If the board of the Gates Foundation never hears honest criticism, and if the board does not reflect diversity in any meaningful way or incorporate the voice of grantees, how is that board supposed to exercise the best judg-

ment? As the Rockefeller Philanthropy Advisors' 2008 report on diversity states, "Inclusiveness [means] sharing of power and decision-making with the entire range of constituents …"[255]

To its credit, the Gates Foundation recently has created several advisory committees to help diversify and guide its grantmaking; yet, the problem of the concentration of power among three trustees persists as a challenge. Advisory committees do not have the same decision-making authority as trustees do and there are questions about whether these committees accurately or adequately reflect the

grantee and constituent perspective. As Scott Page notes, "Diverse people … can handle any contingency owing to their differences, but they can also combine their differences to create even better solutions." In other words, a larger and more diverse board at the Gates Foundation likely would generate more innovative and effective solutions to resolve problems. Excluding the grantee and constituent voices from its decision-making leads to solutions that are not fully-informed by the real needs of the intended beneficiaries of the Gates Foundation's grantmaking.

Ross, president and CEO of the California Endowment states, "Diversity is best understood, prioritized and integrated into the operations of a foundation as a tool for effectiveness in, and responsiveness to, the communities being served."[247]

There is general consensus that the diversity and heterogeneity of the foundation universe results in variable perceptions of effectiveness. Yet, there is less discussion or agreement on the issue of what comprises an authentically diverse board. To address this gap, the Center for Effective Philanthropy (CEP) conducted a rigorous statistical analysis as part of its Foundation Governance Project. In its second report of the Project, CEP found that "once minority membership reaches higher absolute numbers—three or more—ratings of opportunity for influence do not vary between minority and non-minority [board] members."[248] Importantly, as CEP acknowledges in this report, the lack of a single or uniform measure of foundation effectiveness makes any analysis of this important component of foundation governance challenging. Thus, CEP relied on self-reporting from foundation trustees regarding their perceptions of what comprises effectiveness as a proxy measure in this analysis. The findings on board diversity merit a specific caution: while the correlation between the absolute number of minority persons on a board and the minimum number of those members needed to ensure that they feel empowered in board discussions is sound, it has the potential to perpetuate reductionist viewpoints on what diversity comprises. Put differently, just as Page's work on board diversity and effectiveness must be framed in the larger context of social inclusion, so must the CEP findings. It would be counterproductive for boards to assume that once they reach the nominal figure of three "minority" members that there is, in fact, authentic diversity reflected in the board's composition. But the CEP findings do underscore that a board must have a minimum of five people; because a minimum of three non-majority members is needed for them to express their opinions, increasing board size to a minimum of five is a reasonable and achievable benchmark for any grantmaking institution to meet.

Including the grantee voice in decision-making

Grantees are more attuned to the needs of their constituents, understand the local context in which they work and bring other valuable intellectual and human capital to the relationship that funders do not have. This expertise should inform philanthropic decision-making by including these representatives on boards. It is knowledge that increases sector-wide impact and helps foundations better understand on-the-ground realities of the environment in which both parties are working. Some exemplary grantmakers already include grantee or constituent representatives on their boards.

In 2003, NCRP convened representatives from 50 local, national and regional nonprofits including affinity groups, civil rights organizations and community-based organizations. Among the issues raised by participants in their discussion of improving philanthropic practice was diversifying board composition. As the report on the convening states, "Meeting participants particularly cited the need for putting [grantees] on the boards of foundations and for expanding the representation of people of color on foundation boards as high priority tasks ..."[249]

A 2008 survey by Grantmakers for Effective Organizations (GEO) found that only 14 percent of grantmaker respondents indicated that they had delegated power about decisions regarding funding to grantees or representatives of recipient communities.[250] Foundation asset size is associated with the likelihood of engaging grantees or communities served: the larger the foundation, the more likely it is to do so. Even so, GEO's analysis found that only 21 percent of the largest foundations with assets in excess of $400 million reported delegating decision-making.

GEO's survey also found that foundation boards that include members with nonprofit experience are more likely to engage in grantmaking practices that are associated with grantee success. In their sample, respondents with one or more nonprofit representatives on the board were twice as likely to report soliciting anonymous or non-anonymous feedback from grantees. GEO notes that while there is an association between the presence of such board members and these "grantee-friendly" practices, causality is hard to determine. As the report states, it is possible that grantmakers already engaged in such practice are more likely to maintain nonprofit representation on their decision-making bodies if the presence of these members is associated with better decision-making practice.[251]

## TRUSTEE COMPENSATION

Trustee compensation persists as the subject of significant debate and research in philanthropy. The IRS does not provide definitive guidance on how to determine appropriate levels of trustee compensation, noting that "the compensation of officers, directors, trustees, key employees, and others in a position to exercise substantial influence over the affairs of the charity should be determined by persons who are knowledgeable in compensation matters and who have no financial interest in the determination."[257] Media reports continue to demonstrate abuses of trustee fees for personal enrichment and recent research demonstrates high variability across foundations regarding trustee compensation policies and practices. There are two compelling reasons for a grantmaking institution to maintain an uncompensated board: the data do not support proponents of compensation who contend that such policy results in better service; and more importantly, every dollar that goes to excessive trustee compensation is a publicly subsidized dollar that should be used to further the grantmaker's mission. Thus, as a rule, trustees should serve without compensation; this is expected of and true for the vast majority of grantee organizations. The only exceptions should be if the CEO also is a trustee or if the foundation compensates lower-income board members who otherwise would be unable to serve because they cannot afford the time lost from work. As Virginia Esposito of the National Center for Family Philanthropy states, "Foundations are generally averse to supporting that sort of behavior on the nonprofit side, so why do they do it themselves? I would be appalled if a nonprofit that I was thinking to fund paid their trustees, so we should not either."[258]

The 2007 *Principles for Good Governance and Ethical Practice*, issued by the Panel on the Nonprofit Sector convened by the Independent Sector did not rule out compensating board members. The 20th Principle does, however, state that "Board members are generally expected to serve without compensation other than reimbursement for expenses incurred to fulfill their board duties." The conservative Philanthropy Roundtable's president Adam Meyerson challenged the "general expectation" clause when his organization refused to sign on to the *Principles*, asserting that there is no such expectation in the sector. In 2008, William A. Schambra, director of the Bradley Center for Philanthropy & Civic Renewal and

> Philanthropy has an honest reputation that's being tarnished by the actions of a few greedy trustees and staff members who pay themselves far too handsomely .... Foundations have tax-exempt status because they contribute to the greater good. To survive and prosper, they need the public's trust. Excessive compensation drains money away from charity and creates an intolerable stain for the many selfless trustees who work for little or no money.
>
> – Editorial, The Boston Globe, November 2, 2003[256]

senior fellow at the Hudson Institute, synthesized many of the arguments stated by grantee and foundation executives for and against compensation of trustees. As Schambra notes in discussing the Roundtable's response, trustee compensation is a legal practice provided that payments are not excessive and can be considered "'reasonable and necessary to carry out the exempt purposes of the foundation."[259] In contrast, Pablo Eisenberg et al.'s 2003 research notes the potential for self-dealing and abuse that results from variable interpretations of the IRS guidelines that bar trustees from engaging in such practice. As the report states, "According to the IRS, trustees, even family members, can be paid for services to a foundation that are reasonable, necessary and not excessive. There are, however, no firm criteria for evaluating what is reasonable, necessary and not excessive. Such vagueness leaves the door open to potential ethical problems and blatant abuse by trustees."[260] Some grantmaking institutions such as the Charles Stewart Mott Foundation never have compensated board members. As the foundation's president and CEO William White states, "We have never had to pay our board members. There are many, many excellent potential candidates who would love an opportunity to serve on a foundation board free of charge."[261]

Media reports indicate that foundation trustees continue to receive excessive compensation and abuse their positions in other ways. The 2003 *Boston Globe* series concluded that there were many foun-

> We have never had to pay our board members. There are many, many excellent potential candidates who would love an opportunity to serve on a foundation board free of charge.
>
> —William S. White, President and CEO
> Charles Stewart Mott Foundation

dations "whose tax returns show that officers and directors are themselves the principal beneficiaries of foundation assets."[262] For example, the *Globe* found that Paul C. Cabot Jr., principal trustee of the Paul and Virginia Cabot Charitable Trust, paid himself an annual salary of more than $1 million from 1998 to 2001, with an increase in 2001 to finance his daughter's $200,000 wedding. During the same five years, the foundation's assets declined significantly from $14 million to roughly $5 million under Cabot's stewardship while paying out an average of $400,000 a year to grantees. Cabot admitted to the *Globe* that a large proportion of foundation assets was used to maintain his affluent lifestyle.[263] This example demonstrates not only a violation of the public trust but a clear breach of federal laws regarding charitable organizations that apply to private foundations, i.e., that such entities "must ensure that its earnings do not inure to the benefit of any private shareholder or individual" and "must not operate for the benefit of private interests such as those of its founder [or] the founder's family."[264]

More recently, the *Buffalo News*[265] reviewed the tax returns of 80 foundations of variable size and type in a series of articles analyzing foundation grantmaking and expenses in Western New York. The analysis found that 30 (37.5 percent) of these foundations compensated their trustees. The foundations

that provided the highest levels of trustee compensation include the Margaret L. Wendt Foundation and the Oishei Foundation. The article notes that the $124 million Wendt Foundation pays three trustees $156,000 a year while the Oishei Foundation pays its nine trustees a total of more than $300,000 annually. Oishei holds $305 million in assets. Such behavior is an abuse of the public trust and negatively impacts the proportion of foundation assets that are much needed by grantees. In the aggregate, the 80 foundations analyzed spent approximately 25 cents on operating and administration expenses for every dollar awarded in grants. The article highlights the variability in foundation expenses associated with asset size and concludes, "Whether for costly investment advice or trustee costs, [some, mostly smaller, foundations'] operating and administrative expenses, as a percent of their grants, [are] twice the average for foundations between 2002 and 2007."[266] Local context may be an influencing factor in the cost ratios of smaller foundations noted here. In contrast to the *Buffalo News* analysis, the Association of Small Foundations found that most surveyed members usually spend 8 cents for each dollar they pay out in grants.[267]

Smaller samples drawn from the membership of the Council on Foundations indicate that in 2004, 58 percent of independent foundations provided compensation to all or some of their board members, a figure that went up substantially to 83 percent for foundations with assets greater than $500 million.[268] A recent comprehensive analysis by the Urban Institute, the Foundation Center and GuideStar found that roughly 25 percent of all the foundations studied indicated board compensation on their tax filings for at least one of the three years studied. Although some of these foundations did not compensate trustees in each of the three years analyzed, approximately 18 percent did.[269] The report authored by Elizabeth Boris et al. is one of the first thorough analyses of the various factors that influence foundation expense and compensation patterns across different types of foundations with variable asset sizes. The study analyzed influencing factors at 10,000 foundations from 2001 through 2003. Data analyzed included compensation records for more than 50,000 individual staff members, managers, trustees and executives as reported on the 990 and 990 PF forms. The foundations studied represent 16 percent of all independent, corporate and community foundations, and account for 78 percent of all foundation giving and 77 percent of all grantmaking assets. The report thus presents the most accurate available picture of the influential factors for foundation expenses sector-wide.

The analysis shows that compensated board members at independent foundations earned a median salary of $8,000 in the course of the three years studied. But the same research indicates that the median, usually less subject to influential outliers than the mean, still obscures highly compensated board members, whose excessive compensation increased the overall average compensation among independent foundation board members to roughly $15,700 in the three-year study.[270] Trustee compensation among community foundations was rare, but the average among those that did compensate directors was between $5,000 and $7,000. Corporate foundations compensated trustees at rates much lower than either community or independent foundations, but these costs do not include other forms of compensation such as direct payment from the parent corporate company or other monetary recompense for tasks performed for the corporation. Compensation was greater for board members of large foundations with higher annual giving trends.

In 2003, the Center for Public and Nonprofit Leadership at Georgetown University published a study analyzing information on trustee compensation for 176 of the largest private foundations in the United States determined by assets and for 62 smaller U.S. foundations. Pablo Eisenberg et al. analyzed tax returns from 1998 for each foundation and conducted telephone interviews with private foundation representatives to verify the accuracy of the data reported on the 990 PF forms. The results demonstrated that:

1. In the 238 surveyed foundations, a total of $44,891,982 was paid in trustee fees; close to $25 million went to trustees at the large foundations.
2. Fourteen of the large foundations studied paid their trustees more than $100,000 each. Five of the 62 smaller foundations paid their trustees more

than $100,000 each in fees, while nearly half paid $25,000 or more.
3. A subsample of 113 of the large foundations paid trustee fees, and compensation at 18 of these totaled 10 percent or more of administrative costs, while the fees of seven were one-third or more. Further, 22 small foundations provided fees comprising 25 percent or more of administrative costs.[271]

The study concluded that trustee fees should be capped at $8,000 annually per director, emphasizing that this would translate to the equivalent of an annual salary of $96,000. The researchers recommended excluding trustee fees as an allowable expense for foundations to count toward meeting their yearly payout requirements. As Pablo Eisenberg, one of the analysts, stated recently to the *Buffalo News*, "It comes down to a class issue that has not been addressed by the foundation world. It's just an outrageous thing that these wealthy folks should get paid for doing their civic duty."[272] He also noted that trustee fees account for some $300 million annually and that most foundation boards are homogeneous and do not include the types of variable perspectives that many nonprofit boards do.

Some grantmakers contend that paying trustees is necessary because of heightened competition for qualified board members from the private sector, where they receive such fees. For example, John Healy, former president of the Atlantic Philanthropies, stated that the foundation paid its board members "quite handsomely" because "we're asking busy people who have other careers, sometimes in very specialized fields, to give us a lot of time." Similarly, Joel Fleishman, former president of the Atlantic Philanthropic Services Co. Inc., the U. S. program staff of Atlantic Philanthropies, cites this competition for trustees from the private sector and their limited time as the rationale for foundations compensating trustees.[273]

In contrast, foundations such as Charles Stewart Mott, William and Flora Hewlett, David and Lucile Packard, William Penn, Surdna, Rosenberg, George Gund, and the Rockefeller Brothers Fund do not compensate their trustees. Colburn Wilbur, former president of Packard, explained the foundation's policy by stating, "Universities, hospitals and even the largest nonprofits seldom pay trustees; why should the Packard Foundation?" Kirke Wilson, former executive director and president of the Rosenberg Foundation for some three decades, noted that "there is no research supporting the notion that trustee compensation results in higher levels of engagement, better grantmaking or better work."[274] Some smaller foundations including the Baptist Community Ministries, the S. H. Cowell Foundation and the New World Foundation also do not provide trustee fees.[275] This allows them to invest more foundation money towards charitable causes.

In assessing whether compensated trustees provide better service than uncompensated boards, the Center for Effective Philanthropy (CEP) studied the effectiveness of both types of boards. CEP found that paid trustees often were more active outside of the board room than voluntary trustees but concluded that the data could not determine whether there is a causal relationship between more trustee engagement and compensation. The report also concludes that "even if pay were shown to cause the different behaviors described here, it would remain an open question whether this would justify the practice—or whether there are other, equally effective ways to motivate such behavior."[276]

> I believe that poor governance leads to wasted assets, inefficient use of assets, and loss of public trust in the sector. For us to ignore these realities would be shirking our responsibility, our obligation, to assure that assets are used for exempt purposes, and that the billions of dollars of federal tax subsidies Congress has authorized are well spent.
>
> – Steven T. Miller, Commissioner
> Tax Exempt and Government Entities Division of the IRS[277]

In lieu of direct monetary compensation, some grantmaking institutions allow trustees to make discretionary grants with foundation dollars. But this is, in fact, an alternate form of compensation and is not exemplary practice. While this practice at least ensures the dollars still are going to a charitable cause of some kind, there often is little relation between the mission of the foundation and the recipient organization. Some trustees use these discretionary grants to advance their own social standing or to replace monies they would have given from their personal funds.

The IRS guidelines on board compensation are vague, subject to variable interpretations of what is "reasonable," and lead to a lack of consensus across the sector about what this means, even within similar grantmaking institutions. Because of this lack of agreement and the continued abuses documented by the media, as a rule, trustees should serve without compensation with the two exceptions of the CEO or lower-income board members who would be unable to serve otherwise. Especially because most foundation trustees come from affluent backgrounds, there is no defensible rationale for compensation that drains the U.S. civil society sector of needed grant dollars to maximize the social benefit of institutional philanthropy's contributions to its nonprofit partners.

## POLICIES AND PRACTICES THAT SUPPORT ETHICAL BEHAVIOR

In 2008, the IRS revised the 990 form for charitable organizations, including some grantmaking institutions such as community foundations, to include governance information. However, similar changes were not made to the 990 PF form filed by private foundations. Ensuring ethical operations is integral to demonstrating that a grantmaker is using the tax subsidy appropriately, not violating the law, and giving the public a maximum return on its charitable investments. One of the most important things a grantmaking institution can do to build public and regulatory trust in its operations is to maintain appropriate policies and practices that make the prospect of abuse less likely and demonstrate substantive accountability. These policies include but are not limited to: a) maintaining appropriate conflict of interest and whistleblower protection policies; b) establishing reasonable, not excessive, executive compensation; and c) subscribing to and abiding by any of a number of available codes for ethical conduct and good governance.

## Maintaining appropriate conflict of interest and whistleblower protection policies

Several of the Panel on the Nonprofit Sector's principles for good governance align with recommendations made in this chapter. Principle 3 is applicable directly to ensuring that a foundation is carrying out its work ethically and that conflict of interest policies are in place. It states, "A charitable organization should adopt and implement policies and procedures to ensure that all conflicts of interest, or the appearance thereof, within the organization and the board are appropriately managed through disclosure, recusal, or other means."[278]

The most recent IRS guidelines for nonprofit organizational governance state that "the directors of a charity owe it a duty of loyalty [that] requires a director to act in the interest of the charity rather than in the personal interest of the director … In particular, the duty of loyalty requires a director to avoid conflicts of interest that are detrimental to the charity."[279] The same duty of loyalty should apply to conflicts of interest at grantmaking institutions. Ensuring that a conflict of interest policy is in place provides a foundation a range of benefits. It can ensure that there is no self-dealing, a loophole left open by the mid-2000s' regulatory focus on abuses in the charitable sector. By addressing self-dealing, a conflict of interest policy has the potential to curb or prevent abuses from occurring. For example, in 2004, the *New York Times* reported that executives from the J. Paul Getty Trust were being paid retirement packages many times their base salary. Further allegations led the Council on Foundations to investigate whether there was "inappropriate compensation for the foundation's CEO and potential self-dealing"[280] because of a land procurement deal between the Getty Trust and Eli Broad, a billionaire financier and close personal friend of the trust's CEO.[281]

By ensuring compliance with its conflict of interest policy, it is possible that the trust would have avoided public embarrassment and censure by the Council on Foundations. This example also demonstrates the trust's failure to adhere to its role as an ethical steward of its assets as required by the IRS guidelines for ethical operations, specifically that tax exemption is contingent on the organization neither operating for private interests nor engaging in business transactions that do not relate to its tax exempt purpose.

Putting a whistleblower protection policy in place is an important step to ensure that if and when abuses of philanthropy for personal gain are suspected, the employee or trustee knows that she or he can report their superiors without fear of retribution. Similar to adhering to a conflict of interest policy, protecting whistleblowers demonstrates that a grantmaker takes seriously the generous tax subsidies it receives and is committed to eliminating abuses. The media reports discussed earlier demonstrate continued violations of the public trust. These investigative articles would not have been possible had the journalists not granted anonymity to their tipsters. This is one area in which grantmakers could draw lessons from the fourth estate in exercising due diligence that ensures ethical operations. The IRS governance and related topics guidelines for nonprofits "encourages the board of directors to adopt an effective policy for handling employee complaints and to establish procedures for employees to report in confidence any suspected financial impropriety or misuse of the charity's resources."[282] NCRP advocates such policies to ensure that abuses are reported without fear of retribution at grantmaking and grantee organizations alike.

## Establishing reasonable, not excessive, executive compensation

Executive staff are compensated under the IRS stipulation that such compensation is "not excessive and can be considered reasonable and necessary to carry out the exempt purposes" of the foundation. As with the variable interpretation of the terms "reasonable and necessary" in trustee compensation, determining what constitutes "reasonable" compensation for executives of grantmaking institutions remains an area of considerable debate and disagreement.

Numerous factors inform the process for determining an executive's compensation level. Because of regional variations in the cost of employing and retaining high-quality staff, heightened competition for qualified staff who otherwise could work in the private sector, and the huge variations in the cost of conducting a foundation's day-to-day operations, the current mandate that compensation be "reasonable" leaves grantmakers substantial flexibility. It is impossible to determine a single, uniform metric to determine an appropriate level of compensation for foundation executives. But the variable definitions of "reasonable" make it all the more important that grantmakers have clear and transparent processes in place to make compensation decisions. Excessive executive compensation damages the public trust in grantmaking institutions and is an affront to the spirit of philanthropy. For a foundation to increase regulatory and grantee trust in its operations, it should be transparent about the steps taken in determining what it perceives as reasonable and why. By clarifying and publicizing the process and policies used to determine executive compensation, a foundation executive's compensation is contextualized better and abuses of philanthropy for personal gain can be curbed.

The *Chronicle of Philanthropy* notes that the median levels of executive compensation across the nonprofit sector grew at a rate faster than inflation: inflation was 4.1 percent in 2007, while grantee and foundation CEOs received a median compensation increase of 5 percent. As the *Chronicle* highlights, this is the largest increase in a one-year period since the paper's 2002 survey that showed a 7.5 percent increase.[283] Although this analysis emphasizes variability across types of foundations and notes the emerging trend of larger charities hiring leaders with private sector backgrounds as contributing factors, some foundations appear to provide unjustifiably large compensation to their CEOs. Another important finding in the analysis is that many foundation trustees now provide exorbitant bonuses and fringe benefits that supplement even seemingly reasonable executive compensation levels.[284]

Negative publicity that often accompanies excessive compensation has significant consequences for a grantmaking institution. For example, the infamous 1992 scandal about United Way President and CEO William Aramony's theft from the organization continues to haunt United Way chapters nationwide because of the extensive media coverage the incident received. Aramony was convicted in 1995 on 25 counts, including conspiracy to defraud and filing false tax returns; he served seven years in prison. In 2002, upon Aramony's release from jail, the *Nonprofit Quarterly* quoted Bob Beggan—the man in charge of United Way's international work who had reported to Aramony for nineteen years—as stating that he had to travel with a document that explained what had happened because the Aramony scandal came up in other parts of the world.[285]

The same article notes that many local chapters disaffiliated themselves from the national United Way office and filed for name changes, and that local chapters that did not even exist during the early to mid-1990s still must address this scandal in the "Frequently Asked Questions" sections of their web sites. In 2006, Kevin McCarthy, CEO of the United Way of Inland Valley in California, said that he still heard regularly about the Aramony scandal.[286] This egregious example demonstrates how executive largesse and abuse of the public trust hurts the charitable purpose of an organization. More recently, the public scandal surrounding former CEO Gloria Pace King's $2.1 million pension led to outrage among individual donors who withdrew their support, resulting in the United Way of Central Carolinas closing its fundraising campaign in November 2008 some $20 million short of the amount raised in the previous year; the chapter was among the 20 leading fundraising chapters at that time.[287] Excessive executive compensation that brings a grantmaker bad press is especially harmful for grantmaking public charities that rely on raising funds from the public.

Pablo Eisenberg has been a regular critic of the practice of augmenting executive compensation at the expense of talented program officers. He states, "Such compensation practices show how many foundations have begun to borrow the corporate cult of the chief executive, with its increasingly high pay, large benefits, special perks, and separation from the rest of the staff. In many cases, the second-highest ranking official in a foundation ... receives half or less of the CEO's salary, while excellent program officers may get one-third or less of the salary their CEO receives."[288]

The 990 PF form requires data on the compensation provided to all officers, managers, trustees and directors to be listed. A foundation also must report compensation of the five highest paid employees not included in the section on board members and others noted. While these data provide meaningful insight into compensation, the variability in how the information is reported makes comparisons over time challenging. For example, although only 25 percent of foundations employ staff, the data on the PF form vary by year. An employee's name may be reported one way in a given year and differently in another (e.g., John A. Smith can be reported as J. Smith). Uniformity in reporting these data would enhance transparency and allow for longitudinal comparisons, providing better sector-wide trends and benchmarks of accountability and transparency.

## Subscribing to codes of ethical conduct and good governance

The Panel on the Nonprofit Sector's second principle for good governance states: "A charitable organization should have a formally adopted written code of ethics with which all of its directors or trustees, staff and volunteers are familiar and to which they adhere."[289] The

Ford Foundation, for example, makes publicly available on its web site the code of ethical conduct it expects staff to follow.[290] It also publicly discloses its governance practices.[291] Additionally, Ford makes other documents on governance available in three broad areas: the foundation's governing documents; its committee charters and memberships; and the policies and procedures it adheres to.[292] The California Endowment publicly discloses similar information on its web site, including its code of ethics and conflict of interest policy.[293] There likely are many more foundations that follow similar practice, but without centralized data it is not currently possible to determine the proportion of foundations that do so.

There are numerous codes for good governance, accountability, ethical behavior and transparency. The Independent Sector has compiled a list of nearly 100 such standards for nonprofits and foundations.[294] Among those comprising the Independent Sector's compendium are several resources for grantmaking institutions of variable types, including the Council on Foundations and the Minnesota Council on Foundations, Indiana Grantmakers Alliance, Washington Grantmakers and the New York Regional Association of Grantmakers.[295] These publicly available codes of ethical conduct and good governance provide useful tools for grantmaking institutions, and exemplary grantmakers subscribe to and abide by one or more of these sets of principles.

## TRANSPARENCY AND DISCLOSING INFORMATION FREELY

Transparency is integral to ensuring that a grantmaking institution is able to demonstrate that it is making appropriate use of the generous tax subsidies afforded it by the government. The public also has a right and a vested interest to expect a significant level of disclosure about foundation operations. Meaningful transparency can help policymakers and the public discern the extent to which the subsidies afforded foundations actually serve the public good and if a foundation is maximizing its own and the public's return on its charitable contributions. As

Supreme Court Justice Louis Brandeis often is quoted in discussions about transparency and accountability, "Sunlight is said to the best of disinfectants."

NCRP believes that regulation of philanthropy is necessary and important, and that when done properly, it can help foundations achieve their missions and protect the public interest. Although regulation and mandates are among the ways that grantmaking institutions can demonstrate substantive transparency, voluntarily engaging in meaningful transparency by disclosing relevant information publicly is one way that an exemplary grantmaker demonstrates its stewardship of the partly public dollars with which it is entrusted. As Sean Stannard-Stockton, principal and director of Tactical Philanthropy states, "We need to reframe transparency away from some sort of thing that philanthropy is being forced to consider by outside forces and instead celebrate transparency as the mark of an organization that is truly committed to improving the field."[297]

NCRP long has advocated for voluntary information disclosure as one way to help ensure foundation accountability. At the 1980 Council on Foundations annual conference, NCRP presented its first report on foundation accountability, *Foundations and Public Information: Sunshine or Shadow*. The report brought media and foundation attention to sector-wide lax reporting. The increased publicity led to many foundations, including the Pew Memorial Trust and the Rockefeller Foundation, to publish annual reports. Today, most foundations routinely publish such reports and make them publicly available.[298]

In 2008, the IRS revised the 990 form, the tax form all charitable organizations must file, to include information about governance. Steven Miller described the rationale behind the changes to the 990 form as follows: "Despite the absence of explicit federal statutory provisions setting forth clear governance standards, what I am calling jurisdictional gaps, we are not inter-

> By making full and accurate information about its mission, activities, finance, and governance publicly available, a charity encourages transparency and accountability to its constituents.
>
> —Internal Revenue Service, Governance and Related Topics[296]

lopers trying to regulate an area that is beyond our sphere. Rather, the effects of good or bad nonprofit governance cut across virtually everything we see and do in our work. It impacts whether the organization is operated to further exempt purposes and public, rather than private, interests. It dictates whether the organization's executives are compensated fairly or excessively. It influences whether the organization makes informed and fair decisions regarding its investments or its fundraising practices, or allows others to take unfair advantage. The question is no longer whether the IRS has a role to play in this area, but rather what that role will be."[299] Grantmaking public charities now are required to disclose this governance information because they file a 990 form. For private foundations that file the 990 PF form, it is reasonable and fair to expect similar disclosures voluntarily.

access, equity, and diversity, and to end discrimination based on race, ethnicity, gender, sexual orientation, disability, or age."[301] Importantly, this foundation also seeks out grantees that reflect the same diversity values that it employs in its own staffing and board composition. The California Endowment discloses the ethnic and gender breakdown of its staff and trustees. This mirrors the foundation's mission of improving the health of California's multicultural communities.[302] These foundations display a commitment to ensuring inclusive diversity, matching mission with grantmaking and disclosing publicly information that helps build the public trust in philanthropic institutions. Institutional grantmakers should take valuable lessons from such foundations' work on diversity and their willingness to share information openly.

Notably, many grantmakers require their grantees to provide demographic data on staff, including executive leadership and sometimes boards and constituents. Just as the heterogeneity of the foundation world compels accountability to be repositioned without a "one-size fits all" approach, grantee and constituent diversity must be considered

> Some people ... have been raising the issues of philanthropic diversity and inclusiveness as if such calls were new. But these concerns, in fact, have been acknowledged in philanthropic circles for at least three decades.
>
> – Lori Villarosa, Director, Philanthropic Initiative for Racial Equity

There is a void of information that can help the public gauge whether or not taxpayer subsidized dollars are being used to further a foundation's charitable purpose. This results in a lack of substantive transparency. Recent legislation in California highlighted the lack of available information about diversity in foundations. Although the bill, AB 624, eventually was withdrawn by its sponsor, the debate sparked important discussions about diversity in philanthropy and has led to some additional research and to new foundation investments in the capacity of minority-led nonprofits.[300]

Some foundations provide ready access to diversity data. The San Francisco Foundation, for example, sees contextualized diversity as a core value and demonstrates its values by making demographic data on its staff and board publicly available and ensuring that its grants go to truly diverse groups that reflect the communities being served. According to the foundation's policy on diversity, it "actively seeks to promote

variable, subject to local context and non-uniform. Further, if a foundation believes that grantee diversity disclosure is relevant information to inform board decision-making, the same criterion should apply to foundation disclosure of diversity data. As Lori Villarosa, director of the Philanthropic Initiative for Racial Equity, stated in the wake of the debates surrounding AB 624, "Some people ... have been raising issues of philanthropic diversity and inclusiveness as if such calls were new. But these concerns, in fact, have been acknowledged in philanthropic circles for at least three decades."[303] This is an important reminder that diversity is not a new concept for grantmakers; rather, it is a dynamic and salient issue that relates directly to a foundation's own effectiveness. Moreover, it underscores that diversity should be valued and contextualized in the framework of authentic inclusion.

Some foundations have made notable voluntary efforts to share information publicly. Yet, too few foundations engage in real transparency, leading to questions about whether the tax subsidy is being used appropriately. Rigorous self-regulation is valuable for strengthening the public trust in institutional philanthropy and ensuring that grantmakers can withstand any level of scrutiny from the IRS and the public. Sharing significant and relevant information freely is a necessary step. At a minimum, an exemplary grantmaking institution demonstrates transparency and accountability by sharing a range of information including but not limited to:

a. Information about the policies it maintains that promote ethical behavior;
b. Demographic data on its trustees, staff, grantees and the intended beneficiaries of its grants;
c. Information about whether or how it is using its assets in non-grantmaking ways that support its mission;
d. Information about the types of grants it provides; and,
e. Useful information for grant seekers about priorities and application procedures.

By voluntarily disclosing this information freely, an exemplary grantmaker demonstrates that it is an ethical steward of the partially public dollars with which it is entrusted.

### Information that should be voluntarily disclosed

Grantmakers should make comprehensive information about their charitable contributions, governance and management policies publicly available. They also should disclose relevant information about aspects of their other operations to demonstrate substantive accountability. In keeping with the IRS's guidelines for nonprofits, complete and accurate financial statements and accounting reports should be posted on a foundation's web site and made publicly available upon request. Many foundations already do this, but gauging whether an individual foundation implements these policies is a daunting task in the absence of centralized data.

The issue of disclosing demographic data on trustees, staff and grantees is addressed earlier in this chapter under board composition. However, recently, the question of *who* benefits from philanthropy has received substantial attention. In response to the debate sparked by AB 624, the Foundation Center worked with three California regional associations of grantmakers to analyze how much of the state's philanthropic giving benefits communities of color.[304] The report analyzed domestic giving from 1996 to 2005 and found variable trends for giving to benefit the economically disadvantaged and racial or ethnic minorities.[305] Giving that is intended to benefit marginalized groups, broadly defined, is discussed in-depth in Chapter I of this book. The salient point for disclosure however, is that studies like the one referenced above fill a void in sector-wide knowledge about who institutional philanthropy seeks to benefit. In the absence of comprehensive disclosure, there is no way to assess whether a funder is making appropriate use of the generous tax subsidies afforded it or if it is advancing elite interests via patronage grants.

The 990 PF form requires disclosure of the top two program-related investments (PRI) that a foundation makes, and the balance of PRI monies are reported in the aggregate. These usually are below-market loans made to grantee organizations and count toward the qualifying distribution requirement. Beyond this, there are no publicly available data on if and how a foundation is leveraging its assets in ways that support its mission. An increasing number of funders engage in mission investing, a strategy discussed in Chapter IV that seeks both a financial and social return, but there is little publicly available data on this. NCRP encourages those grantmakers who do screen their investments, engage in shareholder activism or seek out proactive mission investments to make such information publicly accessible.

The Foundation Center tracks data on nearly all U.S. grantmakers; it also tracks and analyzes detailed information for more than 1,200 large foundations. A crucial component of the Foundation Center's data collection is the information it gathers on the types of support a foundation provides. Data include information on the proportion of monies granted for direct services, general operating support, continuous funding, leadership development and capacity building, among others. These data allow for closer scrutiny of foundation financial priorities and are the only information available outside of the 990 PF forms that the public, grantees, watchdogs and the media can use to look at private foundations. They also provide grant seekers with valuable information on which grantmakers to approach when looking for particular types of support. There are many benefits to demonstrating transparency through increased disclosure of the types of grants a foundation provides. Some criticize the inherent bias of self-reported data, but two important caveats about the Foundation Center apply: the data are verified against financial records for accuracy, and until such time as more disclosure is mandated, this is an interim step to rebuild the public trust in institutional philanthropy. Finally, foundations themselves can benefit by participating in such voluntary reporting, allowing institutions to assess their own behavior against similarly endowed counterparts to gauge their own effectiveness and policies.

Grant seekers currently can look to specific grantmakers, and to databases such as the ones maintained by the Foundation Center and GuideStar, to find information about what a particular foundation requires to consider a grant application. A recent report by a collaborative of foundations and nonprofits identified variable application procedures as a serious impediment to grantee and funder effectiveness and efficiency.[306] While this may seem obvious, a foundation also should make its application procedures easily available to grant seekers and the public. This will result in efficiency gains for both parties and further demonstrate ethical stewardship. Grantees often are frustrated by how challenging it is to determine the priorities and procedures of various grantmakers.

### Securing anonymous feedback

Third party or neutral external actors often can help foundations elicit the needed anonymous feedback on their performance. Independent consultants present funders with an opportunity to get authentic feedback that is not euphemized because of the threat of lost funding. An important issue that arises in working with independent consultants is where the costs to cover this expense should come from. Because this feedback offers significant improvements for decision-making, foundations should consider seriously whether anonymous feedback should be viewed as a fixed cost in institutional philanthropy.

Some institutional grantmakers already engage in this exemplary practice; for example, the David & Lucile Packard Foundation solicits confidential grantee feedback, which can be provided anonymously or non-anonymously.[307] The foundation also makes its *Grantee Perception Report*, a grantee survey tool developed by the Center for Effective Philanthropy (CEP) to help foundations secure grantee feedback, publicly available on its web site. The James Irvine Foundation also makes the findings of its CEP assessment publicly available on its web site and

has an online form for non-anonymous feedback.[308] Many foundations that have commissioned CEP to conduct these assessments make their findings publicly available.[309] This is a good grantmaker practice of demonstrating accountability and transparency publicly, especially when the results not always are positive.

The Kresge Foundation commissioned CEP to conduct their analysis for grantees and applicants. The findings indicated that Kresge was ranked by survey respondents at or below the 25th percentile on five of CEP's eleven main indicators, including community impact and grantee satisfaction. In response, Kresge president Rip Rapson issued an open letter to the community, noting that while he was disappointed with the report's findings, that he "wanted our partners to help us serve them better. This is the only way we will realize our desire to innovate and improve the bedrock conditions and long-term opportunities for individuals, families and communities in need."[310] Not only does Kresge provide public access to its survey, the foundation developed a multi-year transition guided by nine core values in expanding its grantmaking. As the foundation states on its web site, "We believe we have a moral obligation to recalibrate our grantmaking by elevating the values that have quietly guided us for more than 80 years. In doing so, we hope to contribute more meaningfully to those organizations that most directly advance these values."[311] By incorporating critical feedback in its decision-making, this institutional grantmaker demonstrates responsiveness to external feedback and exemplary stewardship.

Arthur Schmidt, founder of GuideStar, notes that CEP has made a significant contribution to the field by offering its Grantee Perception Report as a tool for institutional grantmakers to solicit anonymous grantee feedback. Yet, Schmidt highlights the tool's limitations because foundations only participate voluntarily and there are significant costs associated with contracting out this work. Like NCRP, Schmidt believes that public disclosure of these reports has sector-wide benefits but that "until the candid views of grantees toward foundation grantmakers are gathered and revealed publicly, the model has limited utility."[312] In sum, exemplary philanthropy solicits authentic grantee feedback, uses that information to inform its decision-making, and is open and transparent about the findings.

Publicly disclosing "failures" is one final area that merits specific attention. As James E. Canales, CEO of the James Irvine Foundation, said, "Given the emphasis in foundations these days on communication, transparency and accountability, it just seems to me that you aren't going to be credible if all you talk about is your successes."[313] The Hewlett and Irvine Foundations each made publicly available reports[314] that documented problems encountered during program implementation. Moreover, both foundations shared this information with the *New York Times*,[315] allowing broad public access to this information. These two foundations demonstrate exemplary voluntary disclosure of relevant information and the importance of substantive accountability and transparency.

## CONCLUSION: SETTING THE BAR FOR PHILANTHROPY AT ITS BEST

As this chapter demonstrated, the partly public nature of foundation dollars makes it incumbent on institutional grantmakers to behave as ethical stewards of the monies with which they are entrusted. The board of a grantmaking institution ultimately is responsible for ensuring legal and regulatory compliance, transparency, accountability and maintenance of policies that promote ethical behavior. Because of the lack of centralized or comprehensive data cited throughout this chapter, it is not possible to determine the proportion of foundations that employ these practices. Yet, some exemplary foundations already do follow these policies and practices, as documented throughout. Based on the analysis presented in this chapter, NCRP advocates that all foundations adopt and implement the three fair and reasonable measures that increase the likelihood of a foundation acting as an ethical steward. As more grantmakers adopt the measures described in this chapter, the social benefit of philanthropy will be maximized and the public trust in institutional grantmaking will be rebuilt.

# Criterion III: Ethics

A grantmaker practicing Philanthropy at Its Best serves the public good by demonstrating accountability and transparency to the public, its grantees and constituents.

a) Maintains an engaged board of at least five people who include among them a diversity of perspectives—including of the communities it serves—and who serve without compensation

b) Maintains policies and practices that support ethical behavior

c) Discloses information freely

## DISCUSSION QUESTIONS

NCRP encourages staff and trustees of foundations and other grantmakers to engage in serious discussions about each criterion and the chapter that elaborates on the criterion. Sample discussion questions are provided here to help get you started.

> Which parts of the chapter did you like the most? Why?

> Which parts did you like the least? Why?

> Is it important to demonstrate accountability and transparency? Why or why not? How and when did we reach this decision? How often do we review our policies regarding these issues?

> Do we feel that the size and diversity of our board could improve? If so, in what ways? If not, what are the barriers to us doing so? Have we considered including the grantee perspective on our board? How do we define diversity?

> How did we establish the compensation policy we have in place for trustees? Why? If we don't compensate trustees, are we ensuring that there's no self-dealing or providing other non-monetary forms of compensation? If yes, how did we determine this is appropriate?

> What policies and practices do we have in place to support ethical behavior? How did we establish our conflict of interest policy? Our whistleblower policy? Who is ensuring compliance with these? How do we set executive compensation? Should we consider adopting new policies, following our current policies more closely or revising our policies to align more with funders with comparable assets and missions?

> What information do we disclose freely to the public? Is that enough? How did we determine that this level of disclosure is appropriate? Do we share demographic information about our board, staff and grantees? Do we have ways to ensure we get authentic feedback? Why or why not?

> What else from this chapter should inform our current grantmaking priorities?

> If we want to make any changes based on this discussion, what will need to happen in order to make those changes? What are the next steps?

# NOTES FOR CHAPTER III: ETHICS

218. He was president of the Minneapolis Foundation when this was written. Quoted in: Emmett D. Carson "A Worst Case Scenario or the Perfect Storm? Current Challenges to Foundation Board Governance," *Responsive Philanthropy*, (Summer 2003).

219. The Internal Revenue Service. "Governance and Related Topics – 501 (c) (3) Organizations," The Internal Revenue Service (February 4, 2003), http://www.irs.gov/pub/irs-tege/governance_practices.pdf.

220. The Foundation Center. *Foundation Growth and Giving Estimates: Current Outlook (2008 Edition)* (New York, NY: The Foundation Center, 2008).

221. Steven T. Miller. "Remarks before the Georgetown Law Center Seminar on Issues in Nonprofit Governance," speech, Georgetown University Law Center, Washington, D.C., April 24, 2008.

222. Christine Ahn. "Democratizing Philanthropy: Challenging foundations and Social Justice Organizations," *Responsive Philanthropy* (Fall 2007).

223. The Internal Revenue Service. *Applying for 501 (c) (3) Tax-Exempt Status: Publication 4220,* (Washington, D.C.: Internal Revenue Service), 2. http://www.irs.gov/pub/irs-pdf/p4220.pdf.

224. Ibid. Adapted from p. 3.

225. Garry W. Jenkins. "Incorporation Choice, Uniformity, and the Reform of Nonprofit State Law," *Georgia Law Review* 41 (2007): 1117.

226. Only private foundations must file a 990 PF form while other grantmakers such as community foundations file the same 990 form as do grantee organizations, leading to variable disclosures among institutional grantmakers.

227. Susan Kraft and David Morse. "Public Scrutiny of Foundations and Charities: The Robert Wood Johnson Foundation Response," in *To Improve Health and Health Care Vol. IX: The Robert Wood Johnson Foundation Anthology*, ed. Stephen L. Isaacs and James R. Knickman (San Francisco, CA: Jossey-Bass, 2006), 213-242.

228. Mark W. Everson, written statement to the U.S. Senate Committee on Finance Hearing on Exempt Organizations: Enforcement Problems, Accomplishments, and Future Direction, April 5, 2005. http://www.irs.ustreas.gov/pub/irs-tege/metest040505.pdf

229. Kraft and Morse, Op. Cit., p.228.

230. See Pablo Eisenberg et al. *Foundation Trustee Fees: Use and Abuse* (Washington, D.C.: The Center for Public and Nonprofit Leadership, Georgetown Public Policy Institute, September 2003).

231. Mark Pacella, testimony before the United States Senate Committee on Finance Hearing on Charity Oversight and Reform: Keeping Bad Things from Happening to Good Charities, June 22, 2004.

232. Rick Cohen, testimony before the Senate Finance Committee Hearing on Charity Oversight and Reform: Keeping Bad Things from Happening to Good Charities, June 22, 2004, http://www.kaisernetwork.org/health_cast/uploaded_files/062

204_senate_charity_transcript.pdf; See also The National Committee for Responsive Philanthropy, *Standards for Foundation and Corporate Grantmaking: An Accountability Statement by the National Committee for Responsive Philanthropy* (Washington, D.C.: National Committee for Responsive Philanthropy, June 2004).

233. Ryan J. Donmoyer and Alison Fitzgerald. "Taking from the Rich, Giving to the Board; Management of Robin Hood's Emergency Assets Raise Eyebrows," *The Washington Post*, July 22, 2007, F07.

234. The Internal Revenue Service. *Applying for 501 (c) (3) Tax-Exempt Status: Publication 4220,* Op. Cit.

235. David Saltzman. letter to Robin Hood Foundation Supporters. Reprinted in John Carney, "Robin Hood Fund Pulls Investments from Hedge Fund Managers," Dealbreaker Blog, posted July 19, 2007, http://dealbreaker.com/2007/07/robin-hood-fund-pulls-investme.php#more (accessed January 14, 2009); See also Ryan J. Donmoyer and Alison Fitzgerald, "Robin hood Ends Investments in Board Members' Funds, (Update 2)" *Bloomberg News*, July 19, 2007, http://www.bloomberg.com/apps/news?pid=newsarchive&sid=a0Qi9IFfhVLQ.

236. Pablo Eisenberg. "Recommendations for the Reform of the Nonprofit Sector," statement to the U.S. Senate Committee on Finance, July 22, 2004.

237. Panel on the Nonprofit Sector. *Principles for Good Governance and Ethical Practice: A Guide for Charities and Foundations* (Washington, D.C.: Panel on the Nonprofit Sector, October, 2007).

238. Eisenberg, 2004, Op. Cit.

239. Ibid.

240. Jessica Chao et al. *Philanthropy in a Changing Society: Achieving Effectiveness through Diversity* (New York: Rockefeller Philanthropy Advisors, 2008).

241. Ibid., pp. 19–20

242. Ibid.; Women comprised a total of 75.8 percent of all foundation staff,; 74 percent of program officers and 51.5 percent of CEOs in 2006.

243. Ibid. p. 21

244. Mary Ellen S. Capek and Molly Mead. *Effective Philanthropy: Organizational Success Through Deep Diversity and Gender Equality* (Cambridge, MA: MIT Press, September, 2007).

245. Effective Philanthropy: Organizational Success through Deep Diversity & Gender Equity, "Defining 'Deep Diversity,'" http://effectivephilanthropybook.org/concepts/deep.html.

246. Scott E. Page, *The Difference: How the Power of Diversity Creates Better Groups, Firms, Schools, and Societies* (Princeton, NJ: Princeton University Press, 2007).

247. Dr. Robert K. Ross. "Diversity in philanthropy achieved through leadership, not mandates," *The Mercury News,* March 12, 2008.

248. Phil Buchanan et al. *Beyond Compliance: The Trustee Viewpoint on Effective Foundation Governance: A Report on Phase II of the Center for Effective Philanthropy's Foundation Governance Project* (Cambridge, MA: Center for Effective Philanthropy, 2005), 3.

249. The National Committee for Responsive Philanthropy. *The Core of the Matter: NCRP's First Convening on the Need to Increase Nonprofit Core Operating Support, June 4, 2003* (Washington, D.C.: National Committee for Responsive Philanthropy, July 21 2003), 11.

250. Grantmakers for Effective Organizations. *Grantmaking Practices that Support Grantee Success: Survey Report* (Washington, D.C.: Grantmakers for Effective Organizations, 2008), 31–32.

251. Grantmakers for Effective Organizations, Op. Cit., p. 39.

252. Sandi Doughton. "Not many speak their mind to the Gates Foundation," *The Seattle Times*, August 3, 2008.

253. Ibid.

254. Ibid. See also http://gateskeepers.civiblog.org/, a watchdog group that monitors the Gates Foundation's activities.

255. Chao et al., Op. Cit.

256. "Firmer foundations," editorial. *The Boston Globe*, November 2, 2003, G10.

257. IRS, February 4, 2003, Op. Cit.

258. Quoted in William A. Schambra. "Board Compensation: To Pay or Not to Pay?" *Philanthropy Roundtable* (January/February 2008): 3.

259. Ibid.

260. Eisenberg et. al. 2003, Op. Cit.. p. 10.

261. Quoted in Schambra, Op. Cit., p. 3.

262. Beth Healy et al. "Some officers of charities steer assets to selves," *The Boston Globe*, October 9, 2003.

263. Ibid.

264. The Internal Revenue Service. *Applying for 501 (c) (3) Tax-Exempt Status: Publication 4220,* Op. Cit.

265. Patrick Lakamp and Mary B. Pasciak. "Why does it goes to much to give Money away? A few foundations spend almost as much on expenses as they do on grants," *The Buffalo News*, December 23, 2008. http://www.buffalonews.com/home/story/530961.html

266. Ibid.

267. The Association of Small Foundations. *2007–2008 Foundation Operations & Management Survey: The tool for small foundation benchmarking* (Washington, D.C.: The Association of Small Foundations, 2007), p. 31. The report notes that these cost ratios would earn most ASF members "a perfect ten rating" using Charity Navigator's metrics. Survey respondents included more than 950 of ASF's 3,145 members.

268. See Schambra, Op Cit.

269. Elizabeth Boris et al. *What Drives Foundation Expenses & Compensation? Results of a Three-Year Study* (Washington, D.C.: The Urban Institute, 2008), 56.

270. Ibid, p. 55.

271. Eisenberg et al. 2003, Op. Cit., pp. 7–9.

272. Lakamp and Pasciak, Op. Cit.

273. Schambra, Op. Cit., p. 2

274. Schambra, Op. Cit., p. 3

275. Eisenberg et al., 2003 Op Cit. p: 21; See also Table 1 of this publication for trustee fees in the sample. Because of the lack of centralized data, there are likely many more foundations that do not compensate trustees. The list of foundations cited here is simply illustrative, demonstrating that regardless of foundation size, some grantmakers already engage in this exemplary practice.

276. Buchanan et al., Op. Cit., p. 11.

277. Steven T. Miller, "Remarks before the Georgetown Law Center Seminar on Issues in Nonprofit Governance," speech, Georgetown University Law Center, Washington, D.C., April 23, 2008.

278. Panel on the Nonprofit Sector, Op. Cit., p. 9

279. Internal Revenue Service, February 4, 2003, Op. Cit.

280. Randy Kennedy and Carol Vogel, "Executive Severance Is a Focus at Getty," *The New York Times*, February 11, 2006.

281. The trust was put on probation by the Council on Foundations in December 2005; membership was restored in mid-April 2006, contingent on the trust providing the council with information regarding management and governance practices. The trust's web site states that it 'strengthened' its conflict of interest policies as part of this process. J. Paul Getty Trust, "J. Paul Getty Trust Membership Status in Council on Foundations Restored; Council on Foundations Lifts Probation," press release, April 17, 2006, http://www.getty.edu/news/press/center/council_on_foundations_release041706.html.

282. Internal Revenue Service, February 4, 2003, Op. Cit.

283. Noelle Barton and Ben Gose. "Executive Pay Outpaces Inflation," *The Chronicle of Philanthropy*, October 2, 2008.

284. Ibid.

285. Matthew Sinclair. "William Aramony is back on the Streets," *The Nonprofit Times*, March 1, 2002.

286. Sharon Hoffman. "For U.S. charities, a crisis of trust: Scandals, accountability problems combine to undermine public support," *NBC News,* November 21, 2006, http://www.msnbc.msn.com/id/15753760/.

287. Eric Frazier. "Charlotte's United Way Spurs Warning to Nation: Agency's probe of pension scandal spurs warning to affiliates elsewhere not to be like Charlotte," *The Charlotte Observer*, December 16, 2008.

288. Pablo Eisenberg. "Excessive Executive Compensation Needs to Be Stemmed," *The Chronicle of Philanthropy*, April 29, 2004.

289. Panel on the Nonprofit Sector, Op. Cit., p. 8.

290. The Ford Foundation. "Staff Code of Conduct and Ethics," http://fordfound.org/pdfs/about/Staff_Code_of_Conduct_and_Ethics.pdf.

291. The Ford Foundation, "Trustee Code of Ethics," http://fordfound.org/pdfs/about/Trustee_Code_of_Ethics.pdf.

292. Ibid.

293. See: The California Endowment. "About Us: Striving to Set the Standard for Accountability and Transparency," http://calendow.org/article.aspx?id=140&ItemID=140.

294. See: Independent Sector. "Compendium of Standards, Codes, and Principles of Nonprofit and Philanthropic Organizations," http://www.independentsector.org/issues/accountability/standards2.html.

295. Ibid.

296. Internal Revenue Service, February 4, 2003, Op. Cit.

297. Sean Stannard-Stockton. "Demonstrating Impact: Philanthropy's Urgent Call to Action," Tactical Philanthropy blog, April 30, 2007, http://tacticalphilanthropy.com/2007/06/demonstrating-impact-philanthropy%E2%80%99s-urgent-call-to-action-2, (accessed January 14, 2009).

298. The National Committee for Responsive Philanthropy. *30 Years: A History from 1976 to 2006,* (Washington, D.C.: National Committee for Responsive Philanthropy, 2007), 9–10.

299. Miller, April 23, 2008, Op. Cit., p.1-2.

300. See, e.g., Lawrence T. McGill, Algernon Austin and Brielle Brian. *Embracing Diversity: Foundation Giving Benefiting California's Communities of Color*, (New York: The Foundation Center, 2008).

301. The San Francisco Foundation. "The San Francisco Foundation Policy on Diversity," http://www.sff.org/about/who-we-are/diversity.

302. The California Endowment, "About Us: Facts & Figures," http://www.calendow.org/Article.aspx?id=1876&ItemID=1876.

303. Philanthropic Initiative for Racial Equity. *Critical Issues Forum, Measuring What We Value, Vol. I* (Washington, D.C.: Philanthropic Initiative for Racial Equity, April 2008), 3. http://www.racialequity.org/docs/final%20layout.pdf.

304. McGill et. al., Op. Cit.

305. Ibid., pp. 2–3.

306. Jessica Bearman. *Drowning in Paperwork, Distracted from Purpose: Challenges and Opportunities in Grant Application and Reporting* (Washington, D.C.: Project Streamline, 2008).

307. The David & Lucile Packard Foundation, "Grantee Feedback," http://www.packard.org/categoryDetails.aspx?RootCatID=2&CategoryID=229.

308. See: The James Irvine Foundation. "Grantee Perception Reports," http://www.irvine.org/evaluation/foundation-wide-assessment/granteeperceptionreports; and The James Irvine Foundation. "Give Us Your Feedback," http://www.irvine.org/contact-us/give-us-feedback.

309. For a comprehensive list of foundations that disclose results publicly, see: The Center for Effective Philanthropy. "Grantee Perception Report: Public Results," http://www.effectivephil-anthropy.org/assessment/assessment_gprpublicreports.html.

310. Rip Rapson. "Grantee Perceptions Essential to the Philosophical and Programmatic Expansion of our Grantmaking," The Kresge Foundation, http://www.kresge.org/content/displaycontent.aspx?CID=139.

311. The Kresge Foundation. "How We Are Changing," http://www.kresge.org/content/displaycontent.aspx?CID=64

312. Arthur "Buzz" Schmidt. "Escaping the Perpetuity Mindset," *The Nonprofit Quarterly* (Fall, 2008).

313. Stephanie Strom. "Foundations Find Benefits in Facing Up to Failures," *New York Times*, July 26, 2007.

314. Gary Walker. *Midcourse Corrections to a Major Initiative: A Report on the James Irvine Foundation's CORAL Experience* (San Francisco: The James Irvine Foundation, 2005); Prudence Brown and Leila Feister. *Hard Lessons about Philanthropy & Community Change from the Neighborhood Improvement Initiative* (Menlo Park, CA: William & Flora Hewlett Foundation, March, 2007).

315. Strom, Op. Cit.

# Chapter IV: Commitment

# Criterion IV: Commitment — At A Glance

A grantmaker practicing Philanthropy at Its Best serves the public good by engaging a substantial portion of its financial assets in pursuit of its mission.

a) Pays out at least 6 percent of its assets annually in grants

b) Invests at least 25 percent of its assets in ways that support its mission

> The purpose of the tax exemption that grantmakers enjoy is to enable them to meet their charitable goals and serve the public interest. When a foundation warehouses assets instead, it eschews its charitable purpose at the expense of taxpayers.

> The foundation payout rate has been a frequent subject of public policy debate. The 1969 Tax Reform Act established a 6 percent payout rate; the rate was reduced to 5 percent in 1976. Since then, many foundations have adopted the legal minimum as a de facto maximum. The variable excise tax foundations pay serves as a disincentive to higher payouts.

> Perpetual philanthropic institutions play a valuable role in sustaining the nonprofit sector and enhancing the common good, as do foundations that decide to spend down their endowments. Paying out at least 6 percent of investment assets in grants is not inconsistent with the goal of perpetuity; some grantmakers that don't have any intention to sunset already do this. These exemplary philanthropic institutions recognize that the civic sector desperately needs additional funding and that tax-exempt foundation dollars have

tremendous impact when given to an effective nonprofit partner.

> A foundation also can use its investment assets to further its mission in ways that go beyond grantmaking. Investment screens, shareholder advocacy and proactive mission investing are three means to diversify a grantmaker's portfolio in support of its mission.

> Research demonstrates that mission investing, generally speaking, yields similar returns to traditional investing strategies. A growing number of funders are practicing mission investing, and the leaders in this field invest 25 percent or more of their assets in these ways.

> Because data on payout and mission investing are neither centralized nor easily available, we cannot say what proportion of the nation's grantmakers meet or exceed these benchmarks. The principle undergirding this criterion is that tax-exempt assets should not be warehoused; rather, they should be deployed in support of the charitable purpose of the foundation. The key is an appropriate balance of payout and mission investing informed by the metrics established here.

# Chapter IV: Commitment

[B]y warehousing endowments, foundations defer funding today's issues for the presumed benefit of funding tomorrow's. As a result, we all face the opportunity cost of leaving today's problems unsolved, and, while we may have a difficult time calculating it, there is certainly a considerable cost in doing so.

—William M. Dietel, Former Chair
F.B. Heron Foundation[316]

The purpose of the tax exemption that private foundations enjoy is to enable them to meet their charitable goals and serve the public interest. When foundations warehouse assets instead, they eschew their charitable purpose at the expense of taxpayers. Foundation perpetuity has been the central issue in discussions regarding foundation payout policies, and investment decisions traditionally have been made with a singular goal of increasing foundation assets. These approaches are shortsighted and fail to realize the significant potential of foundation assets to make positive contributions to society.

Diverse observers have commented on these issues. According to Arthur Schmidt, founder of GuideStar, the proportion of assets that are contributed as grant dollars to maintain a foundation's tax exemption is "not determined by need or opportunity; it is determined only by an arbitrary, statutory payout threshold."[317] Steven T. Miller, commissioner of the Tax Exempt and Government Entities Division of the IRS, articulated the purpose of the tax exemption granted to the U.S. civil society sector when he said that "every charity should make responsible and appropriate use of its resources to achieve its charita-

ble purposes. That is what the tax subsidy is for."[318] Researchers Akash Deep and Peter Frumkin take the concept further and assert that taxpayers are subsidizing future philanthropic giving. As they note, "When a foundation is created today, the burden of lost tax revenue is borne by citizens in the form of a tax expenditure."[319]

The adoption of the legally mandated minimum level of charitable contributions as a foregone maximum results in a significant opportunity cost: it ignores pressing social needs today and diminishes institutional philanthropy's potential impact to maximize its social benefit. When an institutional grantmaker questions seriously the underlying principle that drives its payout policy, it has the potential to maintain its own strategic interests while engaging simultaneously in bold, innovative ways to maximize the social benefit of philanthropic giving. Reaching and maintaining a generous level of payout with a minimum of 6 percent dedicated to grants, ensuring that foundation assets are invested in alignment with its mission, and making investments that maximize the social value of institutional philanthropy are three steps integral to a needed paradigm shift in financial practices that allow a foundation to make the most effective use of its assets and resources.

The total value of foundation assets obviously fluctuates over time, based on many factors. However, assets grew to $670 billion in 2007[320] and generally have shown a rapid and steady progression upwards over time. As Sarah Englehardt, then-president of the Foundation Center, stated in the press release accompanying the 2008 forecast, "Foundations are sometimes confused with individual donors in how their giving will respond to economic fluctuations. In fact, foundations—especially the larger, endowed grantmakers—often engage in long-range planning to ensure that they can maintain relatively stable levels of support for their grantees, regardless of periodic dips in their assets." Bill Gates, co-chair and trustee of the Bill & Melinda Gates Foundation, addressed directly the impact of the current economic crisis on the foundation's payout rate. In his first annual letter published on the foundation's website, he stated, "During the past five years, as the foundation was

As the stock market rose and our understanding of the needs deepened, our Board voted to raise our annual payout to 10 percent, raising our program grants to about $1.2 million per year, double the rate of most foundations. Even after the stock market turned down in the early part of this decade, we reaffirmed our commitment to our grantees by continuing to spend at the same level, thus raising our payout to about 12 percent per year. In recent years, we have realized that such a high payout is not sustainable in the current climate. We have reevaluated yearly, and continue to try to pay out between 7 and 8 percent. However, the markets are so volatile that we will likely have to continue this frequent reevaluation going forward. The challenge is always to maximize our impact on the issues we care about while still enabling us to exist in the longer term.

– Martha A. Toll, Executive Director, Butler Family Fund[323]

growing, we spent a bit over 5 percent of its assets each year in addition to the gift from Warren. There is nothing magic about the 5 percent figure, except that it is the minimum required by the IRS. Our spending in 2008 was $3.3 billion. In 2009, instead of reducing this amount, we are choosing to increase it to $3.8 billion, which is about 7 percent of our assets."[321] Although the Gates Foundation does not seek to exist in perpetuity, this is precisely the type of

bold response that demonstrates how an exemplary grantmaker, regardless of the perpetuity issue, can and should respond to economic turmoil.

This criterion applies primarily to independent foundations, where the concern over warehousing tax-exempt dollars is greatest. Most grantmaking public charities—such as community foundations, public foundations and United Way chapters—pay out at rates well above 6 percent in grants.[322] Mission investing still is an important concept for these entities to consider, but there is less concern that a substantial portion of their assets is not being put toward a charitable purpose than with some private foundations. This chapter first addresses payout and then the ways in which foundations can serve their missions through their investment decisions.

## PAYOUT

Payout has been a frequent subject of debate and continuing dialogue within the philanthropic field. Currently, a private foundation is required to spend a minimum of 5 percent of the fair market value of its total investment assets annually.[324] This includes grants made to nonprofit organizations and qualifying administrative expenses. The 5 percent minimum was established in 1976 and since then many foundations have adopted the minimum as a de facto maximum. Still, there are a sizable number of exemplary foundations, particularly newer and smaller foundations, that pay out at rates higher than the legally-mandated minimum.

### Policy history regarding payout

In 1916, lawmakers and the public were concerned that private foundations were fronts for business enterprises and were shunning their charitable missions in favor of warehousing foundation assets. In response, the Walsh Commission was established following a congressional request to study the socio-economic influence of large foundations. The Walsh Commission proposed a ban on foundation perpetuity, but Congress did not act.[325]

By the early 1960s, the foundation world was growing at the rate of 1,200 new organizations annually.[326] In 1964, the Senate Finance Committee asked the Department of the Treasury to investigate abuse in the field. The investigation found a relatively low level of abuse and recommended a minimum payout rate as a regulatory response to allay government and public concern. The Treasury noted in its report that the public should be able to assume that the charitable deductions foundations enjoy is being offset by the use of the funds to benefit the public good. When private foundations instead retain the funds for "indefinitely long periods,"[327] the public good suffers. Congress took no legislative action.

In 1969, Sen. Russell Long (D-La.), then chairman of the Senate Finance Committee, proposed a 46 percent tax on foundation income and a ten-year time limit on foundations. In response, John D. Rockefeller III and other prominent philanthropists established the Commission on Foundations and Private Philanthropy (informally known as the Peterson Commission after its chair, Peter G. Peterson) to serve as an advocate on behalf of private foundations. The commission researched philanthropic giving in Senator Long's hometown of New Orleans and found that the majority of foundation grants were provided to the Catholic Church, local universities and charities. The commission developed alternatives to a tax on foundations and Peterson convinced Long that imposing a high marginal tax rate on foundations would limit the funds available to help local residents, particularly lower-income residents, leading Long to advocate a minimum payout level instead.[328] The Tax Reform Act of 1969 was an outcome of the commission's findings. Congress mandated a minimum payout rate for private foundations as a result of this act.

The Tax Reform Act required private foundations to pay out whichever was greater—their entire adjusted net income or 6 percent of net investment assets. The 6 percent figure, however, was variable and linked to money rates and investment yields. Using this formula, the payout rate in 1976 would have reached 6.75 percent of total foundation assets, a level that lawmakers had not considered in 1969.[329] In response, Congress eliminated some of the variability in this equation and set minimum payout at the greater of

## QUALIFYING DISTRIBUTIONS AND PAYOUT

Because of the IRS's current policy and expiration of the Deficit Reduction Act, most foundations include numerous expenses as part of their qualifying distributions, detailed in the list below. While IRS form 990 PF lists several types of allowable administrative expenses, a foundation does not necessarily count all expenses of a certain category as designated for its charitable purpose. Below is a list of allowable expenses that a foundation can count toward its qualifying distributions:

> Compensation of officers, directors, trustees, etc.
> Other employee salaries and wages
> Pension plans, employee benefits
> Legal fees
> Accounting fees
> Other professional fees
> Interest
> Taxes
> Occupancy
> Travel, conferences and meetings
> Printing and publications
> Contributions, gifts, grants paid
> Set-asides
> Program related investments

It also is important to note what a foundation cannot count toward its qualifying distributions. Congressional rules disallow investment expenses a foundation incurs from managing its endowment. Such fees include salaries or board meeting costs for investment management purposes; custodial fees; brokerage fees; and investment management fees. Excluding investment management fees, all foundation administrative expenses count toward payout if they are deemed "necessary and reasonable."

entire net adjusted income or a fixed 5 percent of net investment assets.

During the debate leading up to the 1976 change, Eugene Steuerle wrote that the initial proposal in the Tax Reform Act of 1969 had been to require a flat 5 percent payout rate. The Senate rejected this rate and requested that it be 6 percent, which was included in the final law along with the provision for rate adjustment. Arguments against the 6 percent rate included "invasion of corpus" and that market conditions and rates of return at the time did not support such a rate.[330] Steuerle noted that "the answer to the empirical question [of the actual rate of return received by foundations] provides information by which the policy question can be addressed, but the empirical question does not determine the answer to the policy question."[331] Other critics have noted that the 5 percent rule is related less to economic analysis and empirical data than to prolonged political bargaining.[332]

The Economic Recovery Act of 1981 eliminated the "greater of" provision, because requiring foundations to pay out their entire income would reduce real asset value over time.[333] The law ended variable payout rates and since then foundations have been required to

pay out 5 percent of their investment assets. In 1984, the Deficit Reduction Act temporarily limited administrative expenses to 0.65 percent of foundation assets; this reflected a concern that a foundation practically could meet its minimum payout simply by counting its qualifying administrative expenses. The law also put the requirement that administrative expenses be "reasonable and necessary" into the statute. The 0.65 percent maximum administrative expenses requirement expired in 1990, allowing institutional grantmakers to include a range of expenses in determining their qualifying distributions.

Studies demonstrate that 5 percent is not the highest sustainable payout rate and that foundations could pay 7 or even 8 percent and maintain their endowments.[334] NCRP acknowledges that some well-inten-

## TABLE 4.1 MAJOR POLICY PROPOSALS ON PAYOUT

| Year | Policy History | Result |
|---|---|---|
| 1916 | Walsh Commission: Proposed ban on perpetuity | No congressional action |
| 1964 | Department of Treasury investigation | Relatively little abuse found; no legislation |
| 1969 | Sen. Russell Long proposes ten-year maximum life span and a 46 percent tax rate on private foundations | Rockefeller and other private philanthropists establish Peterson Commission to fight Long's proposal Peterson's findings convince Long to drop proposed tax rate and ban on perpetuity |
| 1969 | Peterson Commission findings lead to Tax Reform Act of 1969 | Variable minimum payout established as the greater of: a) Entire net adjusted income or b) 6 percent of net investment assets, adjusted annually based on money rates and investment returns |
| 1976 | Minimum payout reached higher rates than anticipated | Variable minimum payout established as the greater of: a) Entire net adjusted income or b) 5 percent of net investment assets, with no variability |
| 1981 | Economic Recovery Act of 1981: Requiring foundations to pay entire net assets would erode real value of corpus over time | Minimum payout established at 5 percent of net investment assets |
| 1984 | Deficit Reduction Act of 1984: Temporarily limited administrative expenses to 0.65 percent of assets; put requirement that administrative expenses be "reasonable and necessary" into statute. | Qualifying administrative expenses limited to 0.65 percent of assets Expired in 1990 "Reasonable and necessary" requirement remains in statute |
| 2003 | Charitable Giving Act of 2003 (H.R. 7): Would require foundations to exclude administrative costs when calculating qualifying distributions. | No congressional action |

tioned leaders in the sector disagree with these findings and believe honestly that 5 percent is the highest sustainable payout rate. However, NCRP and others believe higher payout and perpetuity are not mutually exclusive. Unless Congress changes the law on this issue, it is up to individual grantmakers to consider carefully their payout policies.

In the early 21st century, Congress again considered changing the statute. The Charitable Giving Act of 2003, also known as H.R. 7, included a provision that would have required private foundations to exclude operating and administrative expenses when calculating annual expenditures to meet the minimum 5 percent payout rule. According to NCRP calculations at the time, this statutory change would have represented a 0.4 percent increase in grantmaking, thereby infusing an additional $4.3 billion annually in grant dollars into the nonprofit sector.[335] The Foundation Center issued a statement in response to NCRP's claim, estimating that the actual amount would be less than half that. Yet, even using the Foundation Center's own calculations, had the increase been a more modest $2 billion, it still would have represented a 17 percent increase in foundation giving to nonprofits.[336] Although the Senate passed the companion bill, the CARE Act (S. 476), Congress did not act on the payout rule prior to the close of session and there was no change to the current statute.

Payout has been the focus of foundation-related policy discussions for nearly 100 years. Table 4.1 summarizes major policy proposals related to payout, the rationale behind each and the outcome of the proposal.

### Studies of foundation payout: influencing factors, contrasting viewpoints

While there appears to be strong convergence around the 5 percent minimum as a foregone maximum among many foundations, there is a movement in the sector by some individual foundations to link payout with mission achievement, often resulting in payout rates significantly higher than the minimum.[337] But the aggregation of payout data that frequently include spend-down foundations, grantmaking institutions with living donors and operating foundations along with private foundations often leads to the perception of a higher rate of grants paid out than actually is true. In other words, the higher payout rates maintained by the many types of foundations aggregated in most payout analyses suggests higher than actual payout rates maintained by most private foundations. For example, a recent article highlights the limitations of perpetuity and the assumption of the 5 percent as a foregone maximum payout rate. In raising pertinent issues for any grantmaker to consider when discussing issues of perpetuity and mission, Arthur Schmidt suggests maximizing the social value of philanthropy as an alternate core guiding principle for this issue.[338] This analysis also notes that once qualifying distribution expenses are accounted for in payout, the average foundation pays out 4 percent in grants.

Three studies that analyzed actual foundation payout data resulted in somewhat contradictory findings. Deep and Frumkin examined the average payout rates and total return on investment for 169 foundations from 1972 to 1996. They found strong convergence around 5 percent payout as a de facto maximum; the sample averaged 4.97 percent payout, despite an average annual return on foundation investment assets of 7.62 percent. Similarly, Cambridge Associates found that in a sample of 33 Michigan foundations, the payout rate was 4.86 percent from 1982–1997. This further illustrates the convergence around the 5 percent minimum as a predetermined maximum following the institution of the statute. Richard Sansing and Robert Yetman's sample comprised 4,239 individual foundations—representing nearly 60 percent of all foundation assets—and focused on the bull market period of 1994–1998. They found that their sample paid out an average of 6.45 percent of investment assets annually, while the assets of foundations in their sample grew at about 17 percent per year.

DeMarche & Associates analyzed investment returns for a hypothetical foundation and concluded that 5 percent may be too high a payout rate for a foundation to exist in perpetuity.[339] Cambridge Associates also concluded that their findings supported a maximum 5 percent payout. These findings merit some robust debate and frank criticism. Foundation growth during the years in which the DeMarche study was conducted was so robust that the researchers acknowledged that foundations could have increased their payout rates to 6.5 percent with minimal to no impact on their corpuses. Moreover, when Perry Mehrling[340] applied his own methodology to DeMarche's hypothetical foundation, he found that over the course of 20 years a payout rate as high as 8 percent would have maintained the foundation's asset size. Yet, DeMarche & Associates insisted that 5 percent was the maximum sustainable payout rate for any foundation seeking to exist in perpetuity.

The studies above focused on determining an appropriate level of foundation payout based on investment returns and existing payout habits. Paul Jansen and David Katz[341] applied an investment concept known as discounting to show that foregoing work on current social problems in favor of storing wealth for future grants is a bad investment strategy for foundations and reduces the value of the original tax-deductible donation. They calculated the present value of future grant investment returns by discounting the returns at a certain rate. From the resulting data, they argued that by paying out at just 5 percent, foundations are foregoing contributing more today and assuming future social problems will be more compelling, but that this is an insufficient justification for low payout rates.

As Mehrling and others have pointed out, treating the legal minimum as a maximum makes it appear that many foundations are doing exactly what Congress wanted to prevent when establishing the minimum—warehousing wealth in perpetuity, thereby defeating "the real social purpose of their privileged tax status."[342] Deep and Frumkin interviewed foundation leaders to understand why more foundations do not pay out at rates higher than 5 percent. Their findings identified three obstacles to payout differentiation:

1. Managerial constraints within staff and board, such as the difficulty of quantifying return on social investment compared with that of the investment portfolio;
2. Conceptual obstacles, such as difficulty of calculating current social benefits versus future social benefits; and
3. Current tax treatment of investment income (the excise tax structure).

More recently, Schmidt highlighted three barriers implicit in the current perpetuity paradigm as limiting institutional philanthropy's social value and strategic potential:

1. Immunity from market and public pressures for accountability;
2. Diminished ability to engage foundation resources, fiscal and human, for optimal resource deployment; and
3. Negative impact on the real social value of institutional philanthropy's assets, resulting in social costs to the charitable sector and society at large.[343]

An important corollary to the third barrier noted above is that it not only has negative consequences for addressing social needs today but also increases the future social costs for when philanthropy does turn its attention to those problems.[344] As Schmidt states, "Any nominal appreciation in the value of a perpetual endowment must be discounted significantly by the cost society incurs (a *social cost of capital*) from the human suffering, environmental degradation and other problems left unresolved today."[345]

In 1999, during the National Network of Grantmakers' (NNG) "1 Percent for Democracy" campaign, NNG asked its members and all other foundations to increase grants payout by 1 percent. NNG found that nearly 83 percent of its 400 individual members agreed that payout should increase, but only a small majority believed that their foundation leadership would support such a change.[346] This, combined with the first barrier identified by Deep and Frumkin, suggests the need for open dialogue within individual foundations and across the foundation world to address the ways in which payout policy affects mission achievement and affects the bottom line of philanthropy: *impact*.

## The foundation excise tax: a disincentive to increasing payout

A persistent and salient policy issue related to payout is the foundation excise tax. Foundations largely are exempt from taxation but they are required to pay certain taxes, including an excise tax on investment income. The current structure of the excise tax is two-tiered: the tax rate is 1 percent but rises to 2 percent for five years if the foundation distributes less in one year than the average of the preceding five years. Two researchers clarify the consequences of this structure with an example: "Suppose over the preceding five years, the foundation spent on average 6 percent of its investment assets in qualifying distributions. This year the foundation has investment assets of $100 million and net investment income of $8 million. If this year's qualifying distributions are less than $6,080,000, then the excise tax is $160,000; if qualifying distributions are $6,080,000 or more, then its tax is $80,000."[347] In other words, should a foundation wish to temporarily pay out at a higher rate, the foundation can expect to pay more excise tax if it reduces its payout in future years. The variable excise tax thus serves as a disincentive for a foundation to increase its payout rate.

Advocates of retaining the excise tax have requested that it be used for its original purpose: to fund IRS oversight of the charitable sector and data services.[348] Others argued that because the excise tax is both a disincentive for varying payout rate and is not being used for its original intent, it should be eliminated.[349] Audit coverage of the sector is historically low, despite the fact that the income from the excise tax—estimated at $500 million annually[350]—far exceeds the budget of the IRS Exempt Organizations Division. The money is diverted to the general treasury, and the remaining funding is not sufficient for the IRS to perform its enforcement duties.[351] The Council on Foundations, NCRP, Independent Sector and the Aspen Institute Nonprofit Sector and Philanthropy Program all have urged Congress to make fixing the excise tax structure a legislative priority.[352]

### Decision-making factors for payout: Perpetuity, spend-down and mission

Often, it is the donor's intent to provide a lasting social benefit to the communal social problems, which are interconnected, structural, complicated and impossible to solve in a lifetime. Thus, many contend that a foundation should be prepared to work toward its mission in perpetuity.[353] Additionally, some argue that professional foundations add value in their grantmaking through their expertise, which makes them more efficient and effective grantmakers than foundations that exist for a relatively short period of time.[354] NCRP recognizes the value of perpetual foundations to civil society and our nation as a whole.

A large number of foundations, however, are choosing to spend down their endowments in lieu of perpetuity. Julius Rosenwald, the former president of Sears, Roebuck & Co., was one of the first philanthropists to question the assumption of foundation perpetuity implicit in much of the sector. He wrote that the goal of perpetuity for private foundations indicated a lack of confidence in the future, and he had absolute confidence in future genera-

tions to meet their own needs. In 1948, nine years before the deadline Rosenwald had imposed, his foundation closed its doors.[355] While the decision to spend down is not unique, the issue of payout and the adoption of 5 percent as a maximum rather than its intended minimum is one that continues to spark dialogue.

> While the decision to spend down is not unique, the issue of payout and the adoption of 5 percent as a maximum rather than its intended minimum is one that continues to spark dialogue. … [T]radition and a lack of consensus in the foundation world are strong barriers to changes in payout policy.

As discussed above, tradition and a lack of consensus in the foundation world are strong barriers to changes in payout policy. In a 2004 discussion of payout moderated by Michael Klausner, many foundation leaders emphasized the importance of matching payout to mission. John Healy, formerly of The Atlantic Philanthropies, criticized foundations for taking perpetuity as "an article of faith," adding that The Atlantic Philanthropies' mission "implies a sense of urgency which compels us to spend down rather than seek perpetuity."[356] Others noted that when the donor establishes the foundation with the intent of contributing to society perpetually, the foundation is compelled to adopt a lower payout rate. Additionally, long-term problems lead a foundation to seek perpetuity in order to provide lasting support for organizations working to solve those problems.

Tying foundation mission explicitly with payout policy appears to be increasing across the sector. Spending down seem to be growing as thousands of new foundations are formed annually. The Bill and Melinda Gates Foundation, with its massive endowment, has committed to sunsetting within 50 years of the death of its last founding trustee.[357] The Gates Foundation's grantmaking accounts for about one in every ten philanthropic dollars.[358] The John M. Olin Foundation was established in 1953 by John M. Olin, president of the Olin industries, a chemical and munitions manufacturing corporation. Olin committed to spending down his foundation during his lifetime; the

Olin Foundation made its last grant in 2005. These examples demonstrate that spending down is a valid option for a foundation to consider when linking payout policy with its mission.

In *Beyond 5 Percent*, Heidi Waleson examined 13 foundations that pay out above the federal minimum; she termed 5 percent payout policies "traditional" foundation practice.[359] Many foundations featured in the report have chosen to spend down in the name of mission and in accordance with donor

> It makes no sense to use 5 percent of your assets to try to promote something, while the other 95 percent might be doing something totally contrary. We try to use 100 percent of our assets to promote our values.
>
> – Victor De Luca, President, Jessie Smith Noyes Foundation[362]

intent, granting between $200 million and $800 million within a few decades. The Lewis B. and Dorothy Cullman Foundation, for example, is committed to ceasing operations within one year of the founder's death. Cullman established his foundation believing that it should benefit society in his lifetime and that future generations would step up to address future social problems. As he put it, "I don't care what people say about me when I'm dead. I won't be around to hear it. Why not get the joy out of spending your money while you're alive?"[360] The Lewis B. and Dorothy Cullman Foundation paid out more than 30 percent of its non-charitable use assets in 2006. Also featured in Waleson's report, the Whitaker Foundation made the decision in 1991 to help start and grow university biomedical engineering departments, spending more than $800 million on achieving its mission and closing down in 2006. This infusion of funding is credited with jump starting the field of biomedical engineering, which now has 80 university departments across the country.[361] This example seems to supersede some of the arguments for preserving foundation assets to address future problems. Many of the foundations in the study enjoyed greater flexibility in spending and financial management when they focused on mission achievement rather than perpetuity.

## MISSION INVESTING

Mission investing (MI) is an effective way for foundations to leverage their non-grantmaking assets to serve their own missions and benefit society. In this criterion, MI is the term used to denote all aspects of a comprehensive mission investment strategy: investment screening, shareholder advocacy and proxy voting, and proactive mission investments. This section reviews how foundations can leverage their endowments and power best as shareholders to achieve their missions and maximize their contributions to the greater public good.

At the F.B. Heron Foundation, which currently is investing 26 percent[363] of its assets in mission investments (MIs), the guiding question that the board adopted when it began developing its MI program was, "Should a private foundation be more than a private investment company that uses some of its excess cash flow for charitable purposes?"[364]

### History of mission investing

The origins of modern socially responsible investing and shareholder activism can be traced back to the early 1970s. The first mutual fund to screen for social issues was started by a group of Methodist clergy in 1971, prior to the Episcopal Church's disinvestment work in South Africa. In 1973, the South Shore Bank, now ShoreBank, became the United States' first private development bank. ShoreBank was created to demonstrate the important role that a regulated bank could play in revitalizing communities marginalized by other financial institutions. It was located in a neighborhood on the south side of Chicago that was dealing with race and class tensions at the time. Today, ShoreBank is an internationally-recognized socially responsible investor. It operates in multiple U.S. cities and internationally and its mission states that it "invests in people and their communities to create economic equity and a healthy environment." The Episcopal Church used shareholder resolutions in the 1970s to pressure companies with business in South Africa during Apartheid to cease operations there.[365]

Shareholder activism through resolutions and proxy voting long has been the realm of pension funds since the ERISA (Employee Retirement Income Security Act) Act of 1974 cited proxy voting and the monitoring of non-financial information as part of good management.[366]

During the 1980s, social investment grew rapidly in the wake of insider trading and environmental degradation scandals. In 1985, the Social Investment Forum documented $40 billion in professionally managed investments with social criteria; by 1991, that figure had grown to an estimated $625 billion.[367] Organizations pressured by the Episcopal Church disinvested in South Africa's companies to demonstrate their values through their investment decisions. Socially responsible investing (SRI) is rooted in a moral concern for the way in which pools of capital are invested and often is described as investing with a "double bottom line."[368] The Social Investment Forum Foundation defines the double bottom line as "[a]n investment seeking financial and social returns."[369]

## Foundations and mission investing

As with SRI,[370] mission investing seeks a double bottom line. In the case of institutional philanthropy, a grantmaker demonstrates its commitment by leveraging its investment assets to achieve its mission using MI. Screening, shareholder advocacy and proactive mission-investing may be used together or alone. For example, screening investments is a simple first step that all foundations easily can take. The three strategies of comprehensive mission-investing in exemplary philanthropy are:

1. *Screens*: Screening traditional investments for social or environmental factors can help a foundation seek corporations whose practices do not conflict with its mission. Screens can be either positive or negative; that is, a screen either can seek out a certain trait such as paying employees a living wage or it can avoid a certain trait such as companies that produce tobacco products.
2. *Shareholder advocacy*: Foundations can leverage stock portfolios to introduce shareholder resolutions and to vote proxies. Foundations also can involve their grantees when appropriate to improve corporate practices.
3. *Proactive mission investing*: Proactively seeking out investment opportunities that advance a foundation's mission such as investing in affordable

housing and providing direct loans to nonprofit organizations.[371]

There is a lack of robust data regarding the extent to which foundations engage in mission investing. However, FSG Social Impact Advisors conducted a study that examined 92 foundations to analyze MI among foundations. In *Compounding Impact: Mission Investing by U.S. Foundations*, Kramer and Cooch defined "mission investing" as "financial investments made with the intention of (1) furthering a foundation's mission and (2) recovering the principal invested or earning financial returns."[372] Mission investments were grouped into two main categories:

1. *Market-rate mission investments*: Investments that account for social and environmental considerations in which a foundation seeks financial returns comparable to average risk-adjusted returns of investments made without regard for such concerns.
2. *Below market-rate mission investments*: Foundation asset investments that seek financial returns below the risk-adjusted average returns. A foundation invests its assets in this way when the goal of the investment cannot be realized using market-rate investments or when it opts to use its non-grant-making funds for charitable objectives over earning a profit. Private foundations also may claim mission-related investments such as program related investments (PRIs),[373] which count for qualifying distributions.[374]

The study found that only 2.6 percent of private foundation assets were allocated to mission investments. The authors contend that despite the lack of robust data and reporting on mission investing in the foundation sector, their findings are indicative of sector-wide trends in this practice. This is partly because the subsample that provided investment details represents 12 percent of all U.S. foundation assets; the subsample that participated in qualitative interviews accounts for 20 percent of foundation assets.[375] However, the study selected foundations that were known to engage in PRI and MI or otherwise recommended it. Complementing this study with preliminary data from a Council on Foundations survey, which found that over 82 percent of foundations "do not take social, environmental or other nonfinancial factors into account when managing … financial

## A PROMINENT GRANTMAKER ADDS NEW MOMENTUM TO FOUNDATION MISSION INVESTING

The W.K. Kellogg Foundation had a $9 billion endowment in 2008 and devoted $100 million to mission investments in the United States and Africa. In Kellogg's case, the development of a mission investment team, comprising program and investment staff, occurred quickly following initial board conversations in January 2007. Three months later, the board agreed to the $100 million allocation, after the team found ample opportunities for mission investments in multiple asset classes. One staff member said, "Few ideas have resonated more completely or more quickly than helping to closely connect investments to our mission."[391]

assets,"[376] suggests that a majority of foundations do not account for mission in their investment decisions. In light of this, the relevant question for exemplary philanthropy is *why* so few foundations match investment strategy with mission.

A significant barrier to higher levels of philanthropic engagement in MI is the perception that only larger foundations have the human and financial capacity to align investments with mission. However, the FSG Social Impact Advisors study referenced above also found that 30 percent of all private foundations making mission investments had total assets of less than $50 million and 9 percent had less than $10 million in assets. Further, smaller foundations comprised 44 percent of all new mission investment dollars in 2005.[377] Mission investment intermediaries can help foundations with little or no staff to develop the expertise and capacity to engage in MI.

Some foundation leaders may view MI as financially riskier and as providing below-market returns. However, data from individual foundations and from the Community Development Fund Index dispel this perception. The Fund Index publishes data annually on the aggregate accomplishments of its funds, which provide financial services to traditionally underserved populations—70 percent of Community Development Financial Institutions (CDFI) clients were lower income in FY 2006.[378] Grantmakers can invest in Community Development Venture Capital funds

(CDVCs) through CDFIs as part of a mission investing program. The CDFI Data Project found that CDVCs had a gross internal rate of return of 15.5 percent in FY 2006. By comparison, the 12-month total return for the S&P 500 in December 2006 was 15.79 percent.[379] Further, Cooch and Kramer analyzed returns on MI loans for foundations in their study. They found that 75 percent of the 28 foundations able to provide data on their loan mission investments had a zero default rate. When three outliers, foundations with high default rates, were removed, this figure jumped to 96 percent.[380]

Individual foundations have shared their success in MI as a way to encourage their peers to follow suit. In 2003, the F.B. Heron Foundation, which allocated 19 percent of its assets to mission investments that year, achieved a total return on investment of 21.07 percent, which was at or above the median rate of return for traditional investments made by foundations.[381] In December 2003, the S&P 500 posted a 12-month return of 28.69 percent.[382] By 2006, the F.B. Heron Foundation had allocated 24 percent of its assets to MI[383] and began aggressively encouraging peers to adopt an MI strategy. It also pioneered the Community Investment Index, a positively screened investment fund with companies that support lower-income communities through workforce development, wealth creation and corporate philanthropy.

In April 2007, the F.B. Heron Foundation partnered with the Annie E. Casey Foundation, the Meyer Memorial Trust Foundation and Cambridge Associates, a reputable independent investment advisor, to launch the "More for Mission Campaign."[384] This campaign challenges foundations to allocate, in the aggregate, 2 percent of their assets for mission investments that would generate some $12 billion more in foundation financial commitments by aligning mission with investing practice. The "More for Mission Campaign" also seeks to build the funder knowledge base of mission investing; to generate a network of foundations committed to mission investing; and to contribute robustly to the knowledge base for investors to leverage their non-grantmaking assets in support of mission.[385] Cambridge Associates formed the Mission Investing Group with the support of these three foundations to provide technical assistance to institutions initiating an investment strategy that aligns with mission. As the F.B. Heron Foundation's president Sharon B. King states, "Harnessing the power of the capital markets for positive social and environmental impact is essential. It is appropriate that tax-advantaged institutions, such as foundations and endowments, begin to invest for mission in a thoughtful and rigorous way."[386] Indeed, the F.B. Heron Foundation's current goal is to increase its mission-related investments to 50 percent of its assets by the end of 2010.[387]

### The case for increased mission investing

The barriers to mission investing are similar to those for increased payout: a lack of motivation at the individual foundation level and a knowledge gap related to the tools needed to implement a mission investing program. Lance Lindblom, president and CEO of The Nathan Cummings Foundation, identifies lack of integration and communication within foundations as a barrier. "The practice in foundations has typically been for the program areas to focus on mission and the investment committee to focus on financial returns, with little—if any— awareness between these silos. And yet, social and economic justice requires an integrated society. Corporations and business cannot be separated from concerns about health, the environment, the arts, about how we live our lives."[388]

Some foundation leadership may not be open to mission investing; this stems primarily from concerns about fiduciary responsibility. Highly risk-averse, directors often are too content to adhere strictly to a "prudent man" approach, which dates back to Harvard University in the 1800s. This approach said that trustees of a foundation or endowment should act as a "prudent man," now a "prudent investor," would when investing his or her own funds.[389] The assumptions implicit in this behavior are reductionist: they presume that a trustee is a rational economic actor with full access to comprehensive knowledge about the entire universe of investment options available to institutional grantmakers. Moreover, unlike the "prudent man," exemplary institutional philanthropy seeks a double bottom line return, financial and social. At a minimum, a foundation is obliged to carry out its stated mission in addition to a social mission that aligns with or supersedes its assessment of financial returns from its investment strategies.

The Uniform Management of Institutional Funds Act of 1972 acknowledged that some risk is unavoidable in any investments. Risk tolerance is both necessary and acceptable so long as the risk does not put the endowment as a whole in jeopardy. The argument that mission investing is too risky does not stand when one considers that foundations have invested in other unconventional stocks such as hedge funds, private equity, international stocks and natural resources.[390] When there is open communication among board and staff leadership, grantmak-

## THE IMPACT OF PROXY RESOLUTIONS

Sometimes, investment managers within foundations may notice discrepancies or conflicts of interest between program goals and investment decisions. In 2002, Caroline L. Williams, chief financial and investment officer for the Nathan Cummings Foundation, noticed that the foundation had given sizable grants to organizations working to hold big agribusiness environmentally accountable, focused on the hog industry. At the same time, the foundation held over $700,000 in shares of Smithfield Foods, the world's largest hog producer and pork processor with an abysmal environmental record. In response, Williams worked with Cummings Foundation president and CEO Lance Lindblom to request a shareholder resolution requiring Smithfield Foods management prepare a report describing the environmental, economic and social impacts of its operations.[392] The Cummings Foundation was joined by Amalgamated Bank and the Sierra Club in issuing a proxy statement asking Smithfield for a report to measure company compliance with the Global Reporting Initiative Sustainability Reporting Guidelines. Because the Securities and Exchange Commission ruled that Smithfield could exclude the resolution from the proxy vote, it did not produce the report, citing the rigid nature of the guidelines.[393] Yet, the proxy had significant impact on Smithfield's voluntary adoption of many elements of the guidelines and increased transparency as evidenced by its production of the 2003 and 2004 Stewardship Reports, and the 2005 and 2007 Corporate Social Responsibility Reports.[394]

ers have found success engaging in MI *and* fulfilling their fiduciary responsibilities.

Although some foundations identify risk-aversion as a reason not to engage substantively in MI, if a foundation does not screen its investments, it runs the risk of public embarrassment should discrepancies like the Cummings example not be dealt with transparently. In 2007, the *Los Angeles Times* investigated the investment practices of the Bill and Melinda Gates Foundation and found that it had large investments that ran contrary to the foundation's global health efforts.[395] Examples of undermining the foundation's long-term goals for short-term financial gain included significant investments in pharmaceutical companies that kept the price of antiretroviral drugs prohibitively high for patients in the developing world where the foundation does much of its AIDS work, and major polluters in developing countries such as oil companies that contributed to health problems among local populations. The Bill and Melinda Gates Foundation owns more than $450 million in stocks in pharmaceutical companies that are considering shareholder resolutions to increase the availability of antiretroviral drugs in less-developed countries.[396] Despite the negative consequences for the foundation's public image from these conflicts of interests, a senior policy officer at the foundation stated that the foundation does not believe it should involve itself in proxy voting because "we want people to understand that the people at the foundation are trying to figure out how to help the people in our areas of focus, and we don't spend our time thinking about the investment portfolio."[397] The Gates Foundation holds its investment assets in the Bill and Melinda Gates Foundation Trust, a separate entity from the Bill and Melinda Gates Foundation.

Discrepancies between a foundation's stated mission and its fiduciary choices raise pertinent issues regarding whether or not it is investing in socially responsible manner that accounts for social and public needs, not only short-term financial gains for an individual endowment. In short, conflicts of interest created by investment strategies negatively impact the social benefit of philanthropy's capital to enhance the common good today and in the future. As Arthur Schmidt notes, "Despite all the good work that foundations do, their perpetuity-at-all-costs mindset ensures that their endowments will constitute a depleting social asset."[398] An exemplary foundation that engages in substantive mission investing is more likely to preserve the social value of its endowment in the long term than one that fails to account for the "social cost of capital" in linking this investing strategy with its decision to continue in perpetuity.[399]

In addition to screening investments, a foundation can establish proxy voting policies rather than automatically voting with management. Foundation leadership may be concerned that voting against management will lead to lower returns.[400] However, studies show the results of shareholder resolutions and engaged proxy voting: honest and reasonably compensated corporate management, socially responsible corporations and independent boards of directors lead to stronger financial returns.[401]

Some grantmakers may think that shareholder resolutions are ineffective. However, a resolution does not have to gain a majority vote to prompt management to act. Modest minority shareholder votes are responsible for such changes in corporate practice as curbing predatory lending, adopting Coalition for Environmentally Responsible Economies (CERES) environmental principles and increasing recycling rates.[402] A survey by the *Chronicle of Philanthropy* found that more than 25 percent of the largest private foundations have integrated environmental or social screening in their investment strategies.[403] Many foundation leaders surveyed by the *Chronicle* stated that they used money managers as delegates for their proxy voting decisions, citing lack of human and financial resources at their foundations to take on this task.[404] In contrast, Victor De Luca, president of the Jessie Smith Noyes Foundation told the *Chronicle* that Noyes employees had reviewed close to 120 shareholder proxy statements in 2005, with De Luca making the final decisions and casting the votes himself.[405] More recently, Noyes reported voting proxies in two portfolios that comprise close to 25 percent of the foundation's investments. In 2008, Noyes voted its proxies with close to 300 companies.[406]

The Educational Foundation of America (EFA) began using negative screens in 1994 and launched a shareholder activism campaign in 1999 to speed Home Depot's phase-out of old growth timber sales. EFA filed the shareholder initiative, which had an impact despite winning only 11 percent of shareholders' votes,[407] while providing support to environmental nonprofits such as the Rainforest Action Network. This dual approach—working from within as an investor and providing support to groups putting external pressure on Home Depot—led to speedier implementation of the no old-growth policy.[408]

Often, foundations lack the internal capacity to manage investments, and hire professional firms instead. In such cases, it is imperative that foundation leadership work with the investment manager and foundation program staff to ensure that the foundation's proxy voting policy is followed and to integrate mission goals into investment strategy. Mission investment intermediaries are one way in which foundations with limited capacity can build a mission investing program. The most common intermediaries are CDFIs, as discussed earlier. In 2005, they achieved substantive measurable impact, all while providing a return to investors. They financed businesses that created or sustained nearly 40,000 jobs; facilitated the creation or renovation of more than 55,000 units of affordable housing; provided more than 11,000 alternatives to payday loans; and helped establish 138,045 first-time bank accounts for lower-income individuals.[409]

Over the past decade, the number of foundations with mission investments has doubled and annual funds invested have tripled.[411] As mission investing expanded beyond the traditional PRI investors, including the Ford Foundation, the David and Lucile Packard Foundation and the John D. and Catherine T. MacArthur Foundation, led in large part by newer foundations such as the F.B. Heron Foundation, others have followed. Moreover, just as socially responsible investing is growing in the business world, current philanthropic interest in raising awareness of an institution's investment decisions on environmental and social impact issues resonates with foundations whose missions seek to improve community-wide benefits and outcomes.

An integrated approach to mission investing incorporates all three strategies: screened investments, shareholder activism and proxy voting, and proactive mission investments. To incorporate MI comprehensively as part of a foundation's investment strategy, a foundation should develop board-level understanding, include investment and program staff, involve grantees in shareholder activism, and enlist experts such as mission investment intermediaries to identify opportunities.[412] As Luther M. Ragin Jr., vice president of investments for the F.B. Heron Foundation, put it, "The approach is not without risk. But if taking well-considered risks for public benefit is not the role of philanthropy, then what is?"[413]

The Needmor Fund, a family foundation with an endowment of close to $30 million at the end of

## LEVERAGING NON-INVESTMENT ASSETS— PUBLIC BENEFIT

In 2001, the Public Welfare Foundation in Washington, D.C., relocated to the Shaw neighborhood, donated space to Manna Community Development Corporation and created meeting spaces for nonprofit organizations. The foundation then partnered with Manna to finance affordable housing construction in the neighborhood. Relocating offices to blighted communities and providing office spaces to grantees are examples of leveraging non-grantmaking, non-investment assets to advance foundation mission and enhancing the public benefit of philanthropy.[410]

2007, first began screening investments in the 1980s when the board raised the issue of investments in companies doing business in South Africa during Apartheid.[414] The Fund provides one example of an integrated approach to foundation MI. Needmor now screens 100 percent of its investment portfolio. In 2000, the foundation—which funds exclusively community organizing groups—collaborated with grantees to introduce resolutions that supported grantees' campaigns directly. The fund also has a strong community development investment program, which has financed homes, provided microloans to impoverished families, developed small businesses, created jobs and financed the construction of community facilities.[415] In 2007, Needmor had 14 percent of its assets invested in market-rate community development programs. Needmor's mission-related investing has grown to incorporate all three MI strategies.

While several exemplary foundations are both making efforts to incorporate mission achievement into asset management and also providing resources to foundations interested in mission investing, mission investing persists as a significant lost opportunity for foundations to enhance their impact. The tools to leverage assets beyond grantmaking, such as market-rate MI, mission investment intermediaries, and engaging in shareholder activism, all are readily available to institutional grantmakers. These are essential components of foundations ensuring that they are doing all they can to meet their missions.

## SETTING THE BAR FOR PHILANTHROPY AT ITS BEST

Most foundations use only a tiny fraction of the financial assets at their disposal to achieve their missions. As this chapter demonstrated, most foundations continue "traditional policies" of paying out only 5 percent of their assets in grants and qualifying distributions each year and do not prioritize the potential mission-advancing power of their investment assets in non-grantmaking ways. Consequently, a significant opportunity for broad, long-term changes and advancing a foundation's mission is lost. Foundations should dedicate substantial portions of their endowments towards achieving their charitable purposes.

By adopting 5 percent as the de facto maximum payout rate, a grantmaker foregoes an opportunity to increase its impact and demonstrate its commitment to using its tax-exempt dollars for a true charitable purpose. Because civil society sector grantees are the means to deliver institutional philanthropy's benefit to the public, the focus should be on how much a funder distributes in grants. Different types and sizes of grantmaking institutions have variable administrative needs, and foundations should be free to cover their administrative costs in whatever manner is most appropriate. But the public interest is served best by focusing attention on how much is paid out in grants. Providing 6 percent of its assets as grants to its nonprofit partners is a reasonable and fair benchmark. Indeed, the following data analysis shows why NCRP chose to focus the metric for this criterion to the percentage of a foundation's assets that are paid out in grants and not on overall payout rates.

By maintaining a generous payout level with 6 percent allocated to grants, an exemplary foundation working within the framework of Philanthropy at Its Best also adds more monies for the civil society sector. Recent commentary and surveys have revealed that while individual foundation staff members often support increased payout, foundation leadership and trustees are not always open to discussing payout in a meaningful way.[416] Foundations that are serious about mission achievement should engage staff, leadership and board members in dialogue regarding payout policy.

In 2008, the Urban Institute's Center on Nonprofits and Philanthropy, the Foundation Center and GuideStar released the final results of the Foundation Expenses and Compensation Project, "the first large-scale, long-term, systematic study of independent, corporate, and community foundations' expense and compensation patterns and the factors behind them."[417] The study analyzed data from the 10,000 largest U.S. grantmaking institutions between 2001 and 2003 and provides a rigorous analysis of various elements of the foundation world's finances, including a range of financial measures that impact foundation expenses such as staffing levels and trustee compensation. In the aggregate, total giving[418] by independent foundations from 2001–2003 comprised $18.3 billion; total independent foundation assets were $312.4 billion. The total number of independent foundations in the study was 8,876.[419] Thus, the aggregate amount of grants provided in the study's timeframe was 5.86 percent of assets. Because these aggregate statistics include spend-down foundations and foundations with living donors, the numbers must be interpreted with caution. Yet, coupled with the study's findings that 29 percent of the 10,000 foundations studied employ staff, which affects charitable administrative expense to qualifying distribution ratios, these findings suggest that many grantmaking institutions in fact pay out at higher levels than the legally mandated minimum 5 percent. However, the study also identified staff employment followed by staff size as the most important variables affecting independent foundation expense levels.[420] This suggests that while a large number of independent foundations pay out grants at rates higher than 5 percent, many such grantmaking institutions likely do not.

An analysis of total grants made and total assets from 2000 to 2005 in the 2008 edition of *The Nonprofit Almanac* provides similar data on grants paid out by independent foundations. Table 4.2 summarizes aggregate total giving for independent foundations.[421]

The data from 2001 to 2003 are especially important because these are years during which the economy was in a recession. Despite the negative impact on foundation asset bases, there was marginal impact on the proportion of grant dollars distributed. Moreover, this timeframe shows a higher level of grant dollars paid out in grants compared to 2000, prior to the impact of the recession. Taken together with the Foundation Center's forecasting for 2008 giving referenced earlier, this suggests that the majority of foundations do, in fact, use long-range planning in determining their payout. Most foundations use a three-year timeframe in determining what level of payout to maintain.

A closer look at the largest independent foundations, those with assets of $10 million or more in 2002–2004, provides some balance to the overall sector trends. These data are summarized in Table 4.3.[422]

The percentage of grants made by the largest independent foundations included in the *Almanac* is disappointingly low. Although such foundations represent 0.3 percent of all foundations analyzed, their assets accounted for 48.4 percent of all independent foundation assets in 2004 and 49.9 percent in both 2003 and 2004. These data indicate that the largest independent foundations are paying out well below 5 percent of their enormous assets in grants. The only year in which this subsample provided more than 5 percent of its total assets in grants was 2002; in 2003 and 2004, the numbers in the table above are similar and below 5 percent.

To contextualize foundation grants paid out better, it is worth noting the amount of total giving *to* foundations as noted in the 2008 edition of *Giving U.S.A.* The data are drawn from 2006 and total estimated giving to foundations, excluding the Buffett payments to the Gates Foundation, was $27.73 billion.[423] Comparing this figure to the amount of giving by foundations for grants in the *Almanac* noted above leads to serious considerations of whether or not the social benefit of philanthropy is being diminished in favor of warehousing foundation assets for the goal of perpetuity. Contrasting giving to foundations with giving by foundations noted by the Foundation Center lends more credence to the argument that philanthropy's perpetuity doctrine is undermining its social potential. Estimated giving by foundations in 2007 was $42.9 billion,[424] less than double the amount of gifts received by institutional grantmakers. To reiterate, NCRP acknowledges the value of perpetual foundations in sustaining the U.S. civil society sector. Yet, the preceding data analysis demonstrates that higher payout rates and perpetuity are in no way mutually exclusive.

Warehousing of partially public dollars does not serve the public interest or advance the social benefits of philanthropy. In light of the data presented in the two studies above, it is clear that many foundations can and do have an all-grants payout rate of more than 5 percent. An exemplary foundation should focus on applying its assets toward fulfilling its mission and using its tax subsidized partially public

## TABLE 4.2 AGGREGATE TOTAL GIVING FOR INDEPENDENT FOUNDATIONS, 2000–2005

| YEAR | GRANTS MADE IN $ MILLIONS | ASSETS IN $ MILLIONS | PERCENTAGE TOTAL GIVING |
|---|---|---|---|
| 2000 | 21,346 | 408,749 | 5.22 |
| 2001 | 23,705 | 403,526 | 5.87 |
| 2002 | 23,254 | 364,143 | 6.39 |
| 2003 | 22,568 | 399,138 | 5.65 |
| 2004 | 23,334 | 425,103 | 5.49 |
| 2005 | 25,199 | 455,570 | 5.53 |

## TABLE 4.3 AGGREGATE TOTAL GIVING OF FOUNDATIONS WITH ASSETS OF $10 MILLION OR MORE, 2002-2004

| YEAR | ASSETS IN MILLIONS | GRANTS MADE IN $ THOUSANDS | ASSETS IN $ THOUSANDS | PERCENTAGE GRANTS MADE |
|---|---|---|---|---|
| 2002 | 250 or more | 10,591,925 | 210,772,484 | 5.03 |
| | 50–249.9 | 5,852,752 | 87,250,757 | 6.71 |
| | 10–49.9 | 5,486,975 | 71,547,145 | 7.67 |
| 2003 | 250 or more | 10,521,494 | 237,735,202 | 4.43 |
| | 50–249.9 | 5,974,240 | 92,458,500 | 6.46 |
| | 10–49.9 | 5,307,777 | 77,346,419 | 6.86 |
| 2004 | 250 or more | 11,306,943 | 254,909,427 | 4.44 |
| | 50–249.9 | 5,732,432 | 100,942,795 | 5.68 |
| | 10–49.9 | 5,362,931 | 82,226,337 | 6.52 |

## TABLE 4.4 FIELD LEADERS IN PROACTIVE MISSION INVESTING[425]

| | |
|---|---|
| The Hutton Foundation | 43.6 percent |
| F.B. Heron Foundation | 26 percent |
| K.L. Felicitas Foundation | 20 percent |
| Community Foundation of Sonoma County | 14 percent |
| Needmor Fund | 14 percent |
| Weeden Foundation | 11 percent |

## TABLE 4.5 FIELD LEADERS IN INVESTMENT SCREENING[426]

| | |
|---|---|
| Gordon and Betty Moore Foundation | 100 percent screened |
| Needmor Fund | 100 percent screened |
| Weeden Foundation | 90 percent screened |
| Jessie Smith Noyes Foundation | 80 percent  screened |
| Nathan CummingsFoundation | 17 percent screened |
| Charles Stewart Mott Foundation | |
| Robert Wood Johnson Foundation | |
| William Penn Foundation | |
| Kresge Foundation | |
| Heinz Endowments | |
| Conservation Land Trust | |
| Educational Foundation of America | |
| Edward W. Hazen Foundation | |
| Max and Anna Levinson Foundation | |
| Merck Family Fund | |
| The Christopher Reynolds Foundation | |
| William Caspar Graustein Memorial Fund | |
| The William Bingham Foundation | |

## TABLE 4.6 FIELD LEADERS IN SHAREHOLDER ACTIVISM[427]

| | |
|---|---|
| Jessie Smith Noyes Foundation | 25 percent of portfolio; close to 300 companies voted on in 2008 |
| Nathan Cummings Foundation | 5 percent of portfolio; filing 16 resolutions in 2009 |
| Camilla Madden Charitable Trust | |
| Conservation Land Trust | |
| Edward W. Hazen Foundation | |
| Lemmon Foundation | |
| Max and Anna Levinson Foundation | |
| Needmor Fund | |
| Wisdom Charitable Trust | |

dollars to advance its charitable purpose. Informed by giving trends for total grants in the analysis above, a grantmaker working in the Philanthropy at Its Best framework maintains a generous payout level with a minimum of 6 percent dedicated to grants for non-profit partners.

The limited mission investing data currently available make gauging sector-wide trends challenging. As noted, the IRS form 990 PF does not collect data on foundation mission investment; foundation self-reporting is the sole source of this information. According to available data, few foundations are engaging in Philanthropy at Its Best in terms of mission investing. However, given the three strategies that will count toward a grantmaker meeting or exceeding this criterion, NCRP believes that all foundations easily can take the minimal step of screening investments, with an eye toward engaging meaningfully in shareholder activism and substantive proactive mission investing.

Several public charities and community foundations, such as the Boston Foundation, Funding Exchange, the Haymarket Fund, the As You Sow Foundation and the Tides Foundation[428] engage substantively in mission investing. While this criterion applies primarily to private foundations, public charities could serve as an important resource for those grantmakers new to this type of investment.

The principle undergirding this criterion is that tax-exempt assets should not be warehoused; rather, they should be put to use in support of the charitable purpose of the foundation. The key is an appropriate balance of payout and mission investing informed by the metrics established in this chapter. For example, a foundation might decide to show its commitment by spending down its assets in the short term but might decide not to engage in mission investing. A foundation that seeks to exist in perpetuity and also practices exemplary philanthropy would pay out 6 percent in grants only while also ensuring that at least 25 percent of its assets are invested in ways that support its mission.[429]

## CONCLUSION

Most foundations use only a tiny fraction of the financial assets at their disposal to achieve their missions. Many foundations continue "traditional payout policies," paying out only 5 percent of their assets in qualifying distributions each year and do not prioritize the potential mission-advancing power of their invest-ment assets in non-grantmaking ways. As a result, a significant opportunity for broad, long-term changes and advancing a foundation's mission is lost. Foundations should dedicate substantial portions of their endowments toward achieving their charitable purposes. As this section demonstrates, warehousing of tax-exempt dollars does not serve the public interest; it shortchanges the social benefit of philanthropy. The many socially-responsible and mission investing mechanisms available to a foundation demonstrate that such investments can minimize risk and provide reasonable returns and do not present high-risk options. By maintaining a generous grants payout and investing a substantial portion of its assets in a manner aligned with its mission, a foundation can increase its impact and demonstrate its commitment to achieving its charitable purpose.

# Criterion IV: Commitment

A grantmaker practicing Philanthropy at Its Best serves the public good by engaging a substantial portion of its financial assets in pursuit of its mission.

a) Pays out at least 6 percent of its assets annually in grants

b) Invests at least 25 percent of its assets in ways that support its mission

DISCUSSION QUESTIONS

NCRP encourages staff and trustees of foundations and other grantmakers to engage in serious discussions about each criterion and the chapter that elaborates on the criterion. Sample discussion questions are provided here to help get you started.

> Which parts of the chapter did you like the most? Why?

> Which parts did you like the least? Why?

> Do you agree that it's important to engage a substantial portion of our financial assets in pursuit of our mission? Why or why not?

> What percentage of our foundation's assets do we pay out in grants each year? How did we establish that percentage? Are we satisfied with that percentage? Why or why not?

> Have we ever considered had an intentional discussion about mission investing? What percentage of our foundation's assets do we invest in accordance with our mission? (Include screening, proxy voting or shareholder activism, and proactive mission investments.)

> How did we establish that percentage? Are we satisfied with that percentage? Why or why not?

> Are there ways we can use other investment assets at our disposal to achieve our mission?

> What else from this chapter should inform our current grantmaking priorities?

> If we want to make any changes based on this discussion, what will need to happen in order to make those changes? What are the next steps?

# NOTES FOR CHAPTER IV: COMMITMENT

316. William M. Dietel. *Mission Stewardship: Aligning Programs, Investments and Administration to Achieve Impact* (New York, NY: F.B. Heron Foundation, 2006).

317. Arthur "Buzz" Schmidt. "Escaping the Perpetuity Mindset," *The Nonprofit Quarterly* (Fall 2008). Schmidt is the founder of GuideStar, founder and CEO of GuideStar International and consults with Southpoint Social Strategies, a management consultant firm that works with nonprofits and their communities to help them reach their goals.

318. Steven T. Miller. "Remarks before Georgetown Law Center Seminar on Issues in Nonprofit Governance," (speech, Georgetown University, Washington, D.C., April 24, 2008), http://philanthropy.com/documents/v20/i14/gtown2008.pdf.

319. Akash Deep and Peter Frumkin. *The Foundation Payout Puzzle* (working paper No. 9, Harvard University, The Hauser Center for Nonprofit Organizations, the Kennedy School of Government June 2001).

320. The Foundation Center. *Foundation Growth and Giving Estimates: Current Outlook (2008 edition)*, (New York, NY: The Foundation Center, 2008).

321. Bill Gates. "2009 Annual Letter from Bill Gates: Page 9: The Economic Crisis," The Bill & Melinda Gates Foundation, http://www.gatesfoundation.org/annual-letter/Pages/2009-economic-crisis.aspx.

322. It is important to note that this payout rate is based on average, across-funds payouts, meaning that while some individual funds at public charities pay out at rates well above 6 percent in grants, others do not.

323. Personal communication with NCRP.

324. According to IRS i990PF (990 instruction form), "A private foundation that is not a private operating foundation must pay out, as qualifying distributions, its minimum investment return. This is generally 5 percent of the total fair market value of its non-charitable assets…" http://www.irs.gov/pub/irs-pdf/i990pf.pdf.

325. Thomas J. Billitteri. *Money, Mission and the Payout Rule: In Search of a Strategic Approach to Foundation Spending* (Washington, D.C.: Nonprofit Sector Research Fund, The Aspen Institute. July 2005).

326. Ibid.

327. Thomas Troyer. "The 1969 Private Foundation Law: Historical Perspective on its Origins and Underpinnings," *Exempt Organization Tax Review* 27 (January 2000): 61.

328. Michael Anft. "How a Foundation Tax Became the Minimum-Payout Rule," *The Chronicle of Philanthropy*, June 26, 2008.

329. Billitteri. Op. cit.

330. Eugene Steuerle. "Distribution Requirements for Foundations", *OTA Paper 12* (Washington, D.C.: U.S. Treasury Department Office of Tax Analysis, May 1976).

331. Ibid.

332. Deep and Frumkin. Op. cit.

333. Jane C. Gravelle. "Minimum Distribution Requirements for Foundations: Proposal to Disallow Administrative Costs," *CRS Report RS21603* (Washington, D.C.: Congressional Research Service, September 5, 2003).

334. See Richard C. Sansing, and Robert J. Yetman. *Prudent Stewards or Pyramid Builders? Distribution Policies of Private Foundations* (working paper no. 02-18, Dartmouth College Tuck School of Business, September 6, 2002); Perry Mehrling, *Spending Policies for Private Foundations: The Case for Increased Grants Payout*, (Washington, D.C.: National Network of Grantmakers, 1999); Heidi Waleson, *Beyond Five Percent: The New Foundation Payout Menu* (New York, NY: Northern California Grantmakers, New York Regional Association of Grantmakers, 2007); and Deep and Frumkin, Op. cit.

335. National Committee for Responsive Philanthropy. *Helping Charities, Sustaining Foundations: Reasonable Tax Reform Would Aid America's Charities, Preserve Foundation Perpetuity and Enhance Foundation Effectiveness and Efficiency* (Washington, D.C.: National Committee for Responsive Philanthropy June 2, 2003).

336. The Foundation Center. *Foundation Center Statement on Source Data Used in NCRP Report and Implications for Findings* (New York, NY: The Foundation Center, June 16, 2003) The Foundation Center paper's estimate was based on 1999 data, when foundation grantmaking totaled $11.57 billion.

337. Cambridge Associates Inc. *Sustainable Payout for Foundations* (Grand Haven, Mich.: Council of Michigan Foundations, April 2000); Deep and Frumkin. Op. cit.; Billitteri. Op. cit.; Waleson. Op. cit.

338. Schmidt. Op. cit.

339. Billitteri. Op. cit., p. 27.

340. Mehrling. Op. cit.

341. Paul J. Jansen and David M. Katz. "For Nonprofits, Time is Money," *The McKinsey Quarterly* (2002): 124.

342. Mehrling. Op. cit.

343. Adapted from Schmidt. Op. cit.

344. Ibid.

345. Ibid., p. 5.

346. Diane Feeney and Terry Odendahl. "Who's Afraid of Increasing Foundation Payout?" *Foundation News & Commentary*, 40 (May/June 1999).

347. Sansing and Yetman. Op. cit.

348. National Committee for Responsive Philanthropy. *A Billion Here, A Billion There: The Empirical Data Add Up* (Washington, D.C.: National Committee for Responsive Philanthropy July 8, 2003).

349. Council on Foundations. *Issue Paper: Excise Tax on Private Foundations* (Washington, D.C.: Council on Foundations, January 2004).

350. Estimate from Steve Gunderson, president and CEO of the Council on Foundations, quoted in Aaron Dorfman, "In Their Own Words: Foundation Trade Association CEOs Brief Their Members on Issues Inside the Beltway," *Responsive Philanthropy* (Fall 2008).

351. Written statement of Mark W. Everson, commissioner of Internal Revenue, before the Committee on Finance, United States Senate, *Hearing on Charitable Giving Problems and Best Practices* (Washington, D.C.: Internal Revenue Service June 22, 2004). http://www.irs.gov/newsroom/article/0,,id=124186,00.html.

352. Ian Wilhelm. "Nonprofit Leaders Debate Foundation Disclosure," *The Chronicle of Philanthropy*, November 7, 2008.

353. Michael Klausner. "Money Talk: Top Foundation Executives Reveal How They Set Payout Rates, Executive Salaries, and Trustee Compensation," *Stanford Social Innovation Review* (Summer 2004): 52.

354. John E. Craig Jr. "In Favor of Five Percent," *Foundation News & Commentary*, 40 (May/June 1999): 23.

355. Billitteri. Op. cit.

356. Klausner. Op. cit.

357. Waleson. Op. cit.

358. This is a conservative estimate; other estimates suggest a higher proportion of the Gates Foundation, between $1 for every $7 or $8, account for all philanthropic dollars in the civil society sector. Moreover, the $30 billion pledge from Warren Buffett to the Gates Foundation is a spend-down commitment. All the money transferred in one year must be spent within that year, i.e., there is no investment of Buffett's gift to the Gates Foundation.

359. Waleson. Op. cit.

360. Ibid.

361. Ibid.

362. Quoted in Emerson, Op. Cit. p. 45.

363. F.B. Heron Foundation. *Impact Across the Mission-Related Investment Portfolio – an overview from F.B. Heron 2007 Annual Report* (New York, NY: F.B. Heron Foundation, 2008), http://www.fbheron.org/documents/ar.2007.mri_impact.pdf; The F.B. Heron Foundation "About F.B. Heron," http://www.fbheron.org/about_heron/index.html.

364. Luther M. Ragin Jr. *New Frontiers in Mission Related Investing* (New York, NY: F.B. Heron Foundation 2003).

365. Amy L. Domini. "What Is Social Investing? Who Are Social Investors?" in *The Social Investment Almanac: A Comprehensive Guide to Socially Responsible Investing*, ed. Peter D. Kindler, Steven D. Lydenberg and Amy L. Domini (New York, NY: Henry Holt and Company 1992), 5.

366. Conrad MacKerron et al. *Unlocking the Power of the Proxy: How Active Foundation Proxy Voting Can Protect Endowments and Boost Philanthropic Missions* (New York, NY: Rockefeller Philanthropy Advisors and As You Sow Foundation, 2004).

367. Joan Shapiro. "The Movement Since 1970," in *The Social Investment Almanac: A Comprehensive Guide to Socially Responsible Investing*, ed. Peter D. Kindler, Steven D. Lydenberg and Amy L. Domini, (New York, NY: Henry Holt and Company 1992), 8.

368. Ibid.

369. Joshua Humphreys. *The Mission in the Marketplace: How Responsible Investing Can Strengthen the Fiduciary Oversight of Endowments and Enhance Philanthropic Missions.* (Washington, D.C.: The Social Investment Forum Foundation, 2007), 19.

370. In current mission-investing discourse, SRI often is used interchangeably with the term "screening," discussed as one of the three strategies of a comprehensive mission investing approach.

371. See Dave Beckwith. "Beyond Grantmaking: Letting our Foundation Assets Work Full-Time," *Responsive Philanthropy* (Summer 2007): 1; Sarah Cooch and Mark Kramer. *Compounding Impact: Mission Investing by U.S. Foundations* (Boston: FSG Social Impact Advisors, March 2007); and Marcy Murninghan. "A New Kind of Voter Education Project: Responsible Equity Ownership & the Public Interest," *Value*, 1 (January 23, 2006): 60.

372. Cooch and Kramer. Op. cit., p. 2.

373. These usually are below-market rate loans made by an institutional grantmaker in support of a specific program.

374. Adapted from Cooch and Kramer, Op. cit., p. 2. For legal guidelines for U.S. Foundations and MI, please see Mark Kramer and Anne Stetson, *A Brief Guide to the Law of Mission Investing for U.S. Foundations* (Boston: FSG Social Impact Advisors, October, 2008).

375. Cooch and Kramer. Op. cit., p. 45.

376. Jed Emerson. "Where Money Meets Mission: Breaking Down the Firewall Between Foundation Investments and Programming," *Stanford Social Innovation Review* (Summer 2003): 41.

377. Cooch and Kramer. Op. cit.

378. *Providing Capital, Building Communities, Creating Impact: Community Development Financial Institutions, 6th Edition* (Arlington, Va.: The CDFI Data Project, 2007).

379. "S&P 500 Monthly Returns," S&P 500 Index Services. Retrieved from http://www2.standardandpoors.com/spf/xls/index/MONTHLY.xls on August 8, 2008.

380. Cooch and Kramer. Op. cit.

381. Ragin. Op. cit.

382. S&P 500 Monthly Returns." Op. cit.

383. Cooch and Kramer. Op. cit.

384. More for Mission Campaign Resource Center. "About Us," More for Mission Investing, http://ec2-enilsson.ath.cx/sites/mfm/default/page/15/about-us; this campaign was formerly known as the "2% for Mission Campaign."

385. Adapted from: http://ec2-enilsson.ath.cx/sites/mfm/default/page/15/about-us.

386. Ibid.

387. "Mission-related Investing at the F.B. Heron Foundation: Data Summary (as of December 31, 2006)," http://www.carleton.ca/ccci/files/MRI%20Data%20Text_12-31-06_wTR.pdf.

388. Emerson. Op. cit.

389. Mark R. Kramer. "Foundation Trustees Need a New Investment Approach," *The Chronicle of Philanthropy*, March 23, 2006.

390. Sarah Cooch and Mark Kramer. "The Power of Strategic Mission Investing," *Stanford Social Innovation Review* (Fall 2007): 43.

391. Steven Godeke with Doug Bauer. *Philanthropy's New Passing Gear: Mission-Related Investing, A Policy and Implementation Guide for Foundation Trustees* (New York, NY: Rockefeller Philanthropy Advisors, 2008).

392. Emerson. Op. cit.

393. Smithfield Foods, Inc. *2003 Stewardship Report: Environment, Employee Safety and Animal Welfare*, http://www.smithfield-foods.com/PDF/SFD_StewardshipReport_03.pdf.

394. Smithfield Foods. "Search Results," http://www.smithfield-foods.com/results.aspx?q=cummings&cx=018443523105461935518%3Arctbpmymf40&cof=FORID%3A11#457.

395. Harvey Lipman. "Meshing Proxy with Mission: Few foundations do much to influence shareholder votes," *The Chronicle of Philanthropy*, May 4, 2006.

396. The example highlighted here is one of many conflicting investment decisions of the Gates Foundation uncovered by the *Los Angeles Times*, other media outlets and watchdogs. Others include investments in Chinese petrochemical companies working with the corrupt and genocidal Sudanese government and large holdings in many financial institutions that contributed to the subprime mortgage crisis.

397. Lipman. Op. cit.

398. Schmidt. Op. cit., p. 5

399. Schmidt. Op. cit.. p. 6.

400. Allessandra Bianchi. "The Other 95 Percent: How a community foundation uses proxy voting to advance its mission," *Stanford Social Innovation Review* (Winter 2005): 63.

401. MacKerron et al. Op. cit., p. 27

402. Ibid.

403. "Stock-Investment Policies at the 50 Wealthiest Private Foundations," *The Chronicle of Philanthropy*, May 4, 2006.

404. Lipman. Op. cit.

405. Ibid.

406. Personal communication between Victor de Luca and NCRP (December, 2008).

407. Godeke. Op. cit.

408. Ibid.

409. Sarah Cooch and Mark Kramer. *Aggregating Impact: A Funder's Guide to Mission Investment Intermediaries* (Boston: FSG Social Impact Advisors, November 2007).

410. Michael Seltzer. "The Funder Next Door: When grantmakers move into the communities they serve," *Stanford Social Innovation Review* (Fall 2005): 72.

411. Cooch and Kramer, November 2007. Op. cit.

412. For more information on MI intermediaries, please see Cooch and Kramer, November 2007. Op. cit.

413. Ragin. Op. cit.

414. Beckwith. Op. cit.

415. Lisa Ranghelli. "Mission-Related Investing," excerpt from *Needmor Fund Program Assessment* (unpublished working paper, 2003).

416. Feeney and Odendahl. Op. cit.; Billitteri. Op. cit.

417. Elizabeth T. Boris et al. *What Drives Foundation Expenses & Compensation? Results of a Three-Year Study* (Washington, D.C.: The Urban Institute, the Foundation Center, GuideStar and Philanthropic Research Inc. 2008): xi.

418. Total Giving is defined as "The total amount paid out by foundations in the form of grants and contributions. [...] For private foundations this figure is taken from Form 990-PF, Part I, line 25, column d." Ibid., p. 71.

419. Ibid., p. 5.

420. Ibid., p. xii.

421. Kennard T. Wing, Thomas H. Pollack, and Amy Blackwood. *The Nonprofit Almanac 2008*. (Washington, D.C.: The Urban Institute Press, 2008): 105–106.

422. Ibid., p. 107.

423. GivingUSA Foundation, *Giving USA 2008: The Annual Report on Philanthropy for the Year 2007* (Indianapolis: The Center on Philanthropy at Indiana University, 2008): 115.

424. The Foundation Center 2008. Op. cit.

425. Cooch and Kramer March 2007. Op. cit.; direct communications with NCRP.

426. List drawn from "Stock-Investment Policies at the 50 Wealthiest Private Foundations." Op. cit.; Humphreys. Op. cit., p. 11; direct communications with NCRP. Foundations that employ a single screen only (such as avoiding tobacco stocks) are excluded.

427. List is drawn from Humphreys. Op. cit.; direct communications with NCRP.

428. Humphreys. Op. cit.

429. As noted in the introduction, public charities' payout rate is based on average, across-funds payouts, meaning that while some individual funds at public charities pay out at rates well above 6 percent in grants, others do not; they also may choose to engage in mission-investing. But the concern with warehousing tax-exempt dollars applies primarily to private foundations.

# Data Appendix

# Data Appendix

To analyze current giving, NCRP worked with a custom dataset developed with the Foundation Center, which includes detailed information on more than 1,200 of the largest foundations in the United States. The search set is based on the Foundation Center's grants sample database, which includes all grants of $10,000 or more awarded to organizations by a sample of 1,172 larger foundations for circa 2004, 1,154 for circa 2005, and 1,263 for circa 2006. For community foundations, only discretionary grants are included. Grants to individuals are not included in the file. International grants are included. The center's grants classification system provides much more detail on current giving trends than other data sources.

To establish fair and reasonable benchmarks for this document, NCRP analyzed giving among these foundations across three years to avoid influential outliers in any single year. The three-year timeframe looks at the most recent years for which data are available. It was selected because a foundation practicing exemplary philanthropy should demonstrate consistency over multiple years. Moreover, many foundations look at three- to five-year time horizons to determine their annual grants allocation. The total sample size was 809 foundations that consistently provided information to the Foundation Center on the issues NCRP analyzed for all three years. There likely are many more foundations that meet the benchmarks established by NCRP based on our data analysis but are not included in our sample. This is because those institutions either do not provide detailed data to the Foundation Center or might not have done so consistently in the timeframe from which the NCRP sample was drawn. In other words, being excluded from this sample or not being listed as

meeting the benchmarks NCRP established does not imply that an individual grantmaking institution is not practicing Philanthropy at Its Best.

The sample had a combined three-year average giving of $14,926,350,872 across 111,218 grants. This figure is the denominator used in NCRP's calculations; if analyzed within giving sub-samples, these figures would be higher and likely overstate the current giving trends. Using the full samples average total giving provides a more comprehensive framework for analyzing the different types of grants. Although some grants are coded for multiple intended beneficiary groups, the total amounts of grantmaking intended to benefit specific populations are not double-counted in the total giving numbers. NCRP also used aggregate statistics from the Foundation Center's annual reports for 1998–2006 as a broader frame in which to analyze our custom dataset. NCRP believes that the three-year combined data set provides the best indicator of current trends in the field. NCRP assumes exclusive responsibility for all data interpretation and metrics established by the data analysis.

## Giving for Marginalized Groups, broadly defined

In the circa 2004–2006 time period from which the NCRP dataset was drawn, in the aggregate, 33.2 percent of all grant dollars were provided for all 11 intended beneficiary groups. That means that approximately $1 out of every $3 granted by larger foundations was intended to benefit communities with the least wealth, opportunity or power and that $2 out of every $3 granted could *not* be classified as benefiting those communities.

Leading the field, 108 foundations or about 13.35 percent of our sample provided at least 50 percent of their grant dollars for the intended benefit of marginalized communities. This is the benchmark for Philanthropy at Its Best. A list of all 108 foundations that NCRP found to currently meet or exceed this benchmark can be found immediately below. As noted earlier, some foundations may meet or exceed this benchmark and still not be listed here. For example, a grantmaker may not be included in the Foundation Center's database or its grants may not be properly coded.

In analyzing the data for the eleven marginalized groups for which it has data, NCRP identified the

## PERCENT OF FOUNDATION GRANT DOLLARS DESIGNATED FOR MARGINALIZED COMMUNITIES IN 2004–2006 NCRP SAMPLE

■ Designated for Marginalized Communities

■ Not Designated for Marginalized Communities

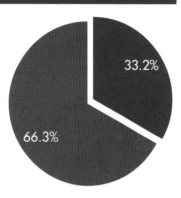

33.2%

66.3%

## PERCENT OF FOUNDATIONS MEETING NCRP'S CRITERIA FOR SUPPORT OF MARGINALIZED COMMUNITIES

■ Foundations Designating 50% or More of Grant Dollars for Marginalized Communities

■ Foundations Designating Less Than 50% of Grant Dollars for Marginalized Communities

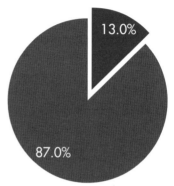

13.0%

87.0%

## FOUNDATIONS MEETING NCRP'S CRITERIA FOR PHILANTHROPY AT ITS BEST SUPPORT FOR MARGINALIZED COMMUNITIES

| | FOUNDATION NAME | STATE | TYPE | % |
|---|---|---|---|---|
| 1 | The James H. and Alice Teubert Charitable Trust | WV | Independent | 100.0 |
| 2 | The John M. Lloyd Foundation | CA | Independent | 100.0 |
| 3 | The Melville Charitable Trust | MA | Independent | 99.7 |
| 4 | The Retirement Research Foundation | IL | Independent | 98.8 |
| 5 | The Corella & Bertram F. Bonner Foundation, Inc. | NJ | Independent | 97.4 |
| 6 | Avon Foundation | NY | Corporate | 97.0 |
| 7 | Lavelle Fund for the Blind, Inc. | NY | Independent | 95.1 |
| 8 | van Ameringen Foundation, Inc. | NY | Independent | 94.5 |
| 9 | Marguerite Casey Foundation | WA | Independent | 92.5 |
| 10 | Oberkotter Foundation | PA | Independent | 91.4 |
| 11 | The Annie E. Casey Foundation | MD | Independent | 86.0 |
| 12 | Northwest Area Foundation | MN | Independent | 84.4 |
| 13 | New York Foundation | NY | Independent | 84.3 |
| 14 | The California Endowment | CA | Independent | 84.2 |
| 15 | The California Wellness Foundation | CA | Independent | 83.8 |
| 16 | Kimberly-Clark Foundation, Inc. | TX | Corporate | 81.2 |
| 17 | Essel Foundation, Inc. | NY | Independent | 79.3 |
| 18 | Tiger Foundation | NY | Independent | 79.2 |
| 19 | Fannie Mae Foundation | DC | Corporate | 78.7 |
| 20 | Moriah Fund | DC | Independent | 78.5 |
| 21 | The Gap Foundation | CA | Corporate | 78.4 |
| 22 | The Gill Foundation | CO | Independent | 77.6 |
| 23 | Fischer Family Foundation | KY | Independent | 77.5 |
| 24 | The F. B. Heron Foundation | NY | Independent | 77.2 |

## FOUNDATIONS MEETING NCRP'S CRITERIA FOR PHILANTHROPY AT ITS BEST
## SUPPORT FOR MARGINALIZED COMMUNITIES (CONTINUED)

| | FOUNDATION NAME | STATE | TYPE | % |
|---|---|---|---|---|
| 25 | The Edna McConnell Clark Foundation | NY | Independent | 76.2 |
| 26 | Kate B. Reynolds Charitable Trust | NC | Independent | 75.7 |
| 27 | Otto Bremer Foundation | MN | Independent | 75.6 |
| 28 | The Kimball Foundation | CA | Independent | 75.6 |
| 29 | Freddie Mac Foundation | VA | Corporate | 75.5 |
| 30 | Great Bay Foundation for Social Entrepreneurship | ME | Independent | 75.2 |
| 31 | B. C. McCabe Foundation | CA | Independent | 74.4 |
| 32 | Con Alma Health Foundation, Inc. | NM | Independent | 72.6 |
| 33 | Jessie Smith Noyes Foundation, Inc. | NY | Independent | 72.3 |
| 34 | The Skillman Foundation | MI | Independent | 71.7 |
| 35 | JEHT Foundation | NY | Independent | 71.5 |
| 36 | Public Welfare Foundation, Inc. | DC | Independent | 71.5 |
| 37 | The Hyams Foundation, Inc. | MA | Independent | 69.5 |
| 38 | California Community Foundation | CA | Community | 69.4 |
| 39 | John D. & Edna Hofer Trust | SD | Independent | 68.2 |
| 40 | The Community Foundation Serving Richmond & Central Virginia | VA | Community | 68.1 |
| 41 | Evelyn and Walter Haas, Jr. Fund | CA | Independent | 67.3 |
| 42 | The Sunshine Lady Foundation, Inc. | NC | Independent | 66.8 |
| 43 | Steven A. and Alexandra M. Cohen Foundation | CT | Independent | 66.5 |
| 44 | The Gamble Foundation | CA | Independent | 66.2 |
| 45 | Eugene and Agnes E. Meyer Foundation | DC | Independent | 65.3 |
| 46 | The Pinkerton Foundation | NY | Independent | 65.3 |
| 47 | The Abell Foundation, Inc. | MD | Independent | 65.2 |
| 48 | The Tudor Foundation, Inc. | CT | Independent | 65.0 |
| 49 | Carrie Estelle Doheny Foundation | CA | Independent | 64.9 |
| 50 | The Winston-Salem Foundation | NC | Community | 64.7 |
| 51 | The Susan Thompson Buffett Foundation | NE | Independent | 64.5 |
| 52 | The Cleo Foundation | CA | Independent | 64.2 |
| 53 | Weingart Foundation | CA | Independent | 64.0 |
| 54 | Lumina Foundation for Education, Inc. | IN | Independent | 63.9 |
| 55 | The Rockefeller Foundation | NY | Independent | 63.8 |
| 56 | Bill & Melinda Gates Foundation | WA | Independent | 63.7 |
| 57 | The Coca-Cola Foundation, Inc. | GA | Corporate | 63.7 |
| 58 | Philip L. Graham Fund | DC | Independent | 63.5 |
| 59 | The Ira W. DeCamp Foundation | NY | Independent | 63.4 |
| 60 | Levi Strauss Foundation | CA | Corporate | 62.9 |
| 61 | Nina Mason Pulliam Charitable Trust | IN | Independent | 62.7 |
| 62 | Altman Foundation | NY | Independent | 62.3 |
| 63 | Manoogian Simone Foundation | MI | Independent | 62.2 |
| 64 | Pleasant T. Rowland Foundation, Inc. | WI | Independent | 62.0 |
| 65 | Raskob Foundation for Catholic Activities, Inc. | DE | Independent | 61.8 |
| 66 | Helena Rubinstein Foundation, Inc. | NY | Independent | 61.1 |
| 67 | Robert Sterling Clark Foundation, Inc. | NY | Independent | 60.4 |
| 68 | Foundation for Child Development | NY | Independent | 59.8 |
| 69 | The Bothin Foundation | CA | Independent | 59.7 |
| 70 | Connecticut Health Foundation, Inc. | CT | Independent | 59.5 |

## FOUNDATIONS MEETING NCRP'S CRITERIA FOR PHILANTHROPY AT ITS BEST SUPPORT FOR MARGINALIZED COMMUNITIES (CONTINUED)

| | FOUNDATION NAME | STATE | TYPE | % |
|---|---|---|---|---|
| 71 | John W. Anderson Foundation | IN | Independent | 58.9 |
| 72 | The Clark Foundation | NY | Independent | 58.4 |
| 73 | Topfer Family Foundation | TX | Independent | 57.8 |
| 74 | Eckerd Family Foundation, Inc. | FL | Independent | 57.6 |
| 75 | Rockwell Fund, Inc. | TX | Independent | 57.2 |
| 76 | The Atlantic Foundation of New York | NY | Independent | 57.1 |
| 77 | The Goldsbury Foundation | TX | Independent | 56.5 |
| 78 | Cisco Systems Foundation | CA | Corporate | 56.2 |
| 79 | Community Foundation for Monterey County | CA | Community | 56.0 |
| 80 | The Prudential Foundation | NJ | Corporate | 56.0 |
| 81 | Kalamazoo Community Foundation | MI | Community | 55.9 |
| 82 | Conrad N. Hilton Foundation | NV | Independent | 55.8 |
| 83 | Norwin S. and Elizabeth N. Bean Foundation | NH | Independent | 55.6 |
| 84 | Bush Foundation | MN | Independent | 54.5 |
| 85 | Lozier Foundation | NE | Independent | 54.4 |
| 86 | W. K. Kellogg Foundation | MI | Independent | 54.3 |
| 87 | Michael Reese Health Trust | IL | Independent | 54.3 |
| 88 | The Sandy River Charitable Foundation | ME | Independent | 54.2 |
| 89 | The Baltimore Community Foundation | MD | Community | 53.9 |
| 90 | Woods Charitable Fund, Inc. | NE | Independent | 53.2 |
| 91 | Helen Bader Foundation, Inc. | WI | Independent | 53.2 |
| 92 | Grousbeck Family Foundation | CA | Independent | 52.7 |
| 93 | Mertz Gilmore Foundation | NY | Independent | 52.3 |
| 94 | The Ford Foundation | NY | Independent | 52.2 |
| 95 | Victoria Foundation, Inc. | NJ | Independent | 52.1 |
| 96 | Amelia Peabody Foundation | MA | Independent | 52.0 |
| 97 | Polk Bros. Foundation, Inc. | IL | Independent | 51.6 |
| 98 | The Case Foundation | DC | Independent | 51.5 |
| 99 | Eva L. and Joseph M. Bruening Foundation | OH | Independent | 51.2 |
| 100 | The Achelis Foundation | NY | Independent | 51.1 |
| 101 | Albert & Bessie Mae Kronkosky Charitable Foundation | TX | Independent | 51.0 |
| 102 | S. H. Cowell Foundation | CA | Independent | 51.0 |
| 103 | F. R. Bigelow Foundation | MN | Independent | 50.5 |
| 104 | The ALSAM Foundation | UT | Independent | 50.5 |
| 105 | McInerny Foundation | HI | Independent | 50.2 |
| 106 | The Morris and Gwendolyn Cafritz Foundation | DC | Independent | 50.1 |
| 107 | Houston Endowment Inc. | TX | Independent | 50.0 |
| 108 | Delaware Community Foundation | DE | Community | 50.0 |

following giving trends across special population groups. The aggregate statistics presented immediately after this analysis are drawn from the Foundation Center's annual reports for 1998–2006 as a broader frame in which to analyze NCRP's custom data. NCRP identified marginalized group-specific field leaders that are listed after the aggregate statistics.

1. **Economically disadvantaged**: In NCRP's sample, 737 of the 809 foundations comprising 91.1 percent of the sample provided at least some grants intended to benefit the economically disadvantaged directly. Within the subset of 737 foundations that provided grants for this intended beneficiary group, the huge variability obscured by aggregated data is stark: for example, the range for

the top ten foundations is 63.4–97.4 percent.

2. **Racial or ethnic minorities**: In analyzing giving trends for racial or ethnic minorities, 664 of the full sample of 809 foundations provided grants intended to benefit this group. The aggregate numbers for grantmaking intended to benefit racial or ethnic minorities as a share of overall giving are disappointingly low: less than 8 percent (7.78) of all grant dollars were intended to benefit racial or ethnic minorities. A disappointingly low proportion, less than 5 percent (4.57), of NCRP's total sample provided 25 percent or more for the intended benefit of racial or ethnic minorities.

3. **Women and girls**: 715 foundations provided grants classified to benefit women and girls. Unsurprisingly, the Avon Foundation tops the list with 96 percent of grant dollars given for the intended benefit of women and girls. The leading 25 foundations as a percentage of grant dollars to benefit women and girls provide between 20.2 and 96 percent.

4. **People with AIDS**: 323 foundations made grants for this population group. Fully 240 foundations comprising this subsample, or roughly three-quarters (74.3 percent), provided less than 1 percent of their grants as intended to benefit people with AIDS. The range of the top ten foundations here is 8.2 to 98.2 percent.

5. **People with disabilities**: 692 foundations of our sample provided grant dollars to benefit people with disabilities. The James and Alice Teubert Charitable Trust leads with 100 percent of grant dollars devoted to this cause. The top 25 funders by the percentage granted to benefit people with disabilities gave from 17.2 to 100 percent of grant dollars.

6. **Aging, elderly, senior citizens**: A total of 555 foundations made grants for this beneficiary group. The Retirement Research Foundation tops the list at 97.8 percent of its grant dollars to benefit the aging and elderly. The top 25 funders by the percentage devoted to this area shows high variability from 9.6 to 97.8 percent.

7. **Immigrants & Refugees**:[430] 385 foundations, some 47.58 percent of our overall sample, provided funds to benefit immigrants and refugees. The range for the top 25 funders in terms of proportion of grants made to benefit immigrants and refugees shows high variability, with a lower bound of 5.8 percent and an upper bound of 40.3 percent.

8. **Crime/Abuse victims**: 536 foundations from our sample provide grants intended to benefit crime or abuse victims. This subsample represents almost two-thirds of our total sample (66.25 percent), indicating that many foundations devote at least some resources to support this vulnerable population group.

9. **Offenders and ex-offenders**: 367 of our 809 foundations provided grants to benefit offenders and ex-offenders. There is huge variability among the top 25 funders, indicating there are very few funders who prioritize giving to this group.

10. **Single parents**: 189 foundations in our sample provided grants to benefit single parents. Only 20 foundations provided 1 percent or more of their grant dollars for single parents, demonstrating that support for single parents is not a high priority for many foundations.

11. **LGBTQ citizens**:[431] 173 foundations or just over 21 percent of our sample provided grants intended to benefit the LGBTQ population. Grantmaking for LGBTQ populations is highly concentrated as demonstrated by the range of the top ten funders for this population group: 2.2 to 61.7 percent.

### AGGREGATE STATISTICS: GIVING BY INTENDED BENEFICIARY GROUP IN THE NCRP SAMPLE COMPARED TO NATIONAL LONGITUDINAL TRENDS

| INTENDED BENEFICIARY GROUP[432] | LOWEST AND HIGHEST SINGLE YEAR PERCENT OF ALL GRANTS AWARDED (1998-2006)[433] | PERCENT OF GRANTS AWARDED IN THE 2004–2006 NCRP SAMPLE |
|---|---|---|
| Economically disadvantaged | 11.7–21.2 | 19.9 |
| Ethnic and racial minorities | 7.0–9.9 | 7.8 |
| Women and girls | 5.2–7.3 | 6.1 |
| People with AIDS | 0.5–5.2 | 3.3 |
| People with disabilities | 2.8–4.0 | 2.9 |
| Aging, elderly, senior citizens | 1.6–2.1 | 1.5 |
| Immigrants and refugees | 0.7–1.1 | 1.0 |
| Crime or abuse victims | 0.8–1.6 | 0.9 |
| Offenders and ex-offenders | 0.3–0.7 | 0.7 |
| LGBTQ | 0.1 | 0.2 |
| Single parents | 0.1–0.2 | 0.1 |
| TOTAL | | 33.2 |

## TOP 25 FUNDERS OF ECONOMICALLY DISADVANTAGED COMMUNITIES
## (AS A PROPORTION OF TOTAL GIVING)

| | FOUNDATION NAME | STATE | TYPE | % |
|---|---|---|---|---|
| 1 | The Corella & Bertram F. Bonner Foundation, Inc. | NJ | Independent | 97.4 |
| 2 | The Melville Charitable Trust | MA | Independent | 91.9 |
| 3 | The Annie E. Casey Foundation | MD | Independent | 78.1 |
| 4 | Northwest Area Foundation | MN | Independent | 74.3 |
| 5 | Fannie Mae Foundation | DC | Corporate | 71.7 |
| 6 | Marguerite Casey Foundation | WA | Independent | 71.7 |
| 7 | The F. B. Heron Foundation | NY | Independent | 71.6 |
| 8 | Tiger Foundation | NY | Independent | 71.0 |
| 9 | John D. & Edna Hofer Trust | SD | Independent | 66.4 |
| 10 | The Kimball Foundation | CA | Independent | 64.7 |
| 11 | The Gamble Foundation | CA | Independent | 63.4 |
| 12 | Kate B. Reynolds Charitable Trust | NC | Independent | 63.3 |
| 13 | The California Endowment | CA | Independent | 61.0 |
| 14 | California Community Foundation | CA | Community | 60.0 |
| 15 | The Rockefeller Foundation | NY | Independent | 58.1 |
| 16 | Kimberly-Clark Foundation, Inc. | TX | Corporate | 57.1 |
| 17 | Freddie Mac Foundation | VA | Corporate | 56.4 |
| 18 | The California Wellness Foundation | CA | Independent | 53.4 |
| 19 | Lumina Foundation for Education, Inc. | IN | Independent | 53.0 |
| 20 | van Ameringen Foundation, Inc. | NY | Independent | 52.7 |
| 21 | The Sandy River Charitable Foundation | ME | Independent | 52.2 |
| 22 | The Ira W. DeCamp Foundation | NY | Independent | 51.9 |
| 23 | The Abell Foundation, Inc. | MD | Independent | 50.9 |
| 24 | The Clark Foundation | NY | Independent | 50.0 |
| 25 | Jessie Smith Noyes Foundation, Inc. | NY | Independent | 49.8 |

## TOP 10 FUNDERS OF ETHNIC AND RACIAL MINORITY COMMUNITIES
## (AS A PROPORTION OF TOTAL GIVING)

| | FOUNDATION NAME | STATE | TYPE | % |
|---|---|---|---|---|
| 1 | Kimberly-Clark Foundation, Inc. | TX | Corporate | 64.5 |
| 2 | Marguerite Casey Foundation | WA | Independent | 56.3 |
| 3 | The Skillman Foundation | MI | Independent | 56.3 |
| 4 | Manoogian Simone Foundation | MI | Independent | 55.7 |
| 5 | Lumina Foundation for Education, Inc. | IN | Independent | 49.7 |
| 6 | Northwest Area Foundation | MN | Independent | 49.1 |
| 7 | New York Foundation | NY | Independent | 46.9 |
| 8 | Jessie Smith Noyes Foundation, Inc. | NY | Independent | 46.4 |
| 9 | The California Endowment | CA | Independent | 46.1 |
| 10 | Moriah Fund | DC | Independent | 43.2 |

## TOP 10 FUNDERS OF WOMEN & GIRLS
## (AS A PROPORTION OF TOTAL GIVING)

| | FOUNDATION NAME | STATE | TYPE | % |
|---|---|---|---|---|
| 1 | Avon Foundation | NY | Corporate | 96.0 |
| 2 | Fischer Family Foundation | KY | Independent | 65.8 |
| 3 | Pleasant T. Rowland Foundation, Inc. | WI | Independent | 62.0 |
| 4 | The Susan Thompson Buffett Foundation | NE | Independent | 51.9 |
| 5 | John W. Anderson Foundation | IN | Independent | 44.6 |
| 6 | Robert Sterling Clark Foundation, Inc. | NY | Independent | 44.1 |
| 7 | B. C. McCabe Foundation | CA | Independent | 40.2 |
| 8 | McAdams Charitable Foundation | RI | Independent | 35.1 |
| 9 | Compton Foundation, Inc. | CA | Independent | 33.1 |
| 10 | The Bristol-Myers Squibb Foundation, Inc. | NY | Corporate | 31.6 |

## TOP 5 FUNDERS OF PEOPLE WITH AIDS
## (AS A PROPORTION OF TOTAL GIVING)

| | FOUNDATION NAME | STATE | TYPE | % |
|---|---|---|---|---|
| 1 | The John M. Lloyd Foundation | CA | Independent | 98.2 |
| 2 | The Bristol-Myers Squibb Foundation, Inc. | NY | Corporate | 37.5 |
| 3 | Irene Diamond Fund | NY | Independent | 32.0 |
| 4 | The Merck Company Foundation | NJ | Corporate | 24.3 |
| 5 | Bill & Melinda Gates Foundation | WA | Independent | 21.5 |

## TOP 5 FUNDERS OF PEOPLE WITH DISABILITIES
## (AS A PROPORTION OF TOTAL GIVING)

| | FOUNDATION NAME | STATE | TYPE | % |
|---|---|---|---|---|
| 1 | The James H. and Alice Teubert Charitable Trust | WV | Independent | 100.0 |
| 2 | Lavelle Fund for the Blind, Inc. | NY | Independent | 64.2 |
| 3 | Oberkotter Foundation | PA | Independent | 90.9 |
| 4 | Essel Foundation, Inc. | NY | Independent | 79.3 |
| 5 | van Ameringen Foundation, Inc. | NY | Independent | 74.5 |

## TOP 5 FUNDERS OF AGING, THE ELDERLY & SENIOR CITIZENS
## (AS A PROPORTION OF TOTAL GIVING)

| | FOUNDATION NAME | STATE | TYPE | % |
|---|---|---|---|---|
| 1 | The Retirement Research Foundation | IL | Independent | 97.8 |
| 2 | The Fan Fox and Leslie R. Samuels Foundation, Inc. | NY | Independent | 39.2 |
| 3 | Mary Stuart Rogers Foundation | CA | Independent | 38.4 |
| 4 | The Atlantic Foundation of New York | NY | Independent | 34.5 |
| 5 | The Ellison Medical Foundation | MD | Independent | 24.6 |

## TOP 5 FUNDERS OF IMMIGRANT & REFUGEE COMMUNITIES
### (AS A PROPORTION OF TOTAL GIVING)

| | FOUNDATION NAME | STATE | TYPE | % |
|---|---|---|---|---|
| 1 | Foundation for Child Development | NY | Independent | 40.3 |
| 2 | New York Foundation | NY | Independent | 30.2 |
| 3 | Moriah Fund | DC | Independent | 19.8 |
| 4 | The California Endowment | CA | Independent | 13.0 |
| 5 | Evelyn and Walter Haas, Jr. Fund | CA | Independent | 12.9 |

## TOP 5 FUNDERS OF CRIME & ABUSE VICTIMS
### (AS A PROPORTION OF TOTAL GIVING)

| | FOUNDATION NAME | STATE | TYPE | % |
|---|---|---|---|---|
| 1 | The Goldsbury Foundation | TX | Independent | 24.7 |
| 2 | The Sunshine Lady Foundation, Inc. | NC | Independent | 18.8 |
| 3 | The Coca-Cola Foundation, Inc. | GA | Corporate | 17.8 |
| 4 | Topfer Family Foundation | TX | Independent | 16.0 |
| 5 | Freddie Mac Foundation | VA | Corporate | 14.7 |

## TOP 5 FUNDERS OF OFFENDERS & EX-OFFENDERS
### (AS A PROPORTION OF TOTAL GIVING)

| | FOUNDATION NAME | STATE | TYPE | % |
|---|---|---|---|---|
| 1 | JEHT Foundation | NY | Independent | 57.7 |
| 2 | Lord Rudolph Spanier Foundation, Inc. | VT | Independent | 20.5 |
| 3 | Open Society Institute | NY | Operating | 18.5 |
| 4 | The Abell Foundation, Inc. | MD | Independent | 15.6 |
| 5 | The Edna McConnell Clark Foundation | NY | Independent | 14.7 |

## TOP 5 FUNDERS OF SINGLE PARENTS
### (AS A PROPORTION OF TOTAL GIVING)

| | FOUNDATION NAME | STATE | TYPE | % |
|---|---|---|---|---|
| 1 | Woods Charitable Fund, Inc. | NE | Independent | 5.4 |
| 2 | Mathile Family Foundation | OH | Independent | 4.0 |
| 3 | Topfer Family Foundation | TX | Independent | 3.1 |
| 4 | The Community Foundation of Greater Chattanooga, Inc. | TN | Community | 2.5 |
| 5 | Albert & Bessie Mae Kronkosky Charitable Foundation | TX | Independent | 2.3 |

## TOP 5 FUNDERS OF LGBTQ COMMUNITIES
### (AS A PROPORTION OF TOTAL GIVING)

| | FOUNDATION NAME | STATE | TYPE | % |
|---|---|---|---|---|
| 1 | The Gill Foundation | CO | Independent | 61.7 |
| 2 | Evelyn and Walter Haas, Jr. Fund | CA | Independent | 16.6 |
| 3 | Arcus Foundation | MI | Independent | 13.7 |
| 4 | Mertz Gilmore Foundation | NY | Independent | 11.9 |
| 5 | The John M. Lloyd Foundation | CA | Independent | 6.4 |

Giving for advocacy, organizing and civic engagement

To look more closely at current giving in advocacy, community organizing and civic engagement, NCRP analyzed disaggregated data in social justice grant-making that we used as a proxy for this work. Grants that meet the social justice definition described in this chapter and in the Foundation Center's publications on social justice grantmaking are included.[434] Because the Center tracks only larger foundations, there very likely are many more foundations—such as the Woods Fund of Chicago and the Liberty Hill Foundation of Los Angeles—that fund social justice work that are not included in our sample. The list drew the leading social justice grantmakers from the Foundation Center's database[435] with sufficient data to be included in our analysis of systems or structural change grants. Some foundations could not be included in the analysis because they did not provide data for all three years.

NCRP's analysis of social justice grantmaking as a share of overall grantmaking demonstrates great variability among the leading U.S. social justice grant-makers. In the aggregate, 682 (84 percent) of our total sample of 809 foundations made at least one social justice related grant during the three-year time period; average giving over three years was $1,549,135,953, comprising 11,958 grants. Though 84 percent of the sample made at least one social jus-

## PERCENT OF FOUNDATIONS MEETING NCRP'S CRITERIA FOR ADVOCACY, ORGANIZING AND CIVIC ENGAGEMENT

 Foundations Designating 25% or More of Grant Dollars for Social Justice

 Foundations Designating Less Than 25% of Grant Dollars for Social Justice

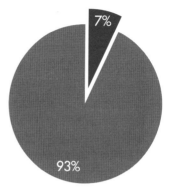

tice grant in the time period analyzed, many did so at very low levels.

Leading the field, 56 foundations, or about 6.9 percent of our sample, provided at least 25 percent of their grant dollars for social justice. This is the benchmark for Philanthropy at Its Best.[436] A list of all 56 foundations that currently meet or exceed this benchmark can be found immediately following. As noted earlier, some foundations may meet or exceed this benchmark and still not be listed here. For example, a grantmaker may not be included in the Foundation Center's database or its grants may not be coded properly.

## FOUNDATIONS MEETING NCRP'S CRITERIA FOR PHILANTHROPY AT ITS BEST SOCIAL JUSTICE GRANTMAKING (AS A PROPORTION OF TOTAL GIVING)

|    | FOUNDATION NAME | STATE | TYPE | % |
|----|-----------------|-------|------|---|
| 1  | The Melville Charitable Trust | MA | Independent | 81 |
| 2  | Moriah Fund | DC | Independent | 76.9 |
| 3  | Marguerite Casey Foundation | WA | Independent | 76.9 |
| 4  | Northwest Area Foundation | MN | Independent | 74.5 |
| 5  | Jessie Smith Noyes Foundation, Inc. | NY | Independent | 70.9 |
| 6  | JEHT Foundation | NY | Independent | 65.5 |
| 7  | The Annie E. Casey Foundation | MD | Independent | 62.6 |
| 8  | Fannie Mae Foundation | DC | Corporate | 62.3 |
| 9  | Mertz Gilmore Foundation | NY | Independent | 61 |
| 10 | The F. B. Heron Foundation | NY | Independent | 60.7 |
| 11 | New York Foundation | NY | Independent | 60.2 |
| 12 | Robert Sterling Clark Foundation, Inc. | NY | Independent | 59.3 |
| 13 | The Gill Foundation | CO | Independent | 55.3 |
| 14 | Public Welfare Foundation, Inc. | DC | Independent | 54.9 |
| 15 | The Ford Foundation | NY | Independent | 54.1 |

## FOUNDATIONS MEETING NCRP'S CRITERIA FOR PHILANTHROPY AT ITS BEST
## SOCIAL JUSTICE GRANTMAKING (AS A PROPORTION OF TOTAL GIVING) (CONTINUED)

| | FOUNDATION NAME | STATE | TYPE | % |
|---|---|---|---|---|
| 16 | Evelyn and Walter Haas, Jr. Fund | CA | Independent | 52.1 |
| 17 | The Rockefeller Foundation | NY | Independent | 48.5 |
| 18 | The John M. Lloyd Foundation | CA | Independent | 48.4 |
| 19 | The California Endowment | CA | Independent | 47.7 |
| 20 | The Commonwealth Fund | NY | Independent | 47.1 |
| 21 | John D. and Catherine T. MacArthur Foundation | IL | Independent | 46.4 |
| 22 | The Fund for New Jersey | NJ | Independent | 45.8 |
| 23 | Z. Smith Reynolds Foundation, Inc. | NC | Independent | 45.3 |
| 24 | Open Society Institute | NY | Operating | 44.4 |
| 25 | Compton Foundation, Inc. | CA | Independent | 43 |
| 26 | Wallace Alexander Gerbode Foundation | CA | Independent | 41.6 |
| 27 | W. K. Kellogg Foundation | MI | Independent | 40.1 |
| 28 | Charles Stewart Mott Foundation | MI | Independent | 37.8 |
| 29 | Bauman Family Foundation, Inc. | DC | Independent | 36.9 |
| 30 | The Hyams Foundation, Inc. | MA | Independent | 36.7 |
| 31 | The John Merck Fund | MA | Independent | 35.7 |
| 32 | Otto Bremer Foundation | MN | Independent | 34.4 |
| 33 | The Overbrook Foundation | NY | Independent | 34 |
| 34 | The Retirement Research Foundation | IL | Independent | 33.4 |
| 35 | The California Wellness Foundation | CA | Independent | 33.2 |
| 36 | Lumina Foundation for Education, Inc. | IN | Independent | 32.8 |
| 37 | Foundation for Seacoast Health | NH | Independent | 31.3 |
| 38 | The Case Foundation | DC | Independent | 30.7 |
| 39 | The Joyce Foundation | IL | Independent | 29.9 |
| 40 | Carnegie Corporation of New York | NY | Independent | 29.5 |
| 41 | van Ameringen Foundation, Inc. | NY | Independent | 29.5 |
| 42 | Levi Strauss Foundation | CA | Corporate | 29.5 |
| 43 | The Atlantic Foundation of New York | NY | Independent | 29.2 |
| 44 | The San Diego Foundation | CA | Community | 28.7 |
| 45 | Citi Foundation | NY | Corporate | 28.4 |
| 46 | The Nathan Cummings Foundation | NY | Independent | 28.1 |
| 47 | Foundation for Child Development | NY | Independent | 27.8 |
| 48 | The Sandy River Charitable Foundation | ME | Independent | 27.5 |
| 49 | William T. Grant Foundation | NY | Independent | 27.1 |
| 50 | John S. and James L. Knight Foundation | FL | Independent | 26.8 |
| 51 | The Coca-Cola Foundation, Inc. | GA | Corporate | 26.4 |
| 52 | The James Irvine Foundation | CA | Independent | 26 |
| 53 | The McKnight Foundation | MN | Independent | 25.9 |
| 54 | S. H. Cowell Foundation | CA | Independent | 25.9 |
| 55 | Alan B. Slifka Foundation, Inc. | NY | Independent | 25.5 |
| 56 | Rockefeller Brothers Fund, Inc. | NY | Independent | 25.3 |

Giving for general operating support

To ensure that our *Criteria for Philanthropy at Its Best* is informed by current practice, NCRP worked with the Foundation Center to produce a custom dataset on general operating support and multi-year funding. The dataset reported disaggregated foundation giving by types of support for a three-year period from circa 2004–2006. The resulting data present a reasonably reliable picture of the percentage of grants or grant dollars each foundation gave based on the two types of support NCRP's analysis identified as associated with positive investments in the health, growth and effectiveness of its grantee partners.

Of the 809 foundations in NCRP's total sample, 617 provided at least some grant dollars for general operating support.[437] In the aggregate, 16.2 percent of grant dollars were provided for general support. The 50 foundations that provided the highest proportion of their grant dollars for general operating support gave more than 90 percent of their grant dollars over all three years for general support. These grantmakers comprise just over 6 percent (6.18) of the total NCRP sample. Within this subsample, 30 foundations provided fully 100 percent of their grant dollars for this type of support. These 30 foundations comprise just below 4 percent (3.70) of the total NCRP sample. Leading the field, 125 foundations, or about 15.5 percent of the NCRP sample, provided at least 50 percent of their grant dollars for general operating support.

## PERCENT OF FOUNDATIONS MEETING NCRP'S CRITERIA FOR GENERAL OPERATING SUPPORT

Foundations Designating 50% or More of Grant Dollars for General Operating Support

Foundations Designating Less Than 50% of Grant Dollars for General Operating Support

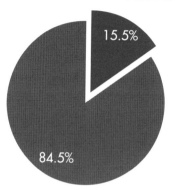

This is the benchmark for Philanthropy at Its Best. It is possible that individual grantmakers that are not included in this list meet the 50 percent benchmark. If a foundation is not included in the lists of "field leaders," this is the result of either not being part of the database from which the NCRP sample was drawn or because that foundation did not provide data consistently over the timeframe of the analysis. It also is possible that a foundation made general support grants that were not coded properly. In short, exclusion does not imply that a grantmaker is not providing the types of support essential to improving effectiveness.

## FOUNDATIONS MEETING NCRP'S CRITERIA FOR PHILANTHROPY AT ITS BEST
## GENERAL OPERATING SUPPORT (AS A PROPORTION OF TOTAL GIVING)

| | FOUNDATION NAME | STATE | TYPE | % |
|---|---|---|---|---|
| 1 | Aspen Foundation, Inc. | NJ | Independent | 100.0 |
| 2 | The Lerner Foundation | OH | Independent | 100.0 |
| 3 | JHJ Foundation, Inc. | NJ | Independent | 100.0 |
| 4 | The William K. Warren Foundation | OK | Independent | 100.0 |
| 5 | Emerson Charitable Trust | MO | Corporate | 100.0 |
| 6 | Comer Science & Education Foundation | IL | Independent | 100.0 |
| 7 | Beatrice P. Delany Charitable Trust | DE | Independent | 100.0 |
| 8 | Jurodin Fund, Inc. | DE | Independent | 100.0 |
| 9 | Mary Stuart Rogers Foundation | CA | Independent | 100.0 |
| 10 | S & G Foundation, Inc. | WY | Independent | 100.0 |
| 11 | Jack N. and Lilyan Mandel Foundation | OH | Independent | 100.0 |
| 12 | The Gottesman Fund | DC | Independent | 100.0 |
| 13 | Covenant Foundation, Inc. | TX | Independent | 100.0 |
| 14 | The Smart Family Foundation | CT | Independent | 100.0 |
| 15 | Manoogian Simone Foundation | MI | Independent | 100.0 |
| 16 | James H. Clark Charitable Foundation | NV | Independent | 100.0 |

## FOUNDATIONS MEETING NCRP'S CRITERIA FOR PHILANTHROPY AT ITS BEST
## GENERAL OPERATING SUPPORT (AS A PROPORTION OF TOTAL GIVING)  (CONTINUED)

| | FOUNDATION NAME | STATE | TYPE | % |
|---|---|---|---|---|
| 17 | The Larry L. Hillblom Foundation, Inc. | CA | Independent | 100.0 |
| 18 | Grousbeck Family Foundation | CA | Independent | 100.0 |
| 19 | John R. McCune Charitable Trust | PA | Independent | 100.0 |
| 20 | Irene W. & C. B. Pennington Foundation | LA | Independent | 100.0 |
| 21 | Mote Scientific Foundation, Inc. | FL | Independent | 100.0 |
| 22 | Essel Foundation, Inc. | NY | Independent | 100.0 |
| 23 | Ann and Robert H. Lurie Foundation | IL | Independent | 100.0 |
| 24 | The MCJ Foundation | NJ | Independent | 100.0 |
| 25 | The Arthur and Rochelle Belfer Foundation, Inc. | NY | Independent | 100.0 |
| 26 | Dick & Betsy DeVos Foundation | MI | Independent | 100.0 |
| 27 | Mitzi & Warren Eisenberg Family Foundation, Inc. | NJ | Independent | 100.0 |
| 28 | The ALS Foundation | UT | Independent | 100.0 |
| 29 | Fischer Family Foundation | KY | Independent | 100.0 |
| 30 | NCC Charitable Foundation | OH | Corporate | 100.0 |
| 31 | Leslie H. Wexner Charitable Fund | NY | Independent | 99.9 |
| 32 | Dan Murphy Foundation | CA | Independent | 99.9 |
| 33 | The Shubert Foundation, Inc. | NY | Independent | 99.6 |
| 34 | Susan & Leonard Feinstein Foundation | NY | Independent | 99.3 |
| 35 | George W. Mergens Foundation | VT | Independent | 99.3 |
| 36 | The Richard and Helen DeVos Foundation | MI | Independent | 99.0 |
| 37 | E. L. and Thelma Gaylord Foundation | OK | Independent | 99.0 |
| 38 | Bradley-Turner Foundation, Inc. | GA | Independent | 99.0 |
| 39 | Pritzker Foundation | IL | Independent | 99.0 |
| 40 | The Mosaic Fund | NY | Independent | 98.1 |
| 41 | Rath Foundation, Inc. | WI | Independent | 97.4 |
| 42 | Boeing-McDonnell Foundation | MO | Corporate | 96.9 |
| 43 | John J. and Mary R. Schiff Foundation | OH | Independent | 96.5 |
| 44 | Lewis B. & Dorothy Cullman Foundation, Inc. | NY | Independent | 96.0 |
| 45 | The Anne and Henry Zarrow Foundation | OK | Independent | 96.0 |
| 46 | The Pinkerton Foundation | NY | Independent | 95.8 |
| 47 | John W. Anderson Foundation | IN | Independent | 94.6 |
| 48 | The Abramson Family Foundation | FL | Independent | 94.5 |
| 49 | S. J. & Jessie E. Quinney Foundation | UT | Independent | 94.1 |
| 50 | Citizens Charitable Foundation | RI | Corporate | 91.8 |
| 51 | Arcus Foundation | MI | Independent | 89.3 |
| 52 | D & DF Foundation | CA | Independent | 89.3 |
| 53 | Orville D. & Ruth A. Merillat Foundation | MI | Independent | 86.3 |
| 54 | Browning-Kimball Foundation | MT | Independent | 86.1 |
| 55 | The MBNA Foundation | DE | Corporate | 84.8 |
| 56 | Duke Energy Foundation | NC | Corporate | 80.7 |
| 57 | J. Roderick MacArthur Foundation | IL | Independent | 80.1 |
| 58 | Mathile Family Foundation | OH | Independent | 79.4 |
| 59 | Mary Flagler Cary Charitable Trust | NY | Independent | 79.1 |
| 60 | The Murphy Foundation | AR | Independent | 78.6 |
| 61 | Boston Foundation, Inc. | MA | Community | 78.3 |
| 62 | Community Foundation of Greater Memphis | TN | Community | 77.7 |
| 63 | Bernard & Irene Schwartz Foundation, Inc. | NY | Independent | 77.2 |

| | FOUNDATION NAME | STATE | TYPE | % |
|---|---|---|---|---|
| 64 | The Dibner Fund, Inc. | CT | Independent | 77.1 |
| 65 | The Flatley Foundation | MA | Independent | 76.8 |
| 66 | Steven A. and Alexandra M. Cohen Foundation | CT | Independent | 76.3 |
| 67 | The Ambrose Monell Foundation | NY | Independent | 74.5 |
| 68 | The Oak Foundation U.S.A. | ME | Independent | 74.4 |
| 69 | Gladys and Roland Harriman Foundation | NY | Independent | 73.9 |
| 70 | Hazel Ruby McQuain Charitable Trust | WV | Independent | 72.2 |
| 71 | Hess Foundation, Inc. | NJ | Independent | 71.2 |
| 72 | BP Foundation, Inc. | IL | Corporate | 70.8 |
| 73 | The John W. Kluge Foundation | MD | Independent | 69.1 |
| 74 | Merrill Lynch & Co. Foundation, Inc. | NY | Corporate | 68.7 |
| 75 | The F. B. Heron Foundation | NY | Independent | 68.6 |
| 76 | The AVI CHAI Foundation | NY | Independent | 67.9 |
| 77 | The Holland Foundation | NE | Independent | 67.1 |
| 78 | Winthrop Rockefeller Trust | AR | Independent | 67.0 |
| 79 | Verizon Foundation | NJ | Corporate | 66.8 |
| 80 | The Carthage Foundation | PA | Independent | 66.3 |
| 81 | The Crawford Taylor Foundation | MO | Independent | 66.3 |
| 82 | Jessie Smith Noyes Foundation, Inc. | NY | Independent | 66.6 |
| 83 | The May Department Stores Foundation | OH | Corporate | 66.0 |
| 84 | The William H. Donner Foundation | NY | Independent | 65.3 |
| 85 | The Marcus Foundation, Inc. | GA | Independent | 64.9 |
| 86 | Public Welfare Foundation, Inc. | DC | Independent | 63.1 |
| 87 | Sue and Edgar Wachenheim Foundation | NY | Independent | 63.0 |
| 88 | Skirball Foundation | NY | Independent | 62.9 |
| 89 | The L. E. Phillips Family Foundation, Inc. | DE | Independent | 62.4 |
| 90 | The Batchelor Foundation, Inc. | FL | Corporate | 62.0 |
| 91 | Ted Arison Charitable Trust | FL | Independent | 62.0 |
| 92 | William K. Bowes, Jr. Foundation | CA | Independent | 61.8 |
| 93 | The Jacob and Hilda Blaustein Foundation, Inc. | MD | Independent | 61.1 |
| 94 | Alan B. Slifka Foundation, Inc. | NY | Independent | 60.7 |
| 95 | Progress Energy Foundation, Inc. | NC | Corporate | 60.6 |
| 96 | The Byrne Foundation, Inc. | NH | Independent | 60.4 |
| 97 | Fannie Mae Foundation | DC | Corporate | 60.1 |
| 98 | Alex Stern Family Foundation | ND | Independent | 60.0 |
| 99 | The Bank of America Charitable Foundation, Inc. | NC | Corporate | 59.6 |
| 100 | Jaquelin Hume Foundation | CA | Independent | 59.0 |
| 101 | The Robert W. Wilson Charitable Trust | NY | Independent | 58.0 |
| 102 | Bauman Family Foundation, Inc. | DC | Independent | 57.7 |
| 103 | The Irving Harris Foundation | IL | Independent | 57.7 |
| 104 | Christian A. Johnson Endeavor Foundation | NY | Independent | 57.6 |
| 105 | Kate B. Reynolds Charitable Trust | NC | Independent | 57.3 |
| 106 | Sarah Scaife Foundation, Inc. | PA | Independent | 56.7 |
| 107 | The Jess & Sheila Schwartz Family Foundation | AZ | Independent | 55.6 |
| 108 | MDU Resources Foundation | ND | Corporate | 55.3 |
| 109 | Kellogg's Corporate Citizenship Fund | MI | Corporate | 55.1 |
| 110 | Amon G. Carter Foundation | TX | Independent | 54.6 |

## FOUNDATIONS MEETING NCRP'S CRITERIA FOR PHILANTHROPY AT ITS BEST GENERAL OPERATING SUPPORT (AS A PROPORTION OF TOTAL GIVING) (CONTINUED)

| FOUNDATION NAME | STATE | TYPE | % |
|---|---|---|---|
| 111 The Thomas and Stacey Siebel Foundation | CA | Independent | 54.4 |
| 112 Thomas & Dorothy Leavey Foundation | CA | Independent | 53.7 |
| 113 Tiger Foundation | NY | Independent | 53.5 |
| 114 The Judy and Michael Steinhardt Foundation | NY | Independent | 53.3 |
| 115 Alabama Power Foundation, Inc. | AL | Corporate | 53.3 |
| 116 The California Wellness Foundation | CA | Independent | 53.0 |
| 117 The William and Flora Hewlett Foundation | CA | Independent | 52.9 |
| 118 Berkshire Taconic Community Foundation | MA | Community | 52.5 |
| 119 J. F Maddox Foundation | NM | Independent | 52.4 |
| 120 U.S. Bancorp Foundation, Inc. | MN | Corporate | 51.9 |
| 121 The Denver Foundation | CO | Community | 51.7 |
| 122 Z. Smith Reynolds Foundation, Inc. | NC | Independent | 51.5 |
| 123 Jay and Betty Van Andel Foundation | MI | Independent | 51.4 |
| 124 Lozier Foundation | NE | Independent | 50.9 |
| 125 The Morris and Gwendolyn Cafritz Foundation | DC | Independent | 50.0 |

## PERCENT OF FOUNDATIONS MEETING NCRP'S CRITERIA FOR MULTI-YEAR FUNDING

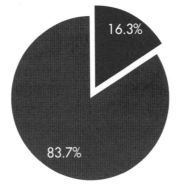

■ Foundations Designating 50% or More of Grant Dollars for Multi-Year Funding

■ Foundations Designating Less Than 50% of Grant Dollars for Multi-Year Funding

### Giving for multi-year support

For multi-year grants, 483 foundations of our 809 foundation sample provided at least one multi-year grant during the three-year time period. Just below 60 percent (59.7 percent) of the total sample provided at least one multi-year grant. This number is disturbing, considering the stated constraints on smaller foundations' ability to provide this type of support. Because the Foundation Center tracks only larger foundations, if smaller foundations were included in the sample, the numbers would be even lower. Interestingly, these findings align with self-reported data from the 2008 GEO survey that found that 60 percent of foundations, regardless of asset size, provided multi-year grants sometimes, often or always.[438] For foundations that made any multi-year grants, the median when measuring multi-year grants as a proportion of overall grantmaking was just below 34 percent (33.7).

Leading the field, 132, or 16.3 percent of the total NCRP sample, provided 50 percent or more of their grant dollars as multiyear grants.[439] This is the benchmark for Philanthropy at Its Best. Once again, we remind readers that just because a grantmaker is not listed here does not necessarily mean it does not meet or exceed this benchmark for multi-year grants. Various reasons cited earlier could lead to their exclusion from this list of field leaders.

## FOUNDATIONS MEETING NCRP'S CRITERIA FOR PHILANTHROPY AT ITS BEST
## MULTI-YEAR FUNDING (AS A PROPORTION OF TOTAL GIVING)

| | FOUNDATION NAME | STATE | TYPE | % |
|---|---|---|---|---|
| 1 | Vermont Community Foundation | VT | Community | 98.7 |
| 2 | W. K. Kellogg Foundation | MI | Independent | 97.1 |
| 3 | The Community Foundation of Louisville, Inc. | KY | Community | 96.0 |
| 4 | William T. Grant Foundation | NY | Independent | 93.3 |
| 5 | Bill & Melinda Gates Foundation | WA | Independent | 93.3 |
| 6 | The Robert Wood Johnson Foundation | NJ | Independent | 91.6 |
| 7 | Josiah Macy, Jr. Foundation | NY | Independent | 91.6 |
| 8 | The California Wellness Foundation | CA | Independent | 90.8 |
| 9 | The Andrew W. Mellon Foundation | NY | Independent | 90.5 |
| 10 | The McKnight Foundation | MN | Independent | 88.8 |
| 11 | John D. and Catherine T. MacArthur Foundation | IL | Independent | 88.3 |
| 12 | Carnegie Corporation of New York | NY | Independent | 87.9 |
| 13 | Lumina Foundation for Education, Inc. | IN | Independent | 87.2 |
| 14 | Hillman Foundation | PA | Independent | 87.1 |
| 15 | Alfred P. Sloan Foundation | NY | Independent | 86.9 |
| 16 | The Bodman Foundation | NY | Independent | 85.7 |
| 17 | Mary Flagler Cary Charitable Trust | NY | Independent | 85.7 |
| 18 | Helen Bader Foundation, Inc. | WI | Independent | 84.8 |
| 19 | John S. and James L. Knight Foundation | FL | Independent | 84.8 |
| 20 | Foundation for Child Development | NY | Independent | 84.1 |
| 21 | The Starr Foundation | NY | Independent | 83.6 |
| 22 | The Joyce Foundation | IL | Independent | 82.8 |
| 23 | Hazel Ruby McQuain Charitable Trust | WV | Independent | 81.6 |
| 24 | Arizona Community Foundation | AZ | Community | 80.4 |
| 25 | Richard and Rhoda Goldman Fund | CA | Independent | 80.2 |
| 26 | Dyson Foundation | NY | Independent | 79.6 |
| 27 | Charles Stewart Mott Foundation | MI | Independent | 79.4 |
| 28 | The Meadows Foundation, Inc. | TX | Independent | 79.0 |
| 29 | The Dallas Foundation | TX | Community | 78.5 |
| 30 | Wallace Alexander Gerbode Foundation | CA | Independent | 78.3 |
| 31 | The Ford Foundation | NY | Independent | 78.2 |
| 32 | The New Hampshire Charitable Foundation | NH | Community | 77.6 |
| 33 | Community Foundation Silicon Valley | CA | Community | 77.0 |
| 34 | The William Penn Foundation | PA | Independent | 77.0 |
| 35 | Triangle Community Foundation | NC | Community | 76.1 |
| 36 | The Achelis Foundation | NY | Independent | 76.0 |
| 37 | The Denver Foundation | CO | Community | 76.0 |
| 38 | ExxonMobil Foundation | TX | Corporate | 75.4 |
| 39 | Omaha Community Foundation | NE | Community | 74.9 |
| 40 | The Cleo Foundation | CA | Independent | 74.8 |
| 41 | The Philadelphia Foundation | PA | Community | 74.7 |
| 42 | Lavelle Fund for the Blind, Inc. | NY | Independent | 74.7 |
| 43 | Meyer Memorial Trust | OR | Independent | 74.6 |
| 44 | Doris Duke Charitable Foundation | NY | Independent | 74.5 |
| 45 | The Greater Des Moines Community Foundation | IA | Community | 74.2 |
| 46 | Arkansas Community Foundation, Inc. | AR | Community | 73.9 |
| 47 | The Clark Foundation | NY | Independent | 73.7 |

## FOUNDATIONS MEETING NCRP'S CRITERIA FOR PHILANTHROPY AT ITS BEST
## MULTI-YEAR FUNDING (AS A PROPORTION OF TOTAL GIVING) (CONTINUED)

| | FOUNDATION NAME | STATE | TYPE | % |
|---|---|---|---|---|
| 48 | The Hamilton Community Foundation, Inc. | OH | Community | 73.7 |
| 49 | The Columbus Foundation and Affiliated Organizations | OH | Community | 73.5 |
| 50 | Santa Barbara Foundation | CA | Community | 73.4 |
| 51 | The Ahmanson Foundation | CA | Independent | 73.2 |
| 52 | Jessie Smith Noyes Foundation, Inc. | NY | Independent | 73.2 |
| 53 | The Gamble Foundation | CA | Independent | 72.4 |
| 54 | The F. B. Heron Foundation | NY | Independent | 72.4 |
| 55 | The William and Flora Hewlett Foundation | CA | Independent | 72.2 |
| 56 | Roy A. Hunt Foundation | PA | Independent | 71.9 |
| 57 | M. J. Murdock Charitable Trust | WA | Independent | 71.7 |
| 58 | The Pittsburgh Foundation | PA | Community | 71.5 |
| 59 | Bush Foundation | MN | Independent | 71.5 |
| 60 | Dorot Foundation | RI | Independent | 71.4 |
| 61 | The Community Foundation for the National Capital Region | DC | Community | 71.4 |
| 62 | The Oregon Community Foundation | OR | Community | 71.2 |
| 63 | Bella Vista Foundation | CA | Independent | 70.9 |
| 64 | The Kimball Foundation | CA | Independent | 70.7 |
| 65 | Boston Foundation, Inc. | MA | Community | 70.6 |
| 66 | The Bolthouse Foundation | CA | Independent | 70.5 |
| 67 | The Rockefeller Foundation | NY | Independent | 70.3 |
| 68 | The Maine Community Foundation, Inc. | ME | Community | 70.3 |
| 69 | MetLife Foundation | NY | Corporate | 70.1 |
| 70 | The Melville Charitable Trust | MA | Independent | 69.9 |
| 71 | The Dayton Foundation | OH | Community | 69.8 |
| 72 | The Reinberger Foundation | OH | Independent | 69.8 |
| 73 | Greater Milwaukee Foundation | WI | Community | 69.4 |
| 74 | F. M. Kirby Foundation, Inc. | NJ | Independent | 69.3 |
| 75 | The Greater Cincinnati Foundation | OH | Community | 69.3 |
| 76 | Ben B. Cheney Foundation | WA | Independent | 69.2 |
| 77 | William Randolph Hearst Foundation | NY | Independent | 69.2 |
| 78 | Berkshire Taconic Community Foundation | MA | Community | 69.0 |
| 79 | AT&T Foundation | TX | Corporate | 68.8 |
| 80 | Community Foundation of Greater Memphis | TN | Community | 68.7 |
| 81 | Evelyn and Walter Haas, Jr. Fund | CA | Independent | 68.6 |
| 82 | The Arthur Vining Davis Foundations | FL | Independent | 68.0 |
| 83 | The San Francisco Foundation | CA | Community | 67.9 |
| 84 | The Henry Luce Foundation, Inc. | NY | Independent | 67.6 |
| 85 | The San Diego Foundation | CA | Community | 67.5 |
| 86 | The Fund for New Jersey | NJ | Independent | 67.3 |
| 87 | The Bothin Foundation | CA | Independent | 67.3 |
| 88 | Hartford Foundation for Public Giving | CT | Community | 67.0 |
| 89 | Hall Family Foundation | MO | Independent | 66.8 |
| 90 | The Retirement Research Foundation | IL | Independent | 66.3 |
| 91 | Rockefeller Brothers Fund, Inc. | NY | Independent | 65.6 |
| 92 | The John M. Lloyd Foundation | CA | Independent | 65.5 |
| 93 | The California Endowment | CA | Independent | 64.7 |

| | FOUNDATION NAME | STATE | TYPE | % |
|---|---|---|---|---|
| 94 | Con Alma Health Foundation, Inc. | NM | Independent | 64.7 |
| 95 | Gannett Foundation, Inc. | VA | Corporate | 64.4 |
| 96 | The Hearst Foundation, Inc. | NY | Independent | 64.4 |
| 97 | The Andy Warhol Foundation for the Visual Arts | NY | Independent | 64.4 |
| 98 | The Minneapolis Foundation | MN | Community | 64.4 |
| 99 | The Ford Family Foundation | OR | Independent | 64.4 |
| 100 | The Annie E. Casey Foundation | MD | Independent | 64.1 |
| 101 | Community Foundation for Southeast Michigan | MI | Community | 63.4 |
| 102 | The Seattle Foundation | WA | Community | 63.0 |
| 103 | Peninsula Community Foundation | CA | Community | 62.8 |
| 104 | The Kovner Foundation | NJ | Independent | 62.8 |
| 105 | The Thomas and Stacey Siebel Foundation | CA | Independent | 62.7 |
| 106 | Lilly Endowment Inc. | IN | Independent | 62.5 |
| 107 | Foellinger Foundation, Inc. | IN | Independent | 62.5 |
| 108 | The Chicago Community Trust | IL | Community | 61.2 |
| 109 | The Cleveland Foundation | OH | Community | 60.4 |
| 110 | The Community Foundation of Western North Carolina, Inc. | NC | Community | 60.2 |
| 111 | Open Society Institute | NY | Operating | 59.7 |
| 112 | The Burton D. Morgan Foundation | OH | Independent | 59.1 |
| 113 | Jessie Ball duPont Fund | FL | Independent | 59.1 |
| 114 | The New York Community Trust | NY | Community | 58.7 |
| 115 | Otto Bremer Foundation | MN | Independent | 58.1 |
| 116 | The William H. Donner Foundation | NY | Independent | 58.0 |
| 117 | McGregor Fund | MI | Independent | 57.5 |
| 118 | Mote Scientific Foundation, Inc. | FL | Independent | 57.2 |
| 119 | The Ella West Freeman Foundation | LA | Independent | 57.1 |
| 120 | The James Irvine Foundation | CA | Independent | 56.1 |
| 121 | The George Gund Foundation | OH | Independent | 56.0 |
| 122 | The Blandin Foundation | MN | Independent | 55.6 |
| 123 | The Skillman Foundation | MI | Independent | 55.2 |
| 124 | The Ave Maria Foundation | MI | Independent | 55.0 |
| 125 | Fannie Mae Foundation | DC | Corporate | 54.8 |
| 126 | Energy Foundation | CA | Independent | 53.7 |
| 127 | The Grainger Foundation Inc. | IL | Independent | 52.9 |
| 128 | Community Foundation of Greater Fort Wayne, Inc. | IN | Community | 51.9 |
| 129 | The Icahn Family Foundation | NY | Independent | 51.7 |
| 130 | Community Foundation of Greenville, Inc. | SC | Community | 51.5 |
| 131 | Helena Rubinstein Foundation, Inc. | NY | Independent | 51.1 |
| 132 | The Bristol-Myers Squibb Foundation, Inc. | NY | Corporate | 50.2 |

## Setting the bar for Ethics and Commitment

The Ethics and Commitment chapters of this book identify specific grantmaking institutions that meet the benchmarks established by these criteria. For numerous reasons, NCRP is unable to provide an accurate analysis of the proportion of funders that meet or exceed the thresholds established in these chapters. For example, to assess the proportion of foundations that do not compensate trustees in any form, including allowing them to make discretionary grants, requires a centralized database that maintains up-to-date data information drawn from the IRS's form 990 PF's and primary data collection conducted to examine foundation financial operations not reflected on the tax form (such as discretionary grantmaking in lieu of monetary compensation). There also is no database that records whether a foundation includes grantee or community representatives on its board of directors. Until such time as these data become available, it is not possible to analyze individual funder practices with rigor and credibility.

The exemplary foundations cited in the Ethics chapter that maintain and implement policies and practices that ensure ethical behavior are drawn from secondary analysis and individual foundation research. Thus, for example, those funders that subscribe to and publicly disclose conflict of interest and whistleblower protection policies are drawn from these sources. Further, there is no way to ensure that a grantmaking institution that maintains these policies in fact implements them. Future NCRP research and analysis from others working in the field may provide some more robust data for analysis of disaggregated data. Regarding disclosure of relevant information, the same issues arise as with maintaining practices and policies that ensure ethical behavior. A final caveat that applies to the benchmarks for these two metrics is that much of the data are qualitative in nature and would require comprehensive analysis of individual annual reports, focus group discussions and telephone interviews to gauge individual grantmaker theory and practice. NCRP or others in the sector may undertake this work at a future point, but in the interim, NCRP encourages more grantmakers to either include this information in annual reports or make the information readily available on funder web sites for public disclosure.

The Commitment chapter establishes a generous payout rate with a minimum of 6 percent of grant dollars allocated for grants only. The narrative presents aggregate statistics on foundation grants drawn from the latest edition of the *Nonprofit Almanac*. NCRP is confident that these data present a reliable picture of sector-wide giving trends across the grantmaking community. At a future date, NCRP may conduct further research by analyzing grants on individual 990 PF forms, but in the interim, the aggregate statistics present a reasonably solid and defensible quantitative supplement to the rationale for why this metric was established at this level.[440] As also noted in the narrative, mission investing, although practiced increasingly by many foundations, is not a required piece of financial information disclosed on either the IRS's 990 or 990 PF forms. Thus, NCRP relied on the FSG Social Impact Advisors' analysis of mission investing and worked with FSG and individual foundation executives and financial managers to secure the detailed mission investing data presented in this chapter. The lack of publicly available mission investing data is a disservice to grantmakers: some exemplary funders are not getting the credit they well might deserve if these data were available publicly. NCRP encourages more grantmaking institutions to provide detailed and comprehensive information on the non-grantmaking ways in which they are advancing their mission. By investing 25 percent of its assets using investment screens, shareholder proxy voting and proactive mission investing, a funder demonstrates exemplary stewardship of the partly public dollars with which it is entrusted. As with the primary data analyses for Values and Effectiveness, not being included as a "field leader" does not imply that a specific funder fails to meet that criterion; rather, it is the result of the problems with data availability noted throughout this appendix.

# NOTES FOR DATA APPENDIX

430. NCRP recognizes that immigrants and refugees are two discrete groups but the current Foundation Center classification system records these two groups together.

431. Lesbian, Gay, Bisexual, Transgendered or Questioning.

432. The Foundation Center refers to these groups as "Special Population Groups."

433. The lower and upper bound figures presented in this table are from various years in the time period of 1998 through 2006; in other words, these bounds do not represent the figures from the start and end years but instead present data on overall giving trends in the full Foundation Center samples for the entire time period.

434. The authors defined social justice philanthropy as "the granting of philanthropic contributions to nonprofit organizations based in the United States and other countries that work for structural change in order to increase the opportunity of those who are the least well off politically, economically, and socially." Importantly, this definition is not intended to convey or support any specific ideological or political position.

435. The search set is based on the Foundation Center's grants sample database, which includes all grants of $10,000 or more awarded to organizations by a sample of 1,172 larger foundations for circa 2004, 1,154 for circa 2005, and 1,263 for circa 2006. For community foundations, only discretionary grants are included. Grants to individuals are not included in the file.

436. The two metrics described in this criterion are not additive. It is assumed that the 25 percent of grant dollars going for advocacy and organizing work will be a subset of the 50 percent of grant dollars going for the intended benefit of marginalized communities.

437. The Foundation Center's grants classification system does not differentiate between unrestricted core support versus negotiated core support; both are included in the general operating support category.

438. Harder+Company. *Grantmaking Practices that Support Grantee Success: Survey Report*, (Washington, D.C.: Grantmakers for Effective Organizations, October 2008), 27. GEO's analysis identified this figure as statistically significant; the p-value for this statistic was <0.001 meaning that the probability that their findings do not reflect reality based on self-reported multiyear funding is less than 1 in 1,000.

439. The two metrics described in this criterion are not additive. For example, a grant that is both multiyear and for general support counts toward meeting both measures.

440. Because the grants data analysis of this section in the chapter presents the data disaggregated by foundation asset size, grantmakers can compare the proportion of their portfolios allocated to grants only with peer institutions to assess their individual performances.

## NCRP STAFF

| | |
|---|---|
| Meredith Brodbeck | COMMUNICATIONS ASSISTANT |
| Julia Craig | RESEARCH ASSISTANT |
| Aaron Dorfman | EXECUTIVE DIRECTOR |
| Kevin Faria | DEVELOPMENT DIRECTOR |
| Niki Jagpal | RESEARCH DIRECTOR |
| Melissa Johnson | FIELD DIRECTOR |
| Kevin Laskowski | FIELD ASSOCIATE |
| Anna Kristina ("Yna") C. Moore | COMMUNICATIONS DIRECTOR |
| Lisa Ranghelli | SENIOR RESEARCH ASSOCIATE |
| Beverley Samuda-Wylder | SENIOR ADMINISTRATIVE ASSOCIATE |

## NCRP BOARD OF DIRECTORS

### OFFICERS

| | |
|---|---|
| David R. Jones | (CHAIR) COMMUNITY SERVICE SOCIETY OF NEW YORK |
| Diane Feeney | (VICE CHAIR) FRENCH AMERICAN CHARITABLE TRUST |
| Dave Beckwith | (SECRETARY) NEEDMOR FUND |
| Rhoda Karpatkin | (TREASURER) CONSUMERS UNION |

### DIRECTORS

| | |
|---|---|
| Marilyn Aguirre-Molina | LEHMAN COLLEGE, CITY UNIVERSITY OF NEW YORK |
| Christine Ahn | KOREA POLICY INSTITUTE |
| Andrea Alexander | CHINOOK WIND ENTERPRISES |
| Lana Cowell | NATIONAL ALLIANCE FOR CHOICE IN GIVING* |
| Louis T. Delgado | INDEPENDENT CONSULTANT* |
| Robert Edgar | COMMON CAUSE |
| Pablo Eisenberg | PUBLIC POLICY INSTITUTE, GEORGETOWN UNIVERSITY |
| Richard Farias | TEJANO CENTER FOR COMMUNITY CONCERNS* |
| Marjorie Fine | CENTER FOR COMMUNITY CHANGE |
| Cynthia Guyer | SAN FRANCISCO SCHOOLS ALLIANCE |
| Judy Hatcher | ENVIRONMENTAL SUPPORT CENTER |
| Priscilla Hung | GRASSROOTS INSTITUTE FOR FUNDRAISING |
| Larry Kressley | PUBLIC WELFARE FOUNDATION* |
| Gara LaMarche | THE ATLANTIC PHILANTHROPIES |
| Pete Manzo | UNITED WAYS OF CALIFORNIA |
| Nadia Moritz | THE YOUNG WOMEN'S PROJECT* |
| Russell Roybal | NATIONAL GAY AND LESBIAN TASK FORCE |
| William Schulz | CENTER FOR AMERICAN PROGRESS |
| Gary Snyder | NONPROFIT IMPERATIVE |
| Helen Vinton | SOUTHERN MUTUAL HELP ASSOCIATION |
| Sherece Y. West | WINTHROP ROCKEFELLER FOUNDATION |
| Jodi Williams | COMMUNITY SHARES OF MINNESOTA* |

### PAST BOARD CHAIRS

| | |
|---|---|
| Paul Castro | JEWISH FAMILY SERVICE OF LOS ANGELES |
| John Echohawk | NATIVE AMERICAN RIGHTS FUND |
| Pablo Eisenberg | PUBLIC POLICY INSTITUTE, GEORGETOWN UNIVERSITY |
| Terry Odendahl | NEW MEXICO ASSOCIATION OF GRANTMAKERS |

*Past NCRP directors who termed off during project finalization.
*Organization affiliation for identification purposes only.*